The MISMEASURE of CRIME

The
MISMEASURE
of CRIME

Clayton J. Mosher
Washington State University, Vancouver
Terance D. Miethe
University of Nevada, Las Vegas
Dretha M. Phillips
Washington State University, Pullman

Sage Publications
International Educational and Professional Publisher
Thousand Oaks ■ London ■ New Delhi

For information:

Sage Publications, Inc.
2455 Teller Road
Thousand Oaks, California 91320
E-mail: order@sagepub.com

Sage Publications Ltd.
6 Bonhill Street
London EC2A 4PU
United Kingdom

Sage Publications India Pvt. Ltd.
M-32 Market
Greater Kailash I
New Delhi 110 048 India

Printed in the United States of America

Library of Congress Cataloging-in-Publication Data

Mosher, Clayton James.
    The mismeasure of crime / by Clayton J. Mosher, Terance D. Miethe, and Dretha M. Phillips.
        p. cm.
    ISBN 0-7619-8711-8 (p.)
        1. Criminal statistics. 2. Criminal statitistics-United States. 3. Victims of crimes surveys. 4. Victims of crime surveys-United States. I. Miethe, Terance D. II. Phillips, Dretha M. III. Title.

    HV6018 .M67 2002
    362.88'0973-dc21   2001058137

02   03   04   05   06   10   9   8   7   6   5   4   3   2   1

Acquiring Editors:	Stephen D. Rutter and Jerry Westby
Editorial Assistant:	Vonessa Vondera
Production Editor:	Claudia A. Hoffman
Copy Editor:	Barbara Coster
Typesetter/Designer:	Denyse Dunn
Indexer:	Molly Hall
Cover Designer:	Michelle Lee

Contents

Exhibits

Acknowledgments

A ll three authors have benefited from the encouragement and ideas of colleagues and teachers too numerous to mention. In particular, we thank James F. Short Jr., one of the pioneers of self-report methodology, who was very supportive of this project and provided reprints of articles and loaned personal copies of books not available in the library. We also thank both Steve Rutter, whose enthusiasm for this project and knowledge of the social sciences contributed tremendously to the final product, and series editor Les Kennedy, who made several useful suggestions. We also acknowledge the contributions of Robert Griffin and Chad Smith, who read and commented on earlier versions of portions of the book.

Dretha Phillips dedicates the book to Ron, her partner when it counts—by any measure.

Chapter One

Introduction

On September 23, 1999, NASA fired rockets that were intended to put its Mars Climate spacecraft into a stable low-altitude orbit over the planet. But after the rockets were fired, the spacecraft disappeared—scientists speculated that it had either crashed on the Martian surface or had escaped the planet completely. This disaster was the result of confusion over measurement units—the manufacturer of the spacecraft had specified the rocket thrust in pounds, whereas NASA assumed that the thrust had been specified in metric system newtons (Browne 2001).

Although measurement is important in the physical sciences, it is equally important in the social sciences, including the discipline of criminology. Criminologists, policy makers, and the general public are concerned about the levels of crime in society, and the media frequently report on the extent and nature of crime. These media reports typically rely on official data and victimization studies and often focus on whether crime is increasing or decreasing.

Both official crime and victimization data indicated that property and violent crime in the United States were in a state of relatively steady decline from the early 1990s to 2000. But in late May 2001, the release of Federal Bureau of Investigation (FBI) official crime data, widely publicized in the media, indicated that crime was no longer declining. This prompted newspaper headlines such as "Decade-Long Crime Drop Ends" (Lichtblau 2001a) and led commentators such as James Alan Fox, dean of the College of Criminal Justice at Northeastern University, to assert, "It seems that the crime drop is officially over. . . . We have finally squeezed all the air out of the balloon" (as quoted in Butterfield 2001a). However, some two weeks after the release of these official data, a report based on victimization data indicated that violent crime had decreased by 15 percent between 1999 and 2000, the largest one-year decrease since the federal government began collecting victimization data in 1973 (Rennison 2001). This prompted headlines such as "Crime Is: Up? Down? Who Knows? (Lichtblau 2001b) and led James Alan Fox to declare, "This is good news, but it's not great news" (as quoted in Bendavid 2001).

How do we reconcile the conflicting messages regarding crime trends from these two sources? First, although most media sources commenting on the FBI data failed to mention this caveat, the official data report was in fact based on preliminary data: "[The report] does not contain official figures for crime rates in 2000" (Butterfield 2001a). Second, and more important, the underlying reason for these differences is that the two data sources measured crime differently. Official crime data are based on reports submitted to the FBI by police departments and measure homicide, rape, robbery, aggravated assault, burglary, car theft, and larceny. Victimization data are based on household surveys that question respondents about their experiences with crime and do not include homicide (for obvious reasons). However, the victimization survey does include questions about simple assaults, which are far more common than aggravated assaults or robberies and thus tend to statistically dominate the report. As Butterfield (2001b) pointed out, simple assaults accounted for 61.5 percent of all violent crimes identified in the victimization survey, and because they had declined by 14.4 percent in 2000 compared with 1999, they accounted for most of the decline in violent crime revealed in the victimization data. In short, and as Alfred Blumstein (as quoted in Butterfield, 2001b) noted, "[The data] are telling us that crime is very difficult to measure."

Statistics and numerical counts of social phenomena, including crime, have become a major fact of modern life. Countries are compared and ranked in terms of statistical information on health, education, social welfare, and economic development. Cities and individuals are compared on similar kinds of social indicators. Geographical areas, social groups, and individuals are judged as relatively high, low, or normal on the basis of various numerical counts. Notice the variability in the following numerical data from a statistical profile of the United States (U.S. Bureau of the Census 1999).

- There were 41,518 injuries associated with a hammer in 1997. There were 44,335 injuries from toilets and 37,401 injuries from televisions in the same year.

- Whooping cough deaths increased from 1,700 to 7,400 from 1980 to 1998. Deaths in the United States resulting from gonorrhea decreased from 100,400 to 35,600 in the same time frame.

- More than 54 percent of U.S. citizens in 1997 were classified as overweight, and 19 percent were considered obese.

- Broccoli consumption increased from 1.4 pounds per capita in 1980 to 5.6 pounds per capita in 1998.

- The proportion of households with a television set increased from 2 percent in 1965 to 85 percent in 1998.

- There were 14 deaths per 100,000 population in the United States by firearms in 1995 compared to 4 deaths from falling per 100,000 population. In contrast, the death rate by firearms in England and Wales was only 0.4 per 100,000, but the death rate from falling was 26 per 100,000.

- The number of offenses known to the police per 100,000 population was 8,836 in the District of Columbia in 1998 and 4,071 in Montana in the same year.

At their face value, each of these types of statistical information may serve as a basis for social action. For example, this information may lead people to exhibit more care when using hammers or toilets, have greater concern with their nagging cough and less concern about particular sexually transmitted diseases, feel good or bad about their weight, invest in broccoli and television production, watch out for firearms in the United States and hazardous walking conditions in Great Britain, and relocate to Montana. It is also not uncommon for this type of numerical data to form the basis of public policy. In fact, public health programs, law enforcement, and other agencies rely on these descriptive statistics to implement various types of reform.

Before taking corrective actions based on statistical information, however, it is important to consider several questions about its accuracy and how the data were collected. These questions about the measurement of social phenomena are often neglected in public discourse, but they ultimately will determine whether corrective action is necessary. For example, one's opinion about the statistics presented above may change when one considers the following questions regarding the measurement of these social facts:

- How are injuries by hammers, toilets, and televisions counted? If a television repairperson hits a television with a hammer and it falls in the toilet and results in an electric shock to the repairperson, is this classified as an injury by a hammer, toilet, or television? Do all agencies classify these injuries the same way? Note that these injury data are calculated from a sample of hospitals with emergency treatment departments. If people are injured by these products and do not go to an emergency ward, their injuries will not be counted. Under these conditions, the number of injuries by hammers, toilets, or televisions may be substantially higher or even lower, depending on how they are counted.

- Does the rise in whooping cough deaths reflect an actual increase in these fatalities or is it due to medical advances in the last decade that have now made it easier to detect whooping cough as a medical problem? Is the dramatic decline in gonorrhea deaths due to improvements in medical care and early detection of this disease or is it due to the reclassification of sexually transmitted disease (STD) deaths by medical personnel (e.g., some STD deaths are now attributed to AIDS)?

- Who establishes the categories of overweight and obesity? Are these self-reported feelings (e.g., "Do you consider yourself to be overweight or obese?"), or are they standardized by height and bone structure? Are the figures of 54 percent overweight and 19 percent obese derived from the entire U.S. population or particular subsets of individuals who went for some type of medical treatment (e.g., diabetes or heart disease, which are associated with obesity)?

- Are we really measuring changes in the human consumption of broccoli or the amount of broccoli purchased per capita? For example, the increase in the last two decades in the number of exotic pets (like iguanas) that eat broccoli may artificially inflate the estimates of human consumption. How are the figures for broccoli consumers who grow their own broccoli counted in data that are derived from grocery stores? Can an increase in a small number of "super" broccoli eaters underlie this increase instead of the apparent rise in the proportion of consumers over time?

- Are uniform standards for the measurement of firearm and falling deaths used within and across the United States and Great Britain? If a person dies a year after the injury occurred, how is the death classified? How are multiple causes counted (e.g., a person is shot and then falls off a building, or a person falls onto a loaded gun)?

- Counts of crime in the District of Columbia include offenses reported to the police at the National Zoo, thereby inflating the crime rate per 100,000 residents. In contrast, complete police data in Montana were not available, so the crime rates had to be estimated. If different jurisdictions use different rules for counting crime and citizens report crime differently in rural and urban areas (which they do), conclusions about the relative danger of the District of Columbia and the safety of Montana may be premature.

As these examples illustrate, numerical measures of crime and other social phenomena have enormous potential to inform social scientists about their theories of human behavior, provide politicians and legislators with an empirical basis for public policy decisions, and help the general public structure their routine activities and how they live their lives. Unfortunately, many people who use these statistics are grossly uninformed about how they are collected, what they mean, and their strengths and limitations.

The goal of this book is to critically examine the various ways in which crime is measured and thereby to instill a healthy skepticism about the accuracy of current methods of counting crime. All social measurement involves human decisions, interpretations, and errors. By examining the sources of error in the measurement of crime, social scientists, legislators, and the general public will be in a better position to understand the utility of current theory and crime control practices that derive from statistical data on crime. In later chapters, we address in considerable detail issues surrounding the three most commonly used measures of crime and delinquency: official data, self-report, and victimization studies. In this introductory chapter, we address the measurement of social phenomena in the context of the key concepts of reliability and validity.

Reliability, Validity, and Sources of Error in the Measurement of Social Phenomena

Stevens (1959) defined measurement as "the assignment of numerals to events or objects according to rule" (p. 25). The initial steps in measurement are to (1) clarify the concept one is interested in and (2) construct what is known as an operational definition of that concept. An individual's social class is often operationally defined by income level, educational attainment is usually measured by years of formal schooling, sexual promiscuity is gauged by number of sexual partners, and political party preference is measured by one's expressed attitudes toward Democrats and Republicans. As illustrated by these examples, the process of operationalization and measurement involves the attachment of a specific meaning to abstract concepts.

The accuracy of many measures of social phenomena, however, is both context and time specific. Sexual promiscuity, for example, was judged by different standards in the Victorian period of the 1800s, the "free love" era of the 1960s, and the current period. Similarly, our working definitions of crime are context and historically specific. Prostitution, alcohol use, and drug use may be differentially evaluated as "serious" crime, depending on the geographic location and historical period, the political circumstances, and the prevailing legal structures. Although illegal in most of the United States, prostitution is legal in certain jurisdictions in the state of Nevada. The consumption and sale of alcohol are legal in the present-day United States, but they were illegal in the 1920s. And although some of the most severe penalties in our criminal code are reserved for users of substances such as cocaine, marijuana, heroin, and methamphetamine, these substances were not illegal in the United States prior to the 20th century. Under these conditions, our choice of a particular working definition and unambiguous indicator of a concept becomes more difficult.

Selecting precise indicators of abstract concepts is a crucial step in attempting to operationalize any social phenomena. Within this process, two fundamental properties of good measurement exist: reliability and validity. Reliability is concerned with questions related to the stability and consistency of measurement over repeat trials, and validity refers to the extent of congruence between the operational definition and the concept it purports to measure.

Reliability and validity are easily demonstrated when we consider the measurement of intelligence. If a test of intelligence sometimes yields a high intelligence quotient (IQ) and at other times a low IQ for the same individual, the test would be considered unreliable because it failed to achieve consistent results over repeated trials. An intelligence test would have questionable validity if there were differences in its ability to accurately measure the intellectual capacity of individuals from different cultures or races or both. In fact, one of the major criticisms of standard intelligence tests is their low validity because they are not culturally sensitive (i.e., the test does not measure intelligence but instead indicates one's adaptation to middle-class culture). Although a valid measure can be unreliable, a reliable measure is not necessarily valid (e.g., a thermometer is a reliable measure of temperature but an invalid measure of social class).

Reliability and Validity in Survey Research

Many of the social measures and indicators we discuss in this chapter and two of the most frequently used measures of crime and delinquency—self-report and victimization studies—rely on surveys of various segments of the general public to collect data and to construct measures. A number of issues related to survey methodology encourage caution in interpreting the results of studies employing this methodology. These include problems in sampling and response rates to surveys, questionnaire format and wording, and interviewer effects.

Survey methodology is based on probability sampling theory. The basic principle is that a randomly selected, relatively small percentage of a population can be used to represent the attitudes, opinions, or behaviors of all people in the population if the sample is selected correctly. The key to being able to generalize to the larger population from a smaller sample is related to a fundamental principle in sampling theory known as equal probability of selection. This simply means that each member of the population has an equal, or at least known, chance of being chosen to participate in the survey. It is instructive to discuss the principles of probability sampling in the context of the frequent public opinion polls conducted in the United States by organizations such as Gallup and Roper.

In telephone surveys conducted by such organizations, the usual goal is to generalize the results of the survey to all adults, 18 years of age and older, living within the continental United States (Newport, Saad, and Moore 1997). However, such surveys generally do not cover individuals living in institutions, including college students who live on campus, armed forces personnel living on military bases, prisoners, hospital patients, and others living in group settings or housing. The procedure organizations such as Gallup use is to obtain a computerized list of all telephone exchanges in the United States, accompanied by estimates of the number of residential households attached to those exchanges. Then, through a procedure known as random digit dialing (RDD), a computer is used to generate a list of telephone numbers. This random digit dialing procedure is important in the context of obtaining a representative sample, because without it, the esti-

mated 30 percent of households in the United States that have unlisted
phone numbers would not be included in the sampling frame.

The typical sample size for public opinion polls is between 1,000 and
1,500 respondents. However, the actual number of people interviewed in a
survey is much less important than adherence to the equal probability of
selection principle. As Newport et al. (1997) note, if respondents are not
selected according to equal probability of selection principles, it would be
possible to conduct a survey with a million people that could turn out to be
less representative of the population than a survey conducted with only
1,000 individuals.

The accuracy of estimates derived from these samples is also based on
probability theory. With the typical sample size of 1,000, the results are
highly likely to accurately represent the true population value within a
margin of error of plus or minus three percentage points. For example, the
results of a Gallup poll released in May of 1998 indicated that 64 percent of
the U.S. public were familiar with the erectile dysfunction drug Viagra,
which had been placed on the market only a few months earlier. This survey
also revealed that 13 percent of the men interviewed indicated they would
like to try the drug within the next year. Interestingly, 15 percent of the
women answered that they would like their husband to try Viagra in the
next year (Saad 1998). The margin of error indicates that the true rating of
women who would like their husbands to try Viagra was somewhere between 12 and 18 percent. If the sample size for this survey was increased to
2,000, the results would be accurate within plus or minus two percentage
points of the true population value, but the cost of conducting the survey
would double.

Another important issue in assessing the reliability and validity of survey
results is related to rates of response—what is also referred to as "contact
and cooperation" (Singer and Presser 1989): the correspondence between
the sample elements selected and those actually interviewed. In recent
years, survey researchers have become concerned about the phenomenon
of declining response rates to surveys, which can result in biased samples
and thereby inaccurate measures or estimates. At least part of the reason for
the general public's lack of willingness to participate in survey research is
the proliferation of entities, both private and government, engaged in survey research. For example, the number of telemarketing firms increased
from 30,000 in 1985 to more than 600,000 in 1995, and according to indus-
try sources, more than 25 million solicitation calls are made in a single day
(Bearden 1998). According to a 1994 study, one in three potential respondents refuses to participate in a survey, and even for respondents who do

participate in surveys occasionally, 38 percent had refused to participate in at least one in the previous year. More generally, it is estimated that from 1990 to 2000, the response rate to telephone surveys declined from approximately 40 percent to 15 percent (Lewis 2000). In most cases, data resulting from surveys with poor response rates can be assumed to be unrepresentative and biased, because the respondents are likely to be self-selected and different in a number of unknown ways from those who do not respond. Unfortunately, many researchers take whatever data they collect, analyze it, and derive conclusions without any consideration of the issue of nonresponse bias. A prime example of the problems that can result from inattention to issues of nonresponse bias occurred in 1985, when the Committee on Health and Long-Term Care issued a report that referred to the abuse of elderly persons in the United States as "a national disgrace." This report cited research claiming that an estimated 4 percent, or 1 million elderly persons, were victims of abuse each year. However, this estimate was based on a survey of 433 elderly residents of Washington, D.C., of whom only 73, or 16 percent of the original sample, responded. Three of these 73 respondents, representing 4.1 percent, reported experiencing some form of psychological, physical, or material abuse. The report then extrapolated from this small and undoubtedly unrepresentative sample to assert that 1 million elderly people were victims of abuse, "thereby constructing a national epidemic out of these three incidents" (Gilbert 1997:112).

The Census Bureau has a high level of respect and is admired for the quality of its data collection policies and procedures. Census Bureau staff are well trained, many of the leading experts in research methodology have direct contact with the national agency, sampling designs are among the most sophisticated in the world, statisticians that work with Census staff possess state-of-the-art knowledge about population estimation, and rigorous pretesting is conducted before actual data collection begins. But even the census, conducted every 10 years in the United States, which is intended to represent a full enumeration of the population, is subject to nonresponse bias and other problems in counting the population.[1] In 1970, the first year that government officials administered the initial part of the census by mail, 83 percent of households returned the questionnaire. In 1980, the rate of return had declined to 75 percent, and by 1990, it was only 65 percent. For the 2000 census, 67 percent of the households that received the form returned it (Holmes 2000). More important, these rates of response vary across geographical regions of the United States and across different sociodemographic categories of the population. Due to nonresponse bias and other problems in enumerating the entire population, it is estimated that the 2000 census did not count between 1.6 and 2.7 percent of black residents and between 2.2 and 3.5 percent of Hispanics. A further 2.8 to 6.7 percent of Native Americans living on reservations were also not counted (Holmes 2001). Interestingly, the population of one town in rural Pennsylvania was missed entirely in the 2000 census. The 14 people who live in the town of Slovenska Nardona Podporna Jednota apparently were not around when the census taker visited—they thought she would come back, but she did not. As a result, the town's population for the year 2000 is listed as zero (*New York Times* 2001). In total, it is estimated that the 2000 census did not count between 6.4 and 8.6 million people living in the United States.

The reverse problem with census data is that of overcounting. It was estimated that more than 4 million people were in fact counted twice in the 2000 census (Holmes 2001). Those who are counted twice tend to be children of divorced parents, college students living away from home who independently fill out census forms but are also listed by their parents, and people with two homes who receive forms in the mail at both of their dwellings. This potentially large overcount is also related to the fact that for the 2000 census, forms were available at convenience stores and government agencies, and respondents were able to provide information over the telephone. The Census Bureau also engaged in a $102 million dollar prime-time advertising campaign to prompt individuals to participate. The issues associated with an accurate enumeration of the population are by no means trivial, because census data are used to determine how seats in the U.S. House of Representatives will be apportioned, to draw congressional and state legislative district boundaries, to allocate state and federal funds, to formulate a wide array of public policies, and to assist with planning and decision making in the private sector.

Reliability and Validity Issues Related to the Questionnaire and Respondents

A number of factors related to the survey instrument itself and the individuals responding to survey questions affect the reliability and validity of results from this method of data collection. Three of these will be covered here: question wording effects, question order effects, and response effects.

Question Wording Effects

A study of wording effects using data from the General Social Survey compared two different versions of questions on government spending priorities and revealed systematic differences in responses. When respondents were asked if they supported increased spending on "welfare," only 32 percent answered in the affirmative. However, when respondents were asked whether there should be "more assistance for the poor," 62 percent favored increased spending (Smith 1989). Another example of the effects of question wording and response options comes from studies examining support for capital punishment in the United States. An opinion poll conducted by Gallup in February of 2001 found that 67 percent of the U.S. population favored capital punishment. However, when interviewers asked whether the penalty for murder should be execution *or* life in prison with no possibility of parole, support for capital punishment declined to 54 percent (Jones 2001).

Question Order Effects

The order in which questions are asked also can have an impact on responses. For example, in a poll conducted before the 2000 U.S. presidential election to determine the popularity of candidates Gore and Bush, respondents were asked to state their preference for president after having responded to a question that asked them to evaluate then President Clinton "as a person." This ordering of questions resulted in a lower level of support for Gore, probably because the question about Clinton reminded respondents of the Monica Lewinsky scandal and led them to disapprove of his vice president as well. However, when the company conducting the poll reordered the questions and surveyed a new sample, support for Gore increased (Harwood and Crossen 2000).

Response Effects

Data from the 2000 census are also relevant to the issue of response effects. One of the most important characteristics of the U.S. population that the census attempts to measure accurately is its racial composition.[2] Although race is a social construct, the racial composition of various jurisdictions in the United States has important implications for economic and social policies. The 2000 census was the first in which people in the United States were allowed to identify themselves as belonging to more than one racial group; the six racial categories created a total of 63 possible racial combinations for respondents to self-identify. Results from the 2000 census indicate that fully 6.8 million people identified themselves as multiracial, and although 93 percent of these classified themselves into only two racial categories, 823 respondents actually checked all six racial categories

(Kasindorf and El Nasser 2001). With respect to the same question, people who indicated that they were "some other race" were asked to write in a particular race. Answers included Bolivian, Bushwacker, Cosmopolitan, and Aryan (Scott 2001).

The American Indian category offers an interesting glimpse into the complications created by the change in census racial classifications. The number of American Indians and Alaska natives who defined themselves only by that category increased by 26 percent between 1990 and 2000. However, when the number of people who claimed they were part Indian is added, the total increased to 4.1 million, representing a 110 percent increase in the number of American Indians since 1990 (Schmitt 2001). However, it is not clear that all of those who identified themselves as Native American legitimately fall into that category. An informal survey conducted by a newspaper in Spokane, Washington, for example, found that some individuals marked the Native American category "as a way to tell the U.S. Census Bureau to mind its own business." Others apparently identified themselves as Native American "because they were born in the United States" (McDonald 2001). More important, racial composition data from the 2000 census will not be directly comparable with previous census figures, and the ability to track the progress of racial groups with respect to their educational, occupational, health, and income characteristics will become far more problematic.

Although it may seem straightforward, even the classification of gender in a census can be ambiguous. In Canada, a transsexual person refused to answer the question, "Are you male or female," on that country's 2001 census. This individual, who was born a male but was taking hormones and had breasts and male genitals, noted that "my gender was not listed" (Raphael 2001).

A related problem has characterized the U.S. census with respect to identifying the number of households occupied by gay couples. In 1990, a person who shared a household with an individual of the same sex and also reported being married created a problem for census data-coders because the Census Bureau did not recognize same-sex marriages. To make the responses consistent, the Census Bureau changed either the person's sex or his or her relationship to the other person, because "if they said they were married and had a spouse of the same sex, the simple thing was to change the spouse's sex. We made them a married couple" (Spencer, quoted in Peterson, 2001). At least partially as a result of changes in this procedure in the 2000 census such that gay and lesbian householders could claim an unmarried partner and then identify his or her sex, there was a "huge increase" (Peterson 2001) in the numbers of gay households identified in 2000.

Errors in questionnaire data are also associated with response styles—the tendency to choose a certain category when responding to a question—regardless of the content of the item. For example, in the frequently used "agree-disagree" format on questionnaires, some respondents may be characterized by an acquiescence response set: the tendency to agree with a question, regardless of its content (Singleton and Straits 1999). A second response style is referred to as social desirability: the tendency to choose those response options most favorable to an individual's self-esteem or in accord with prevailing social norms, regardless of one's real position on the given question. Some have argued that social desirability effects may explain why comparisons of survey data over time reveal a general decline in overt expressions of racially prejudiced attitudes (Quillian 1996).

Additional response problems are related to issues of memory, and in this context, two types of errors can be distinguished: forgetting and telescoping in time. With respect to telescoping, events and behaviors are reported as having happened more recently than they actually did. This form of response error is particularly relevant in the context of self-report and victimization surveys, which are addressed in Chapters 3 and 4 of this book.

The very real possibility also exists that respondents, for a number of different reasons, may be somewhat less than truthful in responding to questionnaires; the evidence regarding lying on questionnaires is well documented. In a 1950 study, Parry and Crossley asked individuals a number of questions in situations where the accuracy of their answers could be assessed. The proportion of honest answers ranged from 98 percent on a question asking whether the respondents had a telephone to approximately 50 percent on one that asked about their voting behavior. McCord (1951) similarly demonstrated that people will sometimes lie when they are asked questions about things that do not exist: one third of his sample claimed they had voted in a special election that in fact never was held. Studies also suggest that between 33 and 45 percent of respondents will lie when they are asked about their level of education, and about half when they are asked whether they have received welfare assistance (Nettler 1978). In addition, some studies have suggested that the tendency to be less than truthful may vary according to the racial/ethnic and gender characteristics of respondents (Mensch and Kandel 1988).

Some surveys of criminal behavior and drug use, which will be addressed in more detail in Chapter 4, have discovered that minority groups have a greater tendency to underreport these behaviors. One explanation of this tendency is that minorities feel more threatened or are made uneasy when asked to report on delinquent activities. Whatever the possible reasons for this underreporting, researchers conducting studies and those reporting on the results of such studies need to be aware of the possibility of biases resulting from these tendencies.

A more general concern with respect to survey research is related to respondents' general knowledge. Public opinion polls have shown that many people in the United States are unaware that there are three branches of government in the United States; significant numbers of the U.S. population believe that Brazil is the capital of Ohio, and approximately 18 percent believe that the sun circles the earth (*USA Today* 1997). In the 1989 General Social Survey, 61 percent of respondents did not feel they were able to rank the social standing of "Wisians." However, 39 percent were able to rank this group, and they provided Wisians with a rather low average rating of 4.12 on a 9-point social ranking scale (*Seattle Post-Intelligencer* 1992). Wisians were a fictitious ethnic group, added by the designers of the General Social Survey to test the honesty of respondents in answering questions.

In short, all data derived from survey research are subject to reliability and validity problems. An intelligent consumer of such data will pay attention to these issues before uncritically accepting the findings from survey research.

Measuring Crime and Deviance

We now move on to a consideration of issues that are more directly relevant to the main topic of this book: the measurement of crime and deviant behavior. We begin with a discussion of the problems associated with measuring crime on college campuses, followed by a consideration of how questionable measures of the extent of drug consumption have been used to create alleged drug "epidemics" with resulting policy changes.

Measuring College Campus Crime

Since the 1990s, numerous states and the federal government have enacted laws requiring colleges and universities to publish crime statistics. The first federal law related to this requirement, known as the Crime Awareness and Campus Security Act, was passed in 1990 (Port and Lesser 1999). As is often the case with legislative proposals in the United States, this law was enacted primarily in response to the occurrence of a single event: the murder of 19-year-old Jeanne Clery at Lehigh University in Pennsylvania in 1986. Clery was a freshman who was assaulted and murdered while asleep in her residence room. When Clery's parents investigated the situation, they discovered that Lehigh University had not informed students about 38 violent crimes that had been committed on the campus in the three years prior to their daughter's murder. The Clerys joined with other campus crime victims and persuaded Congress to enact legislation requiring all colleges and universities to publish statistics on the amount and type of crime on campuses.

As a result of subsequent amendments to this legislation in 1998, institutions must report the incidence of homicide, manslaughter, arson, rape, robbery, aggravated assault, burglary, motor vehicle theft, drug offenses, liquor law violations, and illegal weapons possession. In addition, institutions are required to provide greater detail regarding alleged hate crimes, defined by federal law as incidents that "manifest evidence of prejudice based on race, religion, sexual orientation, or ethnicity." Campuses that do not comply with the legislation face the possibility of fines of up to $25,000 and of losing federal student aid. When data on college crime were first released in the early 1990s, several media outlets invoked rather alarmist language to describe the situation. For example, *U.S. News and World Report* (1994), commenting on the 1993 statistics, alleged that there was an "epidemic" of college campus crime. Similarly, *USA Today* (Henry 1996) referred to "steep increases in crime" in describing the 1994 campus crime statistics. But serious crime on college campuses is exceedingly rare when compared to overall crime rates in the United States—there is less than one homicide for every million students on campus in any given year in the United States.

Problems in the reliability and validity of campus crime data became apparent soon after the federal legislation was enacted. These problems ranged from confusion surrounding how to code particular crimes to outright manipulation of the statistics. A study conducted by the National Center for Education Statistics found that 40 percent of the colleges and universities were using federal definitions of crime to classify their data, 45 percent were using state definitions, and 15 percent were using definitions of their own design (Port and Lesser 1999). A 1997 audit conducted by the U.S. General Accounting Office discovered that only 2 of the 25 colleges examined were correctly reporting their crime statistics. Among other omissions, some colleges were routinely omitting rapes and other sexual assaults that were reported to school officials but not to the police. For example, in September of 1999, the University of Florida admitted withholding 35 rapes from its annual crime reports for the years 1996, 1997, and 1998. Instead of the 12 rapes that were recorded in the official report for this period, the university was aware of 47; however, university officials claimed that they believed that rapes reported to a victims' advocacy group should not be counted (Port and Lesser 1999).

Perhaps the most notorious example of the manipulation of campus crime statistics occurred at the University of Pennsylvania. In 1996, this university reported 18 robberies in its federally mandated campus security report, whereas the police blotter indicated that 181 robberies had occurred. The apparent reason for this gross discrepancy was that the university had chosen to exclude crimes that had occurred on sidewalks and streets that crossed the campus and in buildings it did not own (Port and Lesser 1999).

Anomalies in the officially recorded data and incidents such as the one that occurred at the University of Pennsylvania resulted in further amendments to the legislation. Beginning in 1998, institutions were required to report crimes occurring on public property that was "reasonably contiguous" to their campuses. Not surprisingly, there was initially considerable confusion on the part of university officials regarding what constituted reasonably contiguous property; it has since been defined as public sidewalks, streets, and parking lots adjacent to a campus, or any public property running through the campus.

Comparisons of crime data across college campuses in the United States suggest that universities are not adopting the same definitions of contiguous areas, however. For example, campus police at the University of Washington in Seattle expressed skepticism when the 1998 figures on campus crime were released. In that year, the University of Southern California, located in the middle of a high-crime area of South Central Los Angeles, recorded only 4 assaults, whereas the University of Washington recorded 93 (Rivera 2000). In 1999, the University of Washington's 127 drug arrests placed it fourth in the nation. However, campus police noted that the arrest sometimes involved street people and individuals who wandered onto the campus (Rivera 2001). The perils associated with uninformed comparisons of these data are also revealed when we consider the situation of colleges and universities with branch campuses. The 1997 report for the University of Idaho, located in a rural area of the state, indicated that seven rapes had occurred on campus in that year. However, the rapes had actually occurred at a smaller branch campus of the university, located in Coeur d'Alene. Similarly, Eastern Washington University, located in a largely rural area of Washington state, recorded 74 aggravated assaults in 1997, but the overwhelming majority of these had occurred in a contiguous area of the university's branch campus in the heart of downtown Spokane (deLeon and Sudermann 2000).

Two additional categories of campus crime to examine are those of alcohol and drug arrests. Between 1997 and 1998, alcohol arrests on college campuses increased by 24.3 percent nationally, whereas arrests for violations of drug legislation increased by 11.1 percent. However, campus law enforcement officials attribute these increases to tougher enforcement of existing drug and alcohol guidelines and changes in the previously mentioned reporting categories stipulating that colleges had to include crimes taking place in reasonably contiguous areas.

At the University of Wisconsin, where arrests for alcohol increased from 342 in 1997 to 792 in 1998, the campus police chief claimed that the 132 percent change was due to the university's hiring more campus police officers who were more vigorous in enforcing the laws. At the University of North Carolina at Greensboro, which experienced more than a 700 percent increase in drug arrests between 1997 and 1998, the increases were attributed to the expanded geographical area for which crimes were recorded; of the 132 drug arrests in 1998, 88 occurred on public property near the campus and 17 in residence halls, areas the college had not included in its 1997 report (Nicklin 2000).

There has also been considerable confusion regarding the procedures for counting these drug and alcohol arrests. The University of New Hampshire at Durham was unable to meet the Department of Education's reporting deadline of October 24 for their 1997 and 1998 data. When officials at the university asked the Department of Education how to deal with this problem, they were told to record no offenses for these categories. As a result, an uninformed perusal of the "official data" for the University of New Hampshire would lead one to believe that this campus had no drug arrests in 1997 and 1998 and 124 in 1999, instead of what actually occurred—56 arrests in 1997 and 85 in 1998 (Nicklin 2000).

In addition to the problems outlined above with respect to counting drug and alcohol crimes or offenses, stipulations in the legislation requiring institutions to report the number of campus disciplinary referrals for violations of alcohol, drug, and weapons law violations have created further confusion. In the 1998 report, several institutions placed arrests and referrals in the same category, creating the illusion of a significant increase in arrests. For example, Wake Forest University reported an increase from 8 to 298 for alcohol-related arrests between 1997 and 1998; however, officials at the university claimed they had made only one liquor arrest—the remaining 297 were referrals (Nicklin 2000).

Given all the problems associated with the collection and coding of these data, it makes little sense to engage in cross-campus and over-time comparisons of the campus crime data.

The CAP Index

An alternative measure and ranking of college campuses with respect to their levels of crime has been created by a risk assessment company. This CAP (crimes against persons) index focuses on crime risk in neighborhoods surrounding college campuses and estimates "the risk of crime for the coming year through a sophisticated computer model that compares socio-economic data to past reports of actual crime" (Port and Lesser 1999). Publication of these CAP index rankings of college campuses has attracted considerable controversy, especially in light of the fact that in 1999, four historically black colleges appeared in the top five most dangerous list and seven historically black colleges were rated in the top ten (Wright 2000). In fact, four of these institutions were located in the same urban neighborhood in Atlanta, and officials from the colleges concerned expressed confusion over the rankings. For example, although it experienced no murders, no sexual assaults, only 6 simple assaults and 17 robberies on its campus from 1996 to 1998 inclusive—hardly indicative of a high level of dangerousness—Morehouse College was ranked as the fifth most dangerous campus in the United States, according to this index. In response to criticism of these rankings, the creators of the CAP index claim that the method is 70 to 90 percent accurate in predicting actual levels of crime. However, the company refused to reveal the precise statistical methods used in creating the index—"that would be like Coca-Cola giving away its formula for Coke" was the claim of the chief executive officer of the company. Without the ability to independently verify the reliability and validity of the various components of this index, however, the rankings that result from it must be treated with skepticism.

Drugs and "Drug Epidemics"

Illegal drugs have been a major concern of policy makers in the United States since the beginning of the 20th century. And, as is the case in other areas of social, economic, and crime policies, competing interests rely on both official and unofficial data to support their respective agendas.

Prior to the 1996 presidential election, incumbent President Bill Clinton presented data from victimization surveys to suggest that there had been a 9 percent decrease in violent crime in the United States and claimed that the decline was due to the effectiveness of his administration's crime policies. Republican candidate Bob Dole saw things differently, and used self-report data from the Federal Department of Health and Human Services to blame Clinton for a doubling of drug use among teenagers. However, the questions used in the 1994 survey that led Dole to attack Clinton were very different from those used in previous drug surveys, and the agency could not ensure that it had successfully adjusted for the differences. Even more important, many of the increases in drug use to which Dole referred were not statistically significant. Heroin use by teenagers, for example, superficially doubled from 0.3 percent in 1994 to 0.7 percent in 1995, but the actual number of users in the sample of 4,600 surveyed had increased from only 14 to 32 (Schoor 1996).

An additional example of the confusion that can be caused by uninformed comparisons of drug use statistics comes from the 1999 Report of the Office of National Drug Control Policy. That report claimed that there were 1.5 million people in the United States who had used cocaine in the previous month. However, the same document claimed that 3.6 million people in the United States had used cocaine in the past week (Caulkins 2000). Clearly, these estimates are highly inconsistent and difficult to reconcile. The explanation for the large discrepancy in these estimates is that the first was based exclusively on data from the National Household Survey on Drug Abuse, whereas the latter included data from the Drug Use Forecasting program, which collects self-reports of drug use among arrestees in local jails, who are more likely to use drugs.

Questionable official and unofficial data on drug use are frequently used to justify changes in drug policies. An interesting example of this phenomenon occurred in 2000 and 2001, when the popular media published hundreds of articles on an alleged epidemic in the use of the drug ecstasy (MDMA). A March 5, 2001 editorial, written by former federal drug czar William Bennett (2001), claimed that "while the crack cocaine epidemic of the 1990s has passed, methamphetamine and ecstasy are growing in popularity, especially among the young." Bennett did not provide statistics, official or otherwise, to support his claim of this increase in the use of ecstasy. However, a survey that was widely cited in the media, conducted under the auspices of the Partnership for a Drug Free America, reported that the percentage of teenagers using ecstasy had doubled between 1995 and 2000—from 5 to 10 percent.

Given the paucity of additional self-report data on the use of ecstasy, especially by adults, media sources relied on alternative measures, such as reported seizures of ecstasy tablets, reports of law enforcement officials, and emergency room admission data, to support their claim of an "alarming explosion" (Rashbaum 2000) in the use of MDMA. The commissioner of the U.S. Customs Service claimed that seizures of ecstasy by his agency had increased from 350,000 pills in 1997 to 3.5 million in 1999, then to 2.9 million in just the first two months of 2000. He projected that seizures would amount to 7 or 8 million by the end of 2000. An *Associated Press* article (Hays 2000) suggested that "seizures of the tablets . . . have multiplied like rabbits." An article in *USA Today* (2001a) noted that "ecstasy, a drug once used primarily at nightclubs, has expanded beyond the club scene and is being sold at high schools, on the street, and even at coffee shops in some cities." The source of these claims of ecstasy use spreading to previously unknown contexts was an informal convenience survey of officials in 20 cities in the United States, 80 percent of whom said that ecstasy was "more available than ever."

An additional measure of the alleged increase in ecstasy use came from the federal Drug Abuse Warning Network (DAWN), which tracks hospital room emergency admissions. Rashbaum (2000) reported that mentions of the drug in this source increased from 68 in 1993 to 637 in 1997 (the latest year for which statistics were available).

Despite the questionable validity of the statistics used to document this ecstasy epidemic, in March of 2001, the U.S. Sentencing Commission enacted harsh new penalties for MDMA. These penalties treat ecstasy offenders more severely than cocaine offenders, resulting in a 5-year sentence for individuals selling 200 grams (approximately 800 pills) of the substance and a 10-year sentence for those selling 2,000 grams or more (Lindesmith Center 2001). These legislative changes were enacted despite the opposition of many medical experts and researchers, who argued that the substance was far less likely to cause violence than drugs such as alcohol and was less addictive than cocaine or tobacco. Advocates of the increased penalties argued that these were necessary to curb ecstasy use by teenagers and young adults (*Washington Post* 2001).

Apparently, ecstasy has become a growing problem in Canada as well. In May of 2000, a drug enforcement officer from Toronto claimed, "I believe ecstasy has reached epidemic proportions in this country" (as quoted in Godfrey 2000). Given similar problems with respect to the availability of current statistics on the actual extent of ecstasy use, the Canadian media also relied extensively on seizure figures to support the claim that ecstasy use had increased. In an article appearing in the *National Post*, Grey (2000) reported that seizures of ecstasy in Canada had doubled between 1998 and

1999. Police across the country seized 712,000 ecstasy tablets in 1999, with an estimated street value of between $17.8 and $28.5 million. The article also claimed that it was becoming "common knowledge" among law enforcement officials and researchers that ecstasy was "the drug of choice across demographic lines." In May of 2000, several Canadian newspapers announced that the largest seizure of ecstasy in Canadian history had taken place at Pearson International Airport in Toronto. Police reported that they had seized 170,000 ecstasy tablets, valued at $5 million. However, it turned out that police had made a mathematical error in their calculations, weighing the quantity of pills per pound instead of per kilogram. Thus, the actual seizure was 61,000 tablets, valued at $1.8 million. Ben Soave, a superintendent for the Royal Canadian Mounted Police, noted, "It's one of those unfortunate situations. It was an error that we made and we're only human. So I apologize for that" (as quoted in Alphonso 2000). The ecstasy problem was given further publicity when testimony given at an inquest into the death of a Toronto youth alleged that 13 deaths had been caused by the substance during a three-year period beginning in 1998. Although these ecstasy-related deaths were widely published in the media, it was eventually determined that seven of the deaths were the result of individuals using drug "cocktails," mixtures of heroin, cocaine, and methadone (Freed 2000). Although as of March 2001, no federal or provincial legislation had been enacted in Canada to deal with the ecstasy "problem," a "Raves Act" for the city of Toronto was proposed in May of 2000. This legislation would have defined a rave as a dance event occurring between 2:00 a.m. and 6:00 a.m. for which admission was charged. It would have increased police powers of arrest in situations where drugs were sold at such events and allowed them to terminate the event if illegal acts were occurring (Freed 2000). We need to question whether it is good public policy to change policies based on such questionable data.

To conclude, it is clear that the data we have addressed in this chapter are subject to reliability and validity problems and are also subject to varying interpretations. And although such data are frequently used to draw attention to social problems and issues, to theoretically explain the causes of these problems, and to influence policies to deal with them, it is important to remain critical of the construction of these measures. As Campbell (1971, as cited in Johnston and Carley 1981) argued, "The more any social indicator is used for decision-making, the more subject it will be to corrupting pressures and the more apt it will be to distort and corrupt the social processes it is intended to monitor." More specific to crime data, Gurr (1977) notes that in the interpretation of crime data, it is necessary to "disentangle the social reality of behavioral change from the political and administrative reality of change in the institutions which respond to and record behavioral change" (p. 117).

The Design of This Book

How we measure, but too often mismeasure, crime and delinquency/deviance is the general topic of this book. This chapter introduced the primary constraints on constructing useful measurements of any social phenomena while illustrating those constraints with specific examples from research efforts on crime and deviance. Chapter 2 offers a historical overview of the measurement of crime, paying particular attention to the evolution from official data to self-report studies to victimization surveys. We see that many of the shortcomings characteristic of contemporary data on crime were identified by social scientists writing in the late 1800s and early to mid-1900s. Chapter 3 focuses on official measures of crime based on data compiled by local, state, and federal law enforcement agencies and examines problems associated with the collection and interpretation of these data. Chapter 4 reviews self-reported measures of criminal as well as deviant activity and, in the process, provides an overview of the methodology—survey research—used to collect both self-report and victimization data on crime. Chapter 5 describes victimization surveys in detail, highlighting the advantages as well as the disadvantages of measuring crime on the basis of victim accounts. The final chapter in this book moves us from the realm of describing various measures (and mismeasures) of crime and delinquency/deviance to the province of applying these measures to particular situations. Here we see that accurate and appropriate measurement is absolutely essential in testing explanations or theories of criminal behavior and in developing crime prevention or control policies.

Notes

1. Although the task of enumerating the entire population of a country such as the United States is monumental, consider the situation of China. In that country, with an estimated population of 1.3 billion, the census is conducted through face-to-face interviews by more than 10 million volunteers and government workers. In the past, social and political issues have affected the accuracy of popu-

lation counts in China. Demographers estimate that between 20 million and 100 million people are left out of the count due to evasion of household taxes and child-bearing restrictions, which limit urban families to a single child and rural families to two children if their firstborn is a girl (Chang 2000).

2. In the first U.S. census, conducted in 1790, blacks were counted as three fifths of a person and Native Indians were not counted at all (Anderson and Fienberg 1999).

Chapter Two

The History of
Measuring Crime

*There were, of course, crimes before statisticians occupied this territory,
but it may be doubted whether there were crime rates.*

Porter (1995:37)

The 20th century has been referred to as "the First Measured Century" (Public Broadcasting System 2000). During the past 100 years or so, U.S. citizens became "the most energetic measurers of social life that ever lived. . . . They pioneered the measurement of facets of American life that had never been systematically counted before, such as crime, love, food, fun, religion, and work" (Caplow, Hicks, and Wattenberg 2000). Just a few examples will illustrate the range of topics measured: in 1900, approximately 1 in 6 infants died before his or her first birthday, compared to 1 in 141 in 1999; less than 1 out of 10 men was unmarried in 1900, compared to 1 out of 3 in 1997; only 13 percent of U.S. adolescents completed high school in 1900, compared with 83 percent in 1998; in 1904, there were 69 state and federal prisoners per 100,000 population, whereas the corresponding rate was 462 in 1992.

It is certainly true that the measurement of social phenomena has become more sophisticated and extensive over time. Today's general public is

virtually bombarded with information on an ever-expanding range of topics, yet such measurement has a long history, dating to the beginning of
Greek and Roman civilizations. More to the point here, although the first
national police statistics in the United States were not published until 1930,
alternative measures of crime appeared much earlier, both in the United
States and in other nations.

In this chapter, we discuss the development of statistics on crime, both
cross-nationally and historically. We first address "official" statistics on
crime, examining their sources and how they were often used uncritically
by social scientists and individuals who wrote articles in the popular media
to comment on crime and its causes. We then move to a discussion of how a
growing realization of the inadequacies of these official statistics led to the
development of alternative measures of crime and delinquency. Several
social scientists became concerned about how official crime data were generated, noting that uncritical analyses of these statistics could result in misleading conclusions regarding the causes of crime. In particular, they noted
problems related to the so-called dark figure of crime, that is, crimes
committed by individuals that were not recorded in the official data. These
concerns led first to the development of self-report studies of deviant and
criminal behavior beginning in the 1940s, followed by the emergence of
victimization studies in the 1960s. The use of these alternative measures of
crime data led to important theoretical and policy debates within the discipline of criminology and, some would argue, a fundamental shift in the
focus of criminology as a discipline.

The Early History of Measuring
Social Phenomena and Crime

Number, weight, and measure are the foundations of all exact science;
neither can any branch of human knowledge be held advanced beyond
its infancy which does not, in some way or other, frame its theories or
correct its practice by reference to those elements. What astronomical
records or meteorological registers are to a rational explanation of the
movements of the planets or of the atmosphere, statistical returns are
to social and political philosophy. They assign, at determinate intervals, the numerical values of the variables which form the subject
matter of its reasonings, or at least of such "functions" of them as are
accessible to direct observation; which it is the business of sound theory
so to analyze or to combine as to educe from them those deeper-

seated elements which enter into the expression of general laws. (Herschel 1850, as cited in Duncan 1984:97)

Perhaps the earliest examples of social measurement consist of censuses (taken from the Latin word *censere*, meaning to tax or assess) of the population. These have existed in one form or another for thousands of years; there are records of taxpaying homes recorded in China as far back as 2275 B.C., and Egyptians registered their citizens from as early as 1400 B.C. (Storey 1997). The early Roman census process required individuals to declare their age, family, and property holdings, which allowed the administration to record and rank the jurisdiction's human and property resources. These early censuses were primarily used to determine the number of men available to fight in the military and for tax purposes; the data were not generally used for public policy making, as is common in the current period.

In the 1700s, the purpose of census taking shifted to the creation of a statistical database for studying social and economic trends and, in some cases, developing policies based on these trends. The first census in the United States, conducted in 1790, was different from censuses in other countries that had preceded it in that it was an important part of government and was required by the Constitution. The data for this initial U.S. census were collected by 16 federal marshals, who had considerable difficulty in enumerating the population because residents were concentrated in widely dispersed rural areas. In many cases, the marshals had to use word of mouth to find out about the existence of households in remote areas. Additional problems included a lack of cooperation on the part of residents, who were often suspicious of the questions being asked (*History of the United States Census* 2000).

In addition to census taking in several countries, social data were collected in the context of periodic "surveys" conducted by social scientists. For example, in the 19th century, the British social activists Henry Mayhew and Charles Booth conducted extensive surveys of England's population. Booth's survey sought to investigate "the numerical relation which poverty, misery, and depravity bear to the regular earnings and comparative comfort, and to describe the general conditions under which each class lives" (as cited in Biderman and Reiss 1967).

The first national crime statistics, based on judicial data, were published in France in 1827 (covering the year 1825). These early crime statistics were part of the "moral statistics" movement that emerged in several Western nations in the 1800s. They were also very much a result of the belief that the quantitative techniques being applied to measure phenomena in the physical world could also be applied to the measurement of human phenomena. These data were used in the earliest studies of the spatial and temporal distributions of crime as well as for analyses of the sex, age, income, education, and occupation of criminals.

In France, Adolphe Quetelet, who had originally worked in the field of astronomy, was one of the early moral statisticians who believed that it would be possible to uncover the types of laws and regularities in social phenomena that were emerging from scientific explorations in the natural world. Writing in the 1800s, Quetelet was one of the first commentators to recognize the so-called dark figure of crime. He noted, "All we possess of statistics of crime and misdemeanors would have no utility at all if we did not tacitly assume that there is a nearly invariable relationship between offenses known and adjudicated and the total unknown sum of offenses committed" (as quoted in Sellin and Wolfgang 1964). According to Quetelet (as cited in Coleman and Moynihan 1996), this dark figure was related not only to the seriousness of the crime but also to "the activity of justice in reaching the guilty, on the care with which the latter will take in hiding themselves, and on the repugnance which wronged individuals will feel in complaining, or on the ignorance in which perhaps they will be concerning the wrong which has been done to them" (p. 5).

Based on judicial statistics from France, Quetelet (1842) observed a consistency in crime rates in that country between the years 1826 and 1829 (see Exhibit 2.1). There was 1 accused person for every 4,463 inhabitants over this period, and for every 100 accused, there were 61 individuals "condemned" (in prison). He observed a similar consistency in the ratio between crimes recorded and crimes prosecuted for Belgium between 1826 and 1830. The ratio in that country was 1 accused person for every 5,031 inhabitants. These data led Quetelet to conclude that the ratio of known to unknown offenses was fairly constant over time. However, he was also aware that this ratio of recorded to actual crime would differ according to offense type. He noted that "in a well organized society where the police [are] active and justice is rightly administered, this ratio, for murders and assassinations, will be nearly equal to unity . . . [but] when we look to thefts and offenses of smaller importance, the ratio will become very small, and a great number of offenses will remain unknown, either because those against whom they are committed do not perceive them, or do not wish to prosecute the perpetrator" (p. 82).

In his attempt to explain these crime rates, Quetelet conducted a number of analyses that focused on a variety of factors. Similar to some current theories of crime, he noted the relationship between the consumption of

Exhibit 2.1. Quetelet's Analyses of Crime in France and Belgium

France

Year	Accused Persons	Condemned Persons	Inhabitants/ Accused	Condemned/ Accused	Property Crimes	Person Crimes
1826	6,998	4,348	4,557	62	5,081	1,907
1827	6,929	4,236	4,593	61	5,018	1,911
1828	7,396	4,551	4,307	61	5,552	1,844
1829	7,373	4,475	4,321	61	5,582	1,791
Total/ Average	28,696	17,610	4,463	61	21,233	7,453

Belgium

Year	Accused Persons	Condemned Persons	Inhabitants/ Accused	Condemned/ Accused	Property Crimes	Person Crimes
1826	725	611	5,211	84	536	189
1827	800	682	4,776	85	580	220
1828	814	677	4,741	83	584	230
1829	753	612	5,187	81	550	203
1830	741	541	5,274	73	581	160
Average	767	625	5,031	82	566	200

SOURCE: Quetelet, L. A. J. 1842. Treatise on Man and the Development of His Faculties. Edinburgh: S. W. & R. Chambers.

alcohol and violent crime: "Of 1,129 murders committed in France during the space of four years, 446 have been in consequence of quarrels and contentions in taverns; which would tend to show the fatal influence in the use of strong drinks" (p. 96). Quetelet also emphasized the importance of poverty and relative inequality: "[These factors] give rise to crime, particularly if those who suffer are surrounded by materials of temptation, and are irritated by the continual aspect of luxury and inequality of fortune, which renders them desperate" (pp. 88-9). This impact of inequality was greater in urban areas: "The great cities . . . present an unfavorable subject, because they possess more allurements to passions of every kind, and because they attract people of bad character, who hope to mingle with impunity in the crowd" (pp. 88-9).

Quetelet also examined the importance of "racial" composition, noting that France's population was comprised of three different races—the Celtic, German, and Pelasgian—which were concentrated in different regions of the country. He asserted that the Pelasgian race, located primarily in the southern portion of France, was "particularly addicted to crimes against persons," whereas members of the Germanic race were most likely to be involved in property crimes, apparently because individuals from this group were more commonly engaged in "the frequent use of strong drinks" (p. 90).

Similar to contemporary analyses of crime, Quetelet also examined the correlates of crime, with a particular focus on gender and age. He noted that in France, there were 26 women for every 100 men accused of crimes against property, compared to 16 women for every 100 men accused of crimes against persons (see Exhibit 2.2). He argued that these differences were attributable to the fact that women were "more under the influence of sentiments of shame and modesty, as far as morals are concerned; their dependent state, and retired habits, as far as occasion or opportunity is concerned; and their physical weakness, as far as the facility of acting is concerned" (p. 91). Noting that women were more likely to commit serious violent offenses against intimates as opposed to strangers, Quetelet asserted, "They can only conceive and execute guilty projects on individuals with whom they are in the greatest intimacy; thus, compared with man, her assassinations are more often in her family than out of it."

With respect to the relationship between age and involvement in crime, Quetelet argued that "of all the causes which influence the development of the propensity to crime, or which diminish that propensity, age is unquestionably the most energetic" (p. 92). Similar to current explanations of the age correlate of crime, he suggested that crimes against property were more likely to be committed by those in the younger age groups, whereas crimes against persons evidenced a later age peak; his data from France indicated that these crimes peaked at age 25.

More generally, Quetelet's early studies of the numerical consistency of crimes stimulated theoretical discussions of the causes of crime, contributing in particular to theories that focused on the relative importance of free will versus social determinism in explaining individual criminal behavior. If crime were determined by social forces, then explanations of crime that invoked the free will of individuals were not plausible. He argued that "every thing which pertains to the human species considered as a whole, belongs to the order of physical facts; the greater the number of individuals, the more does the influence of individual will disappear, leaving predominance to a series of general facts, dependent on causes by which society exists and is preserved" (p. 90).

Quetelet was active for nearly half a century in the attempt to measure social phenomena statistically, so much of his work is generally known. Other important and, for their time, innovative studies preceded his work but have not received considerable attention. For example, M. de Guerry Champneuf, who served as director of criminal affairs for the Ministry of

Exhibit 2.2. Male and Female Crime Comparisons (France 1826-29)

Type of Crime	Male	Female	Women to 100 Men
Infanticide	30	426	1,320
Miscarriage	15	39	260
Poisoning	77	73	91
House robbery	2,648	1,602	60
Parricide	44	22	50
Incendiarism of building	279	94	34
Robbery of churches	176	47	27
Wounding of parents	292	63	22
Theft	10,677	2,249	21
False evidence	307	51	17
Fraudulent bankruptcy	353	57	16
Assassination	947	111	12
False coining/counterfeiting	1,669	177	11
Rebellion	612	60	10
Highway robbery	648	54	8
Wounds and blows	1,447	78	5
Murder	1,112	44	4
Violation and seduction	685	7	1

SOURCE: Quetelet, L. A. J. 1842. Treatise on Man and the Development of His Faculties. Edinburgh: S. W. & R. Chambers.

Justice in France from 1821 to 1835, conducted extensive analyses of crime for 86 "departments" in France. Similar to Quetelet, Guerry argued that crime rates were determined by larger societal, as opposed to individual-level, factors. He also recognized the important distinctions between types of crime. He created categories for classifying crimes against property versus crimes against the person, with 17 crimes in each category, and calculated age-sex specific crime rates for each. In contrast to Quetelet, Guerry based his measurement of crime on the number of persons accused of crime, as opposed to convictions. He believed that using convictions, which depended on the decisions and whims of juries, would result in a biased picture of the nature and extent of crime (Coleman and Moynihan 1996). Guerry (as cited in Elmer 1933) also discussed what he thought to be the important correlates and causes of crime, noting, "There is the influence of climate, and there is the influence of seasons, for whereas the crimes against persons are always more numerous in the summer, the crimes against property are more numerous in winter" (p. 64).

Other researchers in the moral statistics tradition included Mayr (as cited in Bonger 1916), who, like Guerry, questioned the use of conviction statistics as measures of crime: "The immorality of a people is determined not by the number of individuals convicted, but by the number of crimes committed; else that people would be most moral in which no offender ever let himself be caught, even if more crimes were committed there than elsewhere" (p. 39). Corne (1868, as cited in Bonger 1916), using court statistics as his data source, attributed an increase in crime that occurred in France between the years 1849 and 1853 to a "better organization of the police" (p. 48). Rettich (as cited in Bonger 1916) criticized existing criminal statistics in Germany and the purported causes of crime that were derived from these data because they did not take into account what we now refer to as white-collar crime: "The worst offenses against property are not committed by the hungry. The merchant who goes into a fraudulent bankruptcy, the banker who embezzles deposits, the worldling who forges drafts, have all taken the step into crime from a life, if not of abundance, at least of a competence" (p. 67).

Judicial statistics were first collected in England in 1805, and more standardized judicial statistics recording indictments and convictions for indictable (more serious) offenses were collected annually beginning in 1834. Commentators on these statistics emphasized the importance of exercising caution in interpreting them. Morrison (1892) argued that it was not possible to determine whether crime was increasing or decreasing in England, due to the fact that crime statistics were handled in an "erratic and haphazard manner" (p. 950). He also noted that a primary cause of increases in crime was changes in legislation that added offenses to the criminal code, whereas at the same time, decreases in crime could be attributed to "the abolition of old penal laws, and the greater reluctance of the public and police to set the law in motion against trivial offenders." The influence of legislative changes on crime rates was also emphasized by du Cane (1893), who noted that offenses against the British Education Acts (which required parents to send their children to school), which were not legislatively mandated prior to 1870, totaled over 96,000 in 1890: "Few people [however] would say that 'crime' was increasing and civilization demoralising us because we now compel parents to send their children to school" (p. 486). Du Cane thus argued that an uninformed comparison of crime rates over the 1870-to-1890 period might conclude that crime had increased, when in reality the increase was due to an expansion in the definition of crime.

The earliest crime statistics published on a statewide basis in the United States were judicial statistics from the state of New York in 1829; statewide prison statistics were first collected in Massachusetts in 1834. By 1905, 25 states had enacted legislation providing for statistics on the number of people prosecuted and convicted in their courts (Pepinsky 1976).

Prior to the development of the Uniform Crime Reports (UCR) system in the United States in 1930, the closest thing to national crime statistics was data on individuals committed to jails, houses of correction, and penitentiaries. These statistics were compiled by the Census Bureau beginning in the 1850s; collection continued in the years 1860, 1870, 1880, and 1890, with separate enumerations in 1904, 1910, 1923, and 1933. Focusing on the number of offenders serving sentences on the date the census was taken, information was collected on the sex, race, age, and length of sentence of offenders, among other things. Due to limitations in the way they were collected within jurisdictions, these data were not particularly useful for measuring levels of crime, let alone for the purposes of making comparisons across jurisdictions.

Federal government attention to more refined criminal statistics began in 1870, when Congress passed a law creating the Department of Justice. One section of this legislation provided that it was "the duty of the Attorney-General to make an annual report to Congress ... [on] the statistics of crime under the laws of the United States, and, as far as practicable, under the laws of the several states" (as cited in Maltz 1977). However, as Maltz notes, this provision was basically ignored by law enforcement officials, and it fell into almost immediate disuse.

In the 1920s, certain jurisdictions and states conducted surveys of the criminal justice system. The first of these was conducted in Cleveland in 1922, and surveys at the state level followed in Illinois, New York, Pennsylvania, California, Virginia, Georgia, Minnesota, Michigan, and Oregon (Robinson 1933). Although these studies provided some important insights into the administration of criminal justice, they too were not particularly useful for the purposes of crime measurement and cross-jurisdictional comparisons.

The Development of Uniform Crime Reports in the United States

The statistics compiled by federal bureaucracies enforcing criminal justice are so deficient and incomparable as to render impossible the answering of a single important question about crime.... Statistics of crime ... are of little value because of the lack of uniformity in the definitions of crime, because of the close relation between police work and politics, because of the lack of comparability among categories employed in reporting, because of varying police practices, and because of the absence of centralized reporting (Tibbits 1932:963).

Despite attempts by the Census Bureau to collect crime statistics based on law enforcement data as early as 1907, it was not until 1930 that such statistics became available at the national level. In 1927, a committee of the International Association of Chiefs of Police (IACP) was formed to examine the feasibility of collecting uniform crime records (IACP 1929). In this period, most crime reports produced by state and municipal agencies were virtually useless for comparative purposes. Definitions of crime were not uniform across jurisdictions or even within states, there were no centralized reporting procedures, law enforcement policies varied across jurisdictions, and crime statistics were frequently used for political purposes. In the 1920s, aside from Massachusetts, no state published any statistics on the total number of arrests, and no state released statistics on crimes known to the police. Virtually the only sources of information in the field of police statistics at this time were the annual reports of individual city police departments, with only 14 cities publishing data covering the more serious offenses that were reported to them (Maltz 1977).

Exhibit 2.3, based on data compiled by Monkkonen (1994), reveals some of the vagaries associated with cross-jurisdictional and longitudinal comparisons of early police arrest data. In 1880, arrests for drunkenness offenses ranged from a low of 1,630 per 100,000 population in Cincinnati, Ohio, to a high of 4,776 in Boston, Massachusetts. By 1915, Boston's drunkenness arrest rate had almost doubled to 8,208, whereas Cleveland, which had a drunkenness arrest rate of 2,191 per 100,000 population in 1880, saw a decline to 378. These vast discrepancies in drunkenness arrest rates over time and across jurisdictions are primarily related to differences in law enforcement activity rather than differences in the actual number of individuals who were arrested because they were drunk. Although they are not as likely to be influenced by police activity, the comparative data on homicide arrests are also interesting to consider. In 1880, Louisville, Kentucky, had the highest homicide rate at 16.2 per 100,000, whereas New Haven, Connecticut, had a rate of 0.0. By 1915, San Francisco's homicide rate had nearly doubled from its 1880 rate to 29.1 per 100,000, and St. Louis saw its rate increase sixfold, from 4.6 to 27.6.

One of the primary motivations for the establishment of the UCR program was to counter media-generated crime waves (O'Brien 1985), and when the IACP began deliberations on the collection of crime data, there were debates about what specific crime statistics would be most useful to

Exhibit 2.3. Arrest Rate Comparisons (per 100,000 Population: Selected Offenses and Cities, 1880 and 1915

City	Total Arrest Rate		Drunkenness Arrest Rate		Homicide Arrest Rate	
	1880	*1915*	*1880*	*1915*	*1880*	*1915*
Baltimore, MD	6,627	6,342	3,633	3,205	81	91
Boston, MA	6,858	12,514	4,776	8,208	30	95
Buffalo, NY	5,809	6,684	1,715	3,128	19	30
Chicago, IL	5,660	4,981	2,841	2,226	24	108
Cincinnati, OH	5,719	6,680	1,630	1,527	55	97
Cleveland, OH	3,679	2,203	2,191	378	34	84
Detroit, MI[a]	3,682	3,030	3,030	NA	95	87
Louisville, KY	3,807	5,323	1,746	3,042	162	231
Milwaukee, WI	2,663	2,718	1,868	1,328	29	19
Newark, NJ	3,694	2,948	1,954	881	22	121
New Haven, CT	7,333	7,001	5,098	3,899	00	20
New Orleans, LA	8,488	10,212	NA	4,108	93	157
New York, NY	5,667	4,091	3,672	1,280	NA	87
Philadelphia, PA[a]	5,230	6,066	3,877	3,539	33	94
Providence, RI	6,205	4,592	4,387	2,848	09	39
Richmond, VA	6,204	8,505	1,948	3,400	47	247
San Francisco, CA[b]	9,003	6,999	4,043	2,987	150	291
St. Louis, MO	4,040	5,413	2,263	1,937	46	276
Washington, DC	9,205	9,684	3,951	4,028	68	83

SOURCE: Adapted from Monkkonen, 1994.
a. 1915 rates based on data from 1914.
b. 1915 rates based on data from 1910.

collect. Some believed that the number of arrests made by the police would be the most useful, but apparently the views of individuals such as August Vollmer, chief of police in Berkeley, California, ultimately held sway. Vollmer maintained that the number of arrests would constitute a false and inadequate measure of crime, because these would be subject to potential bias on the part of the police. Vollmer argued that the only dependable data would be the actual number and types of complaints received by law enforcement officials (Maltz 1977). Hence, the UCR data were based on "crimes known to the police," that is, crimes that were reported to the police by the public.

As a result of the efforts of the IACP, the first monthly report of offenses known to the police was published in January 1930. The association continued monthly publication of these reports until September 1930, when the work was taken over by the Federal Bureau of Investigation (FBI) of the U.S. Department of Justice. In 1931, official crime reports were received from 1,127 cities and towns having a combined population of nearly 46 million, which represented approximately 80 percent of the population of the United States (Tibbits 1932).

Even in the initial years of the UCR, the records were subject to checks for reliability by the FBI, and data from several jurisdictions were eliminated due to irregularities. In addition, some police departments were reluctant to compile and publish reports on the volume of crime in their jurisdictions due to concerns that the data would be used by the public to negatively evaluate their performance (Leonard 1954). The limitations of these data were recognized by the agency that published them. Included in the 1931 UCR publication (as cited in Biderman and Reiss 1967) was the statement, "If it took the highly centralized English government 66 years to get its famous and highly efficient police to report correctly crimes known to the police, it is evident that it will take many years before our decentralized and nonprofessional police forces can be induced to make trustworthy reports of crimes known to the police" (p. 3). Similarly, one issue of the UCR, released in May 1931 (as cited in Maltz 1977), stated that "wide divergences in the total number of particular crimes for various cities of approximately the same population may in some cases not be indicative of a variance in the amount of crime in those cities but may be charged to inadequate record systems or a lack of understanding of the classification on the part of some officials" (p. 38). In subsequent UCRs, caveats such as "in publishing the reports sent in by the chiefs of police in different cities, the Department of Justice does not vouch for their accuracy" were included.

Critics were also aware of the potential misuses of crime statistics by police departments in order to generate additional funding. As the 1930 Wickersham Commission (as cited in Maltz 1977) noted, "It takes but little experience of such criminal statistics as we have in order to convince that a serious abuse exists in compiling them as a basis for requesting appropriations or for justifying the existence of or urging expanded powers and equipment for the agencies in question" (p. 36).

In the early UCR, offenses were classified under 26 separate headings according to their general common-law definitions, and these were then categorized into two broad categories. Seven crimes were selected for inclusion in the initial UCR index. These were murder and nonnegligent manslaughter, rape, robbery, aggravated assault, burglary, larceny, and motor vehicle theft. These offenses were chosen because (1) they constituted offenses that were most likely to be reported to the police, (2) police investigations of such incidents could easily establish that a crime had occurred, (3) these crimes occurred in all geographical areas of the United States, (4) they occurred with sufficient frequency to provide an adequate basis for comparison between jurisdictions, and (5) they were serious by their nature and volume (O'Brien 1985).

Although the number of law enforcement agencies reporting to the UCR increased over time, the practices and procedures of the program essentially remained unchanged until 1958, when a number of modifications were implemented. Included among the changes were the removal of manslaughter by negligence from the criminal homicide category, the limiting of rape offenses to forcible rape, and the exclusion of thefts of property valued at less than $50 from the theft category. One effect of these changes is that historical and cross-jurisdictional comparisons of the number, distribution, and rates of these offense classes cannot be made for the years prior to 1958.

Although improvements were certainly made in the UCR from the time of its implementation in 1930, critics still pointed to problems associated with making cross-jurisdictional and historical comparisons of crime rates. Beattie (1960) noted the difficulties in making cross-state comparisons, first using the example of the ratio of crimes against the person to crimes against property across a number of states. In California, the ratio of crimes against the person to crimes against property was 1 to 7; in New York, 1 to 6.5; in Ohio, 1 to 7. However, the ratio of crimes against the person to crimes against property was 1 to 2 in North Carolina, 1 to 3 in Mississippi, 1 to 22 in Rhode Island, and 1 to 50 in Vermont. Beattie suggested that these vast disparities indicated that states were using entirely different practices in reporting offenses known to the police.

Moving to the level of city comparisons, Beattie used the example of Akron and Canton, adjacent metropolitan areas in Ohio. In 1958, Akron reported three times the forcible rape rate of Canton and more than three times the aggravated assault rate, leading Beattie (1960) to conclude, "It is just not conceivable that crime rates in these metropolitan areas in reality could vary as indicated by these published figures. It is much more likely that the disparities are due to differences in methods of accounting from crimes reported to the police" (p. 55). Beattie further asserted that Los Angeles, which had an efficient police department that collected complete records, was falsely identified as having a high crime rate compared to other cities that were not characterized by similar standards of high-quality record keeping. He also pointed to difficulties in classifying crimes into the various index categories, noting, for example, that with larceny-theft there was no standard basis for assessing the value of stolen property. Thus, comparisons of theft statistics across jurisdictions could be misleading, if not completely meaningless.

The misuse and misrepresentation of UCR data has a long history. In an interesting example of this phenomenon, on January 1, 1962, *U.S. News and World Report* published an interview with J. Edgar Hoover, head of the FBI. Hoover asserted that crime was becoming more serious and frequent in the United States. In support, he noted that between 1950 and 1960, "serious crime" had increased by 98 percent, although the population of the United States grew by only 18 percent. More specifically, Hoover invoked the rather questionable practice of combining all crimes in the crime index to claim that "in 1960, more than 7,700 police departments of this country reported 1,861,300 murders, forcible rapes, robberies, aggravated assaults, burglaries, automobile thefts, and larcenies of $50 or more." The bulk of this total was, however, comprised of more minor crimes such as larcenies. Hoover attributed these increases in crime to a decline in parental authority as well as more general moral standards in the United States. Presaging a view that is popular in explanations of crime today, Hoover also asserted that there was a relationship between exposure to violence in the media and crime: "The highly suggestive, and at times, offensive scenes, as well as the frequent portrayal of violence and brutality on television screens and in motion pictures, are bound to have an adverse effect on young people."

The Dark Figure and Additional Problems with Crime Statistics

[A criminologist] studies the criminals convicted by the courts and is then confounded by the growing clamor that he is not studying the real criminal at all, but an insignificant proportion of non-representative and stupid unfortunates who happened to become enmeshed in technical legal difficulties. (Tappan 1947:96)

Although official data from the UCR and other sources were commonly used by journalists, criminologists, and other social scientists to comment on crime trends and the causes of crime, many commentators began to recognize their potential weaknesses. Beattie (1941) noted that police statistics were manipulable for political purposes and hence questionable in their validity. "Traditionally, police departments are anxious to make a good showing in their annual figures, and there is, therefore, a natural tendency to record and report those facts which show a good administrative record on the part of the department" (p. 21). Vold (1935), commenting on an alleged crime wave in St. Paul, Minnesota, in the early 1930s, suggested that "it has been impossible for the present writer to determine whether this represents an actual increase in serious crime in this part of the country, or merely much needed improvement in police statistics" (p. 802). Sellin (1931) also argued that crime statistics primarily reflected the activity of law enforcement personnel and therefore could not be accepted as indicating particular trends in crime. Indeed, along these lines, Sellin is perhaps best known for his suggestion that "in general, it may be said that the value of a crime rate for index purposes is in reverse ratio to the procedural distance from the commission of crime and the recording of it as a statistical unit" (p. 346).

Early 20th-century criminologists also recognized that crime rates could be affected by the policies and practices of individual police departments. For example, in London, a change in recording practices was implemented in 1932, whereby citizens' reports to the police of thefts that had not previously been recorded in official data were now included. This change resulted in an increase in indictable (more serious) offenses from approximately 26,000 in 1931 to 83,000 in 1932 (Radzinowicz 1945)—an increase of more than 300 percent. Similarly, a change in police administration in New York City in 1950, which led to a modification of recording practices, resulted in increases of 400 percent in robberies, 700 percent in larcenies, and more than 1,300 percent in burglaries over a one-year period (Brantingham and Brantingham 1984).

One of the most influential studies that drew attention to the dark figures of crime and the possibility of criminal justice system biases in generating police and judicial statistics was Robison's (1936) study of delinquent youth in New York state. Robison challenged the common use of juvenile court statistics in examinations of delinquency and was particularly critical of the delinquency area technique adopted by the Chicago School sociologists Shaw and McKay (1931). Shaw and McKay, relying on juvenile court referral data in a number of U.S. cities, found that the highest rates of delinquency occurred in neighborhoods characterized by rapid population change, poor housing, poverty, tuberculosis, adult crime, and mental disorders. In addition, they found that delinquency rates were highest in inner-city or core areas of cities but declined with the distance from the center of the city. They emphasized the importance of social disorganization in explaining how youth in these areas became involved in delinquency. This disorganization was manifested in the alienation of children from their parents and adult institutions, resulting in detachment from informal social controls that would normally produce conformity.

Robison (1936) took issue with Shaw and McKay's studies. She argued that the method used by these sociologists not only was invalid for measuring the extent and nature of juvenile delinquency but also was ineffective for providing theoretical explanations of delinquency and policies for delinquency prevention. The Chicago School studies and others like them had implicitly assumed that the extent of delinquency could be measured accurately through the identification of apprehended delinquents—a questionable assumption, at best. The studies also failed to sufficiently differentiate between different types of delinquency, by generally treating truancy, stealing, and malicious mischief as similar behaviors.

Robison (1936) challenged the commonly held notion that there was a fundamental association between poverty, race/ethnicity, and delinquency, claiming instead that these relationships were due to the differential treatment of individuals of different socioeconomic status and racial/ethnic backgrounds by criminal justice system officials. She argued that the customs of diverse nationality and cultural groups had an impact on which youth would be labeled officially delinquent; therefore, variation in the behavior of parents and authorities confronted with "troublesome children" was potentially more important in determining official rates of delinquency than real differences in the proportion of delinquents in these groups. Robison further noted that "is it not rather a human tendency to regard less critically the behavior of the children who live on the right side of the tracks than that of the urchins who, surprised in suspicious activity, react with an almost reflex furtiveness? The policeman is more prone to suspect the poor man's child of theft and the rich man's child of a prank" (p. 30).

Robison's study combined administrative records of delinquent behavior from a cross section of public schools, family agencies, and agencies that cared for neglected children in New York City. The inclusion of these additional data resulted in an increase in the total number of delinquents from 7,090 (the figure derived from juvenile court records) to 15,898 children who were under the care for the commission of delinquent behavior in 1930. In her analysis of these and other data, she pointed to racial and ethnic differences in the identification and processing of delinquency cases. Referring specifically to official juvenile court data, which indicated that there were seven Catholic youth for each Protestant youth processed and three Catholic to every Jewish, Robison noted that "the same behavior by a boy in a Jewish family, no matter where he lives, has evidently not the same chance of being labeled delinquent and referred to the court as that of a boy in an Italian family. Apparently a misbehaving boy in a Protestant family has even less chance of being referred as delinquent, either to the court or an unofficial agency, than the Italian or Jewish boy, and with Negro boys the chances are still different" (pp. 195-6). In short, Robison's research suggested that reliance on official data to study juvenile delinquency would result in misleading theories about its causes and misguided policy solutions to the juvenile delinquency problem.

Another prominent critic of official crime data was Edwin Sutherland (1947), who made a number of important points regarding the weaknesses in these data. Sutherland was one of the first to note that, for the purposes of comparison, crime statistics needed to be calculated in proportion to the population or some relevant base. He suggested that the rates should be corrected for variations in the age, sex, racial, and urban-rural composition of populations. Underlining the importance of using relevant bases in calculating rates, Sutherland used the example of an increase in convictions for violations of motor vehicle legislation in Michigan from 1,566 in 1912-13 to 27,794 in 1931-32. He noted that the number of cars in Michigan had increased from 54,366 to 1,230,980; using the number of motor vehicles instead of population figures for calculating the conviction rate for these offenses indicated that there had in fact been a significant decline in such convictions over the 20-year period.

Sutherland (1947) also noted that the way the crime index was constructed could result in misleading interpretations of changes in crime over time. Focusing on homicide, he noted that the principal increase in such offenses was primarily due to homicides by negligence, especially in the form of killings related to automobile use. He asserted that the number of homicides by negligence was approximately equal to the number of other criminal homicides. Because the total number of homicides had decreased while the proportion of homicides due to negligence had increased from the 1930s to the 1940s, it followed that the crime of murder had decreased significantly.

Sutherland (1940) is best known for his assertion that explanations of crime were invalid because the official statistics they were based on did not include "white-collar criminals" (p. 4). Defining white-collar crime as "a crime committed by a person of respectability and high social status in the course of his occupation" (p. 4), Sutherland included in this category members of the medical profession—who, he alleged, illegally sold narcotics, provided fraudulent reports and testimony in accident cases, and split fees—and disreputable business and professional men who were "quacks, ambulance-chasers, bucket-shop operators, dead-beats, and fly-by-night swindlers" (p. 4). Although Sutherland's identification of white-collar crime did not lead to changes in how crime was officially counted in the United States, his assertion that crime was committed by individuals in all social classes inspired the work of labeling theorists such as Lemert (1951) and indirectly contributed to the development of self-report measures as alternatives to official measures of crime.

Some commentators also suggest that crimes committed by females, as well as by middle- and upper-class individuals, were underrepresented in official statistics. As early as 1932, a conference sponsored by the White House recognized that official juvenile court data underestimated the extent of female delinquency. One contributor to this debate was psychologist Otto Pollack. As Coleman and Monynihan (1996) note, "While Sutherland had seen the dark figure wearing a collar and tie, Otto Pollack claimed he had seen the dark figure wearing a dress" (p. 11). Pollack's (1951) study of female criminality, while presenting a controversial and rather misguided biopsychological theory of female crime, made an important contribution to the debate on the validity of crime statistics by focusing on the under-representation of females in official data. Pollack argued that female criminality was concealed by the underreporting of offenses committed by women, the lower detection rates of female offenders compared to male offenders, and by the greater leniency shown to women by officials in the criminal justice system, including police, prosecutors, and judges.

The recognition that there was a significant amount of crime that was not recorded in official statistics, whether committed by middle- and upper-class individuals or females, led to the development of the first important alternative measure of crime and delinquency, that is, self-report studies.

Early Self-Report Studies

Discussions of the development of self-report methodology in criminology typically have focused on pioneering studies of researchers such as Wallerstein and Wyle, Porterfield, and Short and Nye. Important precursors to self-report studies, however, were more general developments in the science of survey research and specific refinements in questioning people about their "deviant behavior." Early forerunners of self-report studies of crime and deviance were, in fact, studies examining the sexual behaviors of adults and college youth, many of which focused on sexually deviant behaviors. These studies demonstrated that people would answer questions about private and potentially embarrassing behaviors. For example, in 1897, Havelock Ellis published his then controversial book

Sexual Inversion,[1] which was based on interviews with people in London and Paris regarding their sexual attitudes and behaviors and revealed "the vast, tangled jungle of sex activities which flourish in human bodies" (*Time* 1936).

One of the first studies of sexual behavior in the United States was conducted at the University of Missouri in the late 1920s as part of a course on the family. Included in the survey administered to students were questions about their view of sexual relations, both premarital and extramarital; whether fear, religious convictions, pride, or other forces inhibited their sexual desires; and opinions on divorce and alimony. Although the results of this study were apparently never published, the reactions to it are notable. Two of those who conducted the survey were dismissed from the University of Missouri, and another was suspended for one year. In justifying these actions, a member of the executive board of the university stated, "The time has come for a crusade against such discussions and such literature; for ridding our schools of those who cannot distinguish between legitimate research and cesspool delving and for barring from local libraries volumes which reek with sex appeal" (*Literary Digest* 1929).

As attitudes toward sexual issues became somewhat more liberal in the United States following World War II, several other studies of sexual behavior emerged. In a study of 613 students in Texas, Porterfield and Salley (1946) queried their subjects about their views and behaviors with respect to premarital sex, among other things. Focusing on gender differences in these behaviors, Porterfield and Salley noted that 58.5 percent of the "pre-college" men and 59 percent of the college men in their sample reported involvement in premarital sex, compared to only 1 in 137 (less than 1 percent) of the women.

The best known and most widely publicized of these surveys of sexual behavior and attitudes were those published by Alfred Kinsey and the Institute for Sex Research in the late 1940s and early 1950s. While teaching a course on marriage and the family at the University of Indiana, Kinsey, originally trained as a biologist at Harvard University, began to question his students about topics such as their age at first premarital intercourse, their frequency of sexual activity, and the number of sexual partners they had. He was eventually given funding to conduct more detailed studies of sexual behavior by the Committee for Research in the Problems in Sex, a Rockefeller-funded grant-giving body that operated under the umbrella of the National Research Council. Operating from the premise that "there cannot be sound clinical practice, or sound planning of sex laws, until we understand more adequately the mammalian origins of human sexual behavior" (Kinsey et al. 1953:8), Kinsey's project focused on examining sexual behaviors such as masturbation, heterosexual petting, premarital sexual intercourse, homosexual contact, and animal contact (see Exhibit 2.4). The project resulted in interviews with approximately 18,000 males and females, ranging in age from 2 to 90 years old, and including people from a variety of educational, occupational, and religious backgrounds.

Kinsey (Kinsey et al. 1953) believed that the best method for obtaining information on these issues was to conduct personal interviews[2] with subjects. "We have elected to use personal interviews rather than questionnaires because we believe that face-to-face interviews are better adapted for obtaining such personal and confidential material as may appear in a sex history" (p. 58). He felt that it was easier for interviewers to establish rapport with subjects through this method and that personal interviews made it possible to adapt the wording of each question into the vocabulary and experience of each subject. Recognizing that respondents would be more truthful if they were assured of the confidentiality of their answers, Kinsey and his interviewers recorded answers on special sheets printed with a grid. Kinsey informed his respondents that the information was being recorded using unintelligible codes that only he and his two colleagues would be able to understand. On the other hand, he recognized that respondents might lie in personal interviews, so he embedded a number of checks into his interview schedules to detect individuals who were not being truthful. If contradictions in answers were revealed, then subjects were asked to explain them. If they refused to do so, the interview was terminated, and the information from it was not used (Bullough 1998). Perhaps somewhat unbelievably in the context of the questions being asked, Kinsey (Kinsey et al. 1953) claimed that "unlike the experience of those engaged in public opinion and some other surveys, we find no difficulty in getting our subjects to answer all of the questions in an interview. In the course of 14 years, there have not been more than half a dozen subjects who have refused to complete the records after they had once agreed to be interviewed" (p. 45).

The average interview encompassed approximately 300 questions and required between one and one-half to two hours, but for some respondents who had extensive sexual experience, the number of questions extended to 500 or more. Kinsey and his associates were aware of reliability and validity problems in their data, and used a number of techniques to address these issues. "Retakes" or reinterviews, in which the same questions were asked of respondents, were conducted with 124 males and 195 females 18 months (in most cases) after the original interview had taken place. For the adult females in the sample, the retakes modified the lifetime incidence of re-

Exhibit 2.4. Comparison of Male and Female Sexual Behavior: Selected Variables (Percentages)

Activity	Males	Females
Lifetime incidence of masturbation	93	62
Premarital sexual intercourse	84	50
Erotic responses to same sex	50	28
Sexual contacts with animals	30	15

SOURCE: Adapted from Kinsey et al. (1953).

ported sexual behavior by less than 2 percent; for adult males, there was no activity for which the retakes modified the incidences calculated on the original histories by as much as 3 percent. However, when examining reported frequencies of sexual behavior, there was less reliability. On seven out of the nine items reported by females and on eight out of the nine items reported by males, fewer than 70 percent of the subjects provided identical responses. As an additional check on reliability, Kinsey examined data from 706 pairs of spouses in the sample. He found that the number of identical responses ranged from 39 percent on the maximum frequency of coitus in any single week of the marriage to 99 percent on the use of the male superior position during coitus.

One of the standard methods of organizing data in this period was to create seven-point scales to classify behaviors, and Kinsey used a similar scale to classify individuals as homosexual or heterosexual. He did not trust individuals' self-classification as homosexual or heterosexual, so his only objective indicator was the kind of sexual activities that resulted in the respondent experiencing an orgasm. Although the use of this measure indicated that most in his sample were exclusively heterosexual, it also implied that homosexuality was just another form of sexual activity—a revolutionary assertion in this period, as well as the one that resulted in the most serious attacks on Kinsey and his data. Kinsey's other highly controversial findings challenged prevailing beliefs about the asexuality of women. He found that 40 percent of the females he interviewed had experienced orgasm within the first few months of marriage, 67 percent by the first six months, and 75 percent by the end of the first year. However, he also reported instances in which women failed to reach orgasm after 20 years of marriage (Bullough 1998).

Although critics have questioned several of Kinsey's methods and theories, to suggest that Kinsey's studies were revolutionary is by no means overstating the case. His 1948 book, *Sexual Behavior in the American Male*, which sold for $6.50 and was more than 800 pages long, was published by W. B. Saunders, a respected publishing company that specialized in medical texts. Due to the anticipated popular appeal of the book, the company ordered 25,000 copies, rather than the usual 2,000 or 3,000, and these quickly disappeared (Schwarz 1997).

Kinsey's findings that premarital and extramarital relations, homosexuality, oral sex, masturbation, and a host of other sexual practices were far more common than most people believed were groundbreaking. However, it was his method of data collection that is more important for our purposes. The Kinsey studies were among the first to show that people would report on their "deviant" activities. Other studies, whose researchers were contemporaries of Kinsey, were revealing a similar willingness to report socially "questionable" behaviors via self-administered questionnaires.

One example is the large and sophisticated study of college students' drinking behavior conducted in the late 1940s by researchers at Yale University's Center of Alcohol Studies (Straus and Bacon 1953). The study covered 27 colleges in the United States, which were selected to represent a number of different types of institutions, including public, private, and sectarian institutions; coeducational, exclusively male and female, white and black institutions; urban and rural; those with large and small enrollments; and institutions in different regions of the country. The researchers administered questionnaires to a total of 17,000 college students, and of the 16,300 who filled out the questionnaire, 96.6 percent were used in the analysis.

A few months after their survey operations had begun, Straus and Bacon issued a press release announcing the survey and describing its procedures and purposes. They noted how the popular media's reaction to this study tended to trivialize their efforts. The study was referred to as "Booze Kinsey," and an article in the New Haven, Connecticut, *Journal Courier* in 1949 suggested, "Yale, for some odd reason (maybe they haven't got enough work to do in New Haven), would like to amass a flock of statistics. The snoopers would like to know if rich kids drink more than poor kids, or if the sons of teetotalers lush it up more than the scions of soaks.... Every so often I despair of the work that Satan finds for the idle professional hands to do" (as cited in Straus and Bacon 1953:42-3). The researchers asserted, however, that it was important to conduct this study "against the background of stereotypes, conflicts, problems, and changing patterns of drinking and control" (Straus and Bacon 1953:45).

The questionnaire used by Straus and Bacon contained items about, among other things, students' religious affiliation, family characteristics, frequency of drinking, age when first "tight," "times high, tight, drunk, and passed out," and their opinions about the association between drinking and sexual behavior.

Straus and Bacon (1953) were aware of the potential reliability and validity problems in asking students about their alcohol consumption. Similar to Kinsey, they engaged in extensive checks of each questionnaire to eliminate responses that indicated "insincerity" or inconsistency. They noted that "about 100 students made humorous or sarcastic comments. Most of the latter were male students from one school where a member of the faculty assisting with the distribution of the forms invited attempts at humor with a joking remark at the start" (p. 4). They also realized that there would be variation in the students' knowledge of some issues such as family income and the drinking practices of their parents. Answers to other questions about so-called "measurable facts," such as frequency of drinking, amounts consumed on each occasion or number of times intoxicated, were dependent on memory and other factors in perception that could vary significantly from individual to individual.

Although there is not sufficient space here to enter into a detailed discussion of their results, several of the findings from this study are worth noting. Straus and Bacon found that 20 percent of the males and 39 percent of the females identified themselves as abstainers from alcohol. Male students were much more likely to have become tight than females (see Exhibit 2.5). Consumption of alcohol for most of the students took place in homes or public places such as restaurants, taverns, bars, or night clubs, as opposed to college dorm rooms and other on-campus sites. Beer was the most common alcoholic drink consumed by males, and wine was more commonly consumed by females. Straus and Bacon also noted that most students began drinking before they entered college. Of those who drank, approximately half had begun drinking by the age of 17. The reasons for drinking varied somewhat according to the type of beverage consumed, although these were generally related to issues of sociability.

As survey methodology in general, and self-report methodology in particular, progressed in sophistication and acceptability, researchers began to focus more on the measurement of criminal and deviant behavior. One of the pioneering studies in this genre was that of Porterfield (1946), who compared the self-reported delinquent behavior of 337 college students with that of 2,049 "alleged delinquents" who had appeared in the juvenile court in Fort Worth, Texas. Porterfield noted that those in the officially delinquent sample had been charged with a total of 55 specific offenses, ranging from "shouting spit wads at a wrestling match" to murder. How-

Exhibit 2.5. College Students' Drinking (1953): First Drink Before or After Entering College (Percentages)

First Drink	Men	Women
Before entering college	79	65
After entering college	21	35

**Male Students Ascribing Importance to Each of
12 Reasons for Drinking, by Type of Beverage Most Frequently Used**
(Percentage ascribing some or considerable importance to each reason)

Reason for Drinking	Beer	Wine	Spirits
To get along better on dates	36	15	36
To relieve fatigue or tension	56	47	55
To be gay	66	41	63
To relieve illness	26	26	28
To comply with custom	65	53	66
Because of enjoyment of taste	77	65	72
In order not to be shy	27	26	24
As an aid in meeting crises	8	12	12
For a sense of well-being	18	21	28
As an aid to forgetting disappointments	29	18	23
To get high	53	24	42
To get drunk	16	9	17

Number of Times Student Drinkers Have Become Tight (Percentages)

Occasions	Men	Women
Never	20	51
1-5 times	25	32
6-15 times	18	9
16-50 times	17	4
51-100 times	5	0
100 or more	4	—
Have been tight, frequency not stated	11	4

SOURCE: Adapted from Straus and Bacon, *Drinking in College*, Copyright © 1953. Used by permission of Yale University Press.

ever, the study also revealed a significant amount of delinquent activity on the part of the sample of college students. "One well-adjusted ministerial student said he had indulged in 27 of the 55 offenses," and a few of the college students allegedly even confessed to committing murder. Presaging the findings of self-reported studies conducted in the 1960s and later years, however, Porterfield acknowledged that although the offenses of the college students were as serious as those committed by the official delinquents, they were probably not committed as frequently. Porterfield (1946) surmised that the official delinquents had been labeled as such due to inherent biases in the operations of the criminal justice system and characterized the juvenile delinquent as "a friendless young person who does not live in a good home or in a college dormitory . . . but who has offended some part of a rather peevish and irresponsible community, and been charged with the necessity for being responsible and other than peevish himself" (p. 205).

Murphy, Shirley, and Witmer (1946) similarly questioned the validity of official data on juvenile delinquency and took as their point of departure the fact that a considerable number of juveniles who violated the law did not appear in official criminal statistics. Studying a group of 114 officially delinquent boys, they grouped delinquency into three categories of seriousness: (1) violations of city ordinances, including such "offenses" as shining shoes or vending without a license, street ball playing, hopping streetcars, swimming or fishing or both in forbidden places, and violating curfew laws; (2) minor offenses, involving behaviors such as truancy, petty stealing, trespassing, running away from home, and sneaking into movies; and (3) more serious offenses, involving acts such as breaking and entering, larceny-theft, assault, drunkenness, and sex offenses.

To measure the extent to which their subjects engaged in these offenses, Murphy, Shirley, and Witmer (1946) engaged in a group consultation with youth case workers and reviewed the youth's self-reported delinquency to determine whether he engaged in these offenses rarely (denoting a frequency span of from 1 to 3 offenses per year), occasionally (4 to 9 offenses per year), or frequently (more than 10 times per year). Based on these data, they estimated that the 114 boys had committed a minimum of 6,416 infractions of the law during a five-year period (covering the ages between 11 and 16). Supporting their contention that there existed a large dark figure of unrecorded delinquency, the researchers noted that only 95 of these violations became a matter of "official complaint." The authors noted the implications of their study for official measures of crime: "So frequent are the misdeeds of youth that even a moderate increase in the amount of attention paid to it by law enforcement authorities could create a semblance of a 'delinquency wave' without there being the slightest change in adolescent behavior" (p. 696).

Wallerstein and Wyle (1947) conducted a self-report study of delinquent behavior using a sample of 1,698 adult men and women in New York City, focusing on the delinquent behavior these subjects had committed before they reached the age of 16. The mailed questionnaire listed 49 separate offenses, and 99 percent of their sample reported committing at least 1 delinquent act. Men admitted to an average of 18 crimes and women to an average of 11. Perhaps even more surprising, 64 percent of the males and 29 percent of the women in the sample reported committing at least 1 of the 14 felonies included in the list of offenses.

Further developments in self-report methodology were associated with the work of James F. Short Jr. and Ivan Nye (Nye and Short 1957; Nye, Short, and Olson 1958; Short and Nye 1957-58). These researchers began their project with a critique of existing criminological theories that had examined the relationship between juvenile delinquency and socioeconomic status based on official data. Similar to the earlier observations of Robison (1936), they asserted that studies using court records, police files, and other official measures were adequate for measuring official delinquency but were unreliable as indexes of delinquent behavior in the general population.

In one of their studies, Short and Nye (1957-58) administered a questionnaire to samples of the general population of adolescents who were attending school and to a sample of "official delinquents" who were institutionalized in training schools. The questionnaire included a total of 23 items, and from these, they created a delinquency index consisting of 7 items. Respondents were asked if they had committed the following acts since beginning grade school: (1) defied parents' authority (to their face), (2) taken little things (worth less than $2) you didn't want or need, (3) driven a car without a driver's license or permit, (4) skipped school without a legitimate excuse, (5) bought or drank beer, wine, or liquor (including drinking at home), (6) purposely damaged or destroyed public or private property that did not belong to you, and (7) had sexual relations with a person of the opposite sex. For each one of these items, involvement in the behavior was divided into four categories: (1) did not commit the act, (2) committed the act once or twice, (3) committed the act several times, and (4) committed the act very often.

In analyses of their data, Nye, Short, and Olson (1958) found only weak relationships between delinquency and social class. For example, they noted that heterosexual relations were most frequently engaged in by lower-class boys in their sample, but purposely damaging or destroying property was committed most frequently by upper-class boys and girls. However, the researchers did recognize the limitations of their study in that not all adolescents were in school. School dropouts, who would not have been questioned in their surveys, may well have been more delinquent than those in school and may have been disproportionately concentrated in the lower class.

Short and Nye were also aware of potential reliability and validity problems in measuring crime and delinquency through self-reports. They were especially concerned that the institutionalized delinquents they included in their samples would attempt to manipulate the interview situation. To assess the extent of lying on the questionnaires, Short and Nye (1957-58) included a number of trap questions, which were designed to identify both overreporting and underreporting of delinquency. They argued that if respondents indicated they had never told a lie and had never disobeyed their parents, they were presenting an "over-conformist" image; respondents who were identified as such were excluded from the analyses. On the other hand, some noninstitutionalized respondents in their study reported that they had committed all the offenses on the checklist; such individuals were also excluded because it was believed that "such a person would not be at large." Such attention to the potential methodological weaknesses in these early self-report studies has been of considerable value to those who continue to conduct research using this methodology.

Despite the inclusion of relatively trivial "offenses," Short and Nye's work and other early self-report studies were important both methodologically and substantively. They demonstrated that people would report having committed delinquent acts and that the alleged negative relationship between social class and delinquent behavior was not as strong as extant criminological theory purported it to be. As Hindelang, Hirschi, and Weis (1981) noted, "Much like the Kinsey studies before them, the Short/Nye studies revolutionalized ideas about the feasibility of using survey procedures with a hitherto taboo topic. They also eventually led to a revolution in thinking about the substance of the phenomenon itself" (p. 23).

Erickson and Empey (1963) also took issue with the use of official data to measure delinquency. They argued that such behavior was not an attribute but was instead a phenomenon that was distributed along one or more continua. Their study involved personal interviews with males aged 15 to 17 in Utah and included four subsamples: (1) 50 high school boys who had never appeared in court, (2) 30 boys who had been to court once, (3) 50 repeat offenders who were on probation, and (4) 50 incarcerated offenders. Erickson and Empey suggested that the face-to-face interview method was the most effective in uncovering delinquent behavior because it allowed interviewers to provide more complete and reliable data, especially given a lack of literacy among some of their subjects. They also asserted that this method allowed for more accurate estimates of the frequency of involvement in delinquent behavior than the standard method of having subjects respond to predetermined categories such as "none," "a few," or "a great many times." However, interviewers in the Erickson and Empey study encountered problems because some respondents were reluctant to reveal their involvement in offenses and the fact that some more habitual offenders had committed the offenses so frequently that they could not accurately estimate the number of times.

Similar to the findings of previous self-report studies, Erickson and Empey (1963) noted that the number of violations admitted to by their respondents was "tremendous." Three types of offenses were most common: theft (a total of 24,199 offenses), traffic violations (23,946), and the purchase and drinking of alcohol (21,698). In more than 90 percent of the cases, these offenses were undetected and not acted on by any official agency. Although the amount of hidden delinquency in this sample was significant, they found that boys who had been labeled as officially delinquent had committed a far greater number of delinquent acts than those who had not been so labeled.

Gold's (1966) self-report study began by noting that in one Michigan city, boys who lived in the poorer sections of town and were apprehended by police were four to five times more likely to be officially labeled delinquent than boys from the wealthier sections of town who were involved in the commission of the same types of offenses. This study relied on interviews with 522 13- to 16-year-old boys and girls living in the school district, who were matched with interviewers on the basis of race and sex. The self-report instrument contained a total of 51 questions that asked youth about offenses they had committed during the previous three years. Aware of the possibility that his respondents might conceal their delinquent activities, Gold also interviewed a "criterion" group of 125 young people for whom he already had collected reliable information on their delinquency from official data. In addition, he interviewed peers of the respondents in order to gather independent information on delinquent acts that they had witnessed or had been described to them by the respondents.

Using these data, Gold concluded that 72 percent of the youth provided self-reported delinquency information that was consistent with information provided by the informants, 17 percent were identified as "outright concealers," and the remaining 11 percent were "questionables." More important for measures of delinquency and for theories of delinquent behavior, and in contrast to several of the earlier self-report studies, Gold (1966) concluded that crime was, in fact, inversely related to social status. The lower-status young people in this study were found to commit delinquent acts more frequently than higher-status adolescents. However, this relationship existed only among boys.

An additional development with respect to reliability checks of self-reports of deviant behavior was associated with the work of Clark and Tift (1966). These researchers conducted a study of 45 white males enrolled in a sociology course at a midwestern U.S. university in which respondents were asked to report their frequency of commission of a number of delinquent behaviors. The subjects were also given a polygraph test to check the veracity of their reports. Clark and Tift found that self-reports of delinquent behavior were accurate when a wide range of behaviors was considered simultaneously, but that there was differential validity on specific questionnaire items.

The first National Youth Survey (NYS), conducted in 1967 (Williams and Gold 1972), drew on interviews and official records of 847 13- to 16-year-old boys and girls. In this study, respondents were given the following instructions: "Here is a set of things other kids have told us they have done. Which of them have you done in the past three years, whether you were caught or not?" Respondents were asked to report whether they had never engaged in the activity, whether they had done it just once in the previous three years, or whether they had done it more than once. Williams and Gold found that 88 percent of the teenagers they interviewed confessed to committing at least one chargeable offense in the three years prior to the interview. They concluded that "if the authorities were omniscient and technically zealous, a large majority of American 13- to 16-year-olds would be labeled juvenile delinquents" (p. 213).

The Williams and Gold study was one of the first to focus in some detail on racial differences in self-reported delinquency. The researchers discovered that black females were not more frequently or seriously delinquent than white females, and black boys were not more frequently delinquent than white boys. However, black males reported involvement in more serious forms of delinquency than whites. For example, when involved in theft, blacks stole more expensive items, and when involved in assaults, they tended to inflict more serious injury.

Victimization Surveys

Another method of measuring crime that arose in response to the limitations of official data is the victim survey. Although not commonly identified as such in the literature, one of the first studies of this nature was conducted by Fitzpatrick and Kanin (1957), who investigated sexual aggressiveness in dating relationships on a university campus. Questionnaires were distributed to 291 females in 22 university classes, asking them about their experiences with males in dating relationships. Of the respondents, 55.7 percent reported that they had been "offended at least once during the academic year at some level of erotic intimacy," 20.9 percent had experienced forceful attempts at intercourse, and 6.2 percent had experienced "aggressively forceful attempts at sexual intercourse in the course of which menacing threats or coercive infliction of pain were employed."

The primary motivation for the development of comprehensive national surveys of crime victims in the United States was the recognition of the limitations in official measures of crime. In response to apparently escalating crime rates and urban unrest in several U.S. cities in the late 1960s, the President's Commission on Law Enforcement and Administration of Justice (1968) was impaneled in 1965 to develop policy and recommendations concerning the crime problem. The President's Commission noted that "one of the most neglected subjects in the study of crime is its victims" and found that much of the information needed to formulate policy recommendations with respect to the rising crime problem was not available. The President's Commission also noted that official statistics were problematic because many crimes were not reported to the police, and a number of administrative and organizational factors were believed to affect the reporting of these statistics in particular jurisdictions.

Both the deficiencies of official data and developments in the methodology of large-scale sample surveys provided the President's Commission with the impetus for developing victimization surveys. The initial efforts involved three separate studies: a pilot study in Washington, D.C., a second-stage study in three U.S. cities, and a national survey.

The Washington, D.C., pilot study was conducted during the spring of 1966. Working from a probability sample of homes in three police precincts, 511 interviews were completed with individuals who were asked to report whether they had been a victim of a list of crimes since New Year's Day, 1965. This study contributed to the methodological sophistication of subsequent victimization studies. It also demonstrated that household surveys would provide a different picture of crime than that derived from police statistics. Depending on the type of crime, the pilot study found that there were from 3 to 10 times as many criminal incidents reported by victims than were recorded in official data (President's Commission 1968).

The second-stage study was designed to elicit criminal victimizations experienced by businesses and organizations in selected high-crime areas in

Boston, Chicago, and Washington, D.C., and to measure household victimizations among residents in Boston and Chicago. This study similarly found that there was much more crime than was reported in official statistics.

The third victimization study sponsored by the President's Commission was a national survey conducted by the National Opinion Research Center, in which one respondent was interviewed in each of 10,000 households. This study revealed that approximately twice as many incidents of personal violence, and more than twice as many individual property victimizations, were estimated to have occurred than were recorded in the UCR. These data indicated that although many people experienced crime, many chose not to report it to the police. This survey also examined nonreporting of victimizations and the reasons individuals did not report offenses they had experienced. Nonreporting was found to vary across offenses, ranging from a high of 90 percent for consumer frauds to a low of 11 percent for automobile thefts. Most of those who did not report their victimizations to the police felt either that the incident was private or that the police could not do anything about the offense (President's Commission 1968).

The National Opinion Research Center victimization study reported a number of findings that were of interest to criminologists and policy makers. For example, the highest rates of victimization were found in the lower-income groups, nonwhites were victimized disproportionately by all index crimes except theft over $50, and the rates of victimization for men were almost three times higher than those for women.

Early reports also recognized the need for caution in the interpretation of victimization data, however, and pointed to a number of methodological problems. For example, in noting the higher rates of burglary, larceny, and auto theft committed against men, the President's Commission suggested that this was primarily an artifact of the survey methodology, whereby offenses committed against the household were assigned to the head of the household, which, in most cases, was a male. There was also recognition of the problems of telescoping and recency effects in the interview data. For instance, Biderman (1967) noted that the distribution of incidents reported for the national survey had a "bulge" at the beginning of the 12-month period for which the respondents were asked to report, as well as a larger bulge at the recent end of the distribution. These bulges suggested that respondents were remembering some crimes that they had been the victims of before the 12-month reference period as well as being more likely to recall crimes that they had experienced recently. The studies also revealed that people interviewed about crimes affecting their households mentioned incidents they had experienced personally in considerable disproportion to incidents affecting others who lived with them—that is, they were more likely to report their own victimization experiences as opposed to those of their family members. As Biderman (1967) noted, the inefficiency of asking about others' victimization experiences was underscored by the finding that there was not a positive relationship between the number of individuals in the household and the number of incidents reported by the respondent.

The initial victimization surveys also revealed an interesting finding with respect to the education of respondents: those who were college-educated reported more frequent victimization experiences than others. But as Biderman (1967) noted, this may have been an artifact related to the "productivity" of respondents: those with higher levels of education may have had better memories of events.

Although these initial victimization surveys were thus characterized by several methodological problems that will be explored in more detail in Chapter 5, they were important in establishing the victimization survey as an alternative to official measures of crime.

Summary and Conclusions

Accurate counts of various social phenomena have been important to policy makers and citizens alike since at least early Greek and Roman times. Still, the century just passed may well be "the first measured century," because more and more numbers are used to characterize more and more facets of our lives. Historically, measures of crime and delinquency are among those that have the greatest potential for generating controversy.

As described in this chapter, the earliest measures of crime were derived from official statistics. Concern over the reliability and validity of official counts led to the development of self-report and victimization measures— the earliest examples of which likewise evidenced limitations. Nonetheless, those pioneering official, self-report, and victimization studies served as the basis for more recent developments and refinements in crime measurement.

Chapters 3, 4, and 5 critically examine each of these data sources—official statistics, self-report studies, and victimization surveys—in turn, with the goal of identifying its role in providing accurate measures of crime and delinquency.

Notes

1. When Ellis published this book, he was arrested by the London police and all copies of the volume were seized. It was not until 1936 that individuals other than doctors and laywers in the United States were allowed to legally purchase the book (*Time*, March 9, 1936).

2. Apparently some individuals, falsely claiming that they were part of the Kinsey research project, attempted to conduct telephone interviews with unsuspecting subjects. "At many points in the United States within the past five years, there have been imposters who posed as interviewers connected with the present project. In most instances they operated through telephone calls" (Kinsey et al., 1953:58). In response to this problem, Kinsey notes, "It should be understood that our staff never conducts interviews over the telephone."

Chapter Three

Official Crime Data

The statistics of crime and criminals are known as the most unreliable and difficult of all statistics. First, the laws which define crimes change. Second, the number of crimes actually committed cannot possibly be enumerated. This is true of many of the major crimes and even more true of the minor crimes. Third, any record of crimes, such as arrests, convictions, or commitments to prison, can be used as an index of crimes committed only on the assumption that this index maintains a constant ratio to the crimes committed. This assumption is a large one, for the recorded crimes are affected by police policies, court policies, and public opinion.

Sutherland (1947:29)

Official crime data are those that derive from the normal functions of the criminal justice system. These official counts of crime include police reports of offenses and arrests, charges filed by prosecutors, criminal complaints and indictments, imprisonment data, and prison releases.

Although official data come from a number of different sources, both the volume and nature of recorded crime incidents change dramatically through successive stages of criminal justice processing. A funnel analogy is often used to describe how both the number of offenders and the number of criminal offenses decrease significantly as one moves from police statistics to imprisonment data. Of all offenders and offenses known to the police, only a proportion are subject to arrest. Only some of those subject to arrest will be prosecuted in courts, and of these, only some will be convicted. A smaller proportion still will be incarcerated. The most inclusive official measure of crime thus involves police reports of criminal incidents.

This chapter examines the nature and scope of police statistics on crime. We begin with a description of the crime reporting procedures in the United States. We then summarize historical trends in crime rates and the characteristics of offenders that derive from police reports. The chapter concludes with a discussion of the various problems associated with using police data as a measure of crime.

Uniform Crime Reports in the United States

As discussed in Chapter 2, prior to 1930, police reports of crime in the United States were not collected or compiled in any systematic way across jurisdictions. Some large cities kept yearly counts of reported crime incidents and persons arrested, whereas other cities did not formally record such information. The classification of crime also varied widely across jurisdictions, with different community standards and legal definitions affecting how crimes were defined and whether particular activities would be recorded as crimes in official data. Public tolerance and law enforcement activities toward lynchings, abortion, spouse abuse, drug and alcohol use, dueling, and other forms of mutual combat varied widely both within and between southern and northern states. Both comparisons across jurisdictions and estimates of historical trends in crime are extremely hazardous prior to 1930 because of the lack of uniformity in definitions of crime and in the collection of police data on crime incidents.

In developing the Uniform Crime Reporting (UCR) program in the late 1920s, the International Association of Chiefs of Police (IACP) recognized that not all crimes are equally important. They therefore focused on seven types of crime that were prevalent, generally serious in their nature, widely identified by victims and witnesses as criminal incidents, and most likely to be reported to the police. The original seven major index crimes, or what are also referred to as Part I offenses, include murder and manslaughter, forcible rape, robbery, aggravated assault, burglary, larceny, and motor vehicle theft. The reporting of other offenses (referred to as Part II or nonindex offenses) is not mandatory for police departments that participate

Exhibit 3.1. Part I and Part II Offenses in the UCR Classification

Index Crimes

Part I Offenses	*Part II Offenses*
Violent Crime	Other Assaults
Murder and Nonnegligent	Forgery and Counterfeiting
Manslaughter	Fraud
Forcible Rape	Embezzlement
Robbery	Stolen Property, Buying, Receiving, Possessing
Aggravated Assault	Vandalism
Property Crime:	Weapons, Carrying, Possessing, etc.
	Prostitution and Commercialized Vice
Burglary	Sex Offenders (except forcible rape and prostitution)
Larceny-Theft	Drug Abuse Violations
Motor Vehicle	Gambling
Arson	Offenses Against the Family and Children
	Driving Under the Influence
	Liquor Laws
	Drunkenness
	Disorderly Conduct
	Vagrancy
	All Other Offenses (except Traffic)
	Suspicion
	Curfew and Loitering Law Violations
	Runaway

SOURCE: Uniform Crime Reports.

in the UCR program. A list of Part I and Part II offenses is presented in Exhibit 3.1.

Although the number of police departments participating in the UCR program has increased over time, the program remained essentially unchanged in its content and structure from its inception in 1930 until 1958. During this period, the FBI published crime data according to the size of the jurisdiction and did not provide reports of a national rate of crime because there was insufficient coverage of the entire country. Changes in 1958 included (1) the use of a composite crime index of all Part I offenses in the UCR, (2) the elimination of negligent manslaughter and larceny under $50 as Part I crimes, (3) the removal of statutory rape from UCR counts, and (4) the estimation and publication of crime rates for the entire United States.

Further changes to the UCR program, involving the development of state-level officials to serve as intermediaries between local police departments and the FBI, were implemented in the 1970s. There are currently 44 states with special UCR programs that provide technical assistance within their state and submit data to the federal UCR program. The number of law enforcement agencies reporting to the UCR has almost doubled since the introduction of these state programs.

In 1979, arson was added to the UCR crime index as a Part I offense. This was in response to an apparently growing problem with this crime. In the United States in 1977, arson was reported to account for approximately one quarter of all fires and "perhaps about 750 deaths and possibly many more" (Simpson 1978). Senator John Glenn (1978) was instrumental in having arson classified in the UCR, noting, "A criminal could steal a car in New York and drive it to New Jersey and his crime would be noted in the FBI charts. But let that same criminal torch a house or business—causing untold property damage and ruined lives—and his crime of arson will never make the charts. That's a ridiculous situation" (p. 15). Despite protestations of FBI officials who believed it would be difficult to properly classify arson incidents in the UCR (Renshaw 1990), Glenn's argument that including arson as a Part I crime would focus national attention on a solution to the problem ultimately held sway.

The most fundamental change in the UCR program in the last three decades involves the movement toward what is known as a national incident-based reporting system (NIBRS), the special features of which will be addressed later in this chapter.

Although participation in the UCR program is voluntary, the proportion of law enforcement agencies participating is remarkably high. A total of 16,788 state, county, and city law enforcement agencies, covering more than 272 million inhabitants, submitted crime reports under the UCR system in 1999. A total of 97 percent of the U.S. population is covered by this data source, with participation rates slightly lower in cities outside metropolitan areas (90 percent) and in rural areas (87 percent).

Data Collection Procedures Under the Uniform Crime Reports Program

Crime data under the UCR program are collected on a monthly basis from participating local law enforcement agencies or the state UCR programs. The FBI provides report forms, tally sheets, and self-addressed envelopes to local agencies. These agencies complete the forms and return them directly to the FBI.

A national reporting system such as the UCR that relies on the cooperation of local and state agencies requires the development and establishment of standard operating procedures and uniform practices. Accordingly, the FBI has gone to considerable lengths to standardize these reporting procedures through the provision of training services and data collection manuals to local agencies.

According to the *UCR Reporting Handbook* (1984), basic minimum standards in several areas are required for agencies providing data for the UCR program. First, a written record is made of each crime upon receipt of a complaint or a call for service. A follow-up system is used to examine whether reports are promptly submitted in all cases. Second, crime reports are checked to see that all offenses submitted in the UCR program conform to the UCR classification of offenses. Third, all records and statistical reports are closely supervised by the agency administrator. Periodic inspections are made to ensure strict compliance with the standard rules and procedures.

Classifying and Scoring Criminal Offenses in the UCR Program

Two essential components of the UCR data system involve the classifying and scoring of criminal offenses. Classifying crime offenses in the context of the UCR refers to the process of translating offense titles used in particular local and state laws into the standard UCR definitions for Part I and Part II offenses. Depending on the particular classifications used in individual jurisdictions, this conversion process may be more or less ambiguous for certain offenses. Scoring of criminal offenses, in contrast, refers to counting the number of offenses after they have been classified under the UCR typology and entering the total count on the appropriate form. Uniformity in both classifying and scoring criminal offenses across jurisdictions is essential for maintaining the integrity of the UCR.

The *UCR Reporting Handbook* provides reporting agencies with detailed definitions and general rules for the classification and scoring of criminal offenses. The classification of offenses into particular UCR categories is based on the facts that underlie an agency's investigation of the crime. The UCR program distinguishes between crimes against persons (i.e., criminal homicide, forcible rape, robbery, and aggravated assault) and crimes against property (i.e., burglary, larceny-theft, motor vehicle theft, and arson). Under the UCR scoring rules, one offense is counted for each offense in crimes against persons, and one offense is counted for each "distinct operation" in crimes against property. Motor vehicle thefts are an exception to the property-counting rule in that one offense is counted for each stolen vehicle.

Given that UCR definitions of criminal offenses are a crucial element in the standardization of reporting practices, it is important to look more closely at how major criminal offenses are defined and counted under the UCR scheme. As described in the methodological appendix to the 1999 UCR Report and the 1984 *UCR Reporting Handbook*, crimes against persons are defined as follows:

1. *Criminal homicide* involves two subtypes of offenses. Murder and nonnegligent manslaughter are defined as "willful (nonnegligent) killing of one human being by another." The second type of criminal homicide involves manslaughter by negligence, which is defined as "the killing of another person through gross negligence." Although manslaughter by negligence is a Part I crime, it is not included in the calculation of the crime index.

2. *Forcible rape* is defined as "the carnal knowledge of a female forcibly and against her will." It involves two categories: (a) rape by force and (b) attempts to commit forcible rape. These offenses are restricted to female victims, and they are classified as forcible regardless of the age of the victim. Statutory offenses (no force used, victim under the age of consent) are excluded.

3. *Robbery* is defined as "the taking or attempt to take anything of value from the care, custody, or control of a person or persons by force or threat of force or violence and/or by putting the victim in fear."

4. *Aggravated assault* is defined as an "unlawful attack by one person upon another for the purpose of inflicting severe or aggravated bodily injury." This type of assault is usually accompanied by the use of a weapon or by means likely to produce death or great bodily harm. Simple assaults are excluded.

The crimes against property included in the UCR are as follows:

1. *Burglary* is the unlawful entry of a structure to commit a felony or theft. Attempted forcible entry is included in this category.

2. *Larceny-Theft* involves the "unlawful taking, carrying, leading, or riding away of property from the possession or constructive possession of another." Larceny-theft is subclassified into the following categories: (a) pocket picking (i.e., theft from a person by stealth), (b) purse snatching that involves no more force than necessary to snatch the purse from the

person's custody, (c) shoplifting, (d) thefts of articles from motor vehicles, (e) thefts of motor vehicle parts and accessories, (f) thefts of bicycles, (g) thefts from buildings, (h) thefts from coin-operated devices or machines, and (i) all other larceny-theft not specifically classified. Attempted larcenies are included in this category.

3. *Motor vehicle theft* is the theft or attempted theft of a self-propelled vehicle that runs on land surface and not on rails. Motorboats, construction equipment, airplanes, and farming equipment are specifically excluded from this category.

4. *Arson* involves "any willful or malicious burning or attempt to burn, with or without intent to defraud, a dwelling house, public building, motor vehicle or aircraft, personal property of another, etc." Fires of suspicious or unknown origin are excluded from the UCR.

Sources of Ambiguity

Coding crimes into these categories can be a complex process. The FBI provides training to local reporting agencies and presents numerous examples in the *UCR Reporting Handbook* (FBI 1984) to illustrate the rules for classifying and scoring criminal offenses. However, there are several sources of ambiguity in the definition and coding of even the UCR Part I offenses that call into question the uniformity of reporting practices across jurisdictions. In fact, it is not unreasonable to assume that all the index crimes are subject to considerable variability in counting and scoring across individual reporting units. The primary sources of variability include differences across local jurisdictions in their interpretation of crime incidents, the "hierarchy rule," the diligence of record keeping, and the adequacy of follow-up procedures.

In the specific case of homicide, the main obstacle to uniform reporting and counting involves the follow-up procedures, the timing of police investigations and UCR filing, and definitional ambiguity in the classification of accidental killings and justifiable homicides. For example, the recording of situations of aggravated assaults that become murders because the victim dies as a result of the assault assumes equal diligence and detailed record keeping across reporting agencies in conducting follow-up investigations and correctly adjusting multiple monthly returns. Some less reliable agencies may simply count the aggravated assault and fail to record the subsequent death of the victim as a murder. Depending upon when in the investigative process the UCR incident is filed, a deadly shooting involving two juveniles playing with a gun may be classified as accidental (i.e., manslaughter by negligence) or willful killing (i.e., murder and nonnegligent manslaughter). Similarly, the killing of an individual by a law enforcement officer or private citizen in the course of the commission of a felony by that individual is a justifiable homicide under the UCR, but some local agencies violate UCR procedures and count such incidents as criminal homicides. Such differences in classification are not likely to be identified in the record-checking procedures used by the FBI.

The major source of ambiguity in the definition and classification of forcible rape involves what constitutes "carnal knowledge of a female forcibly and against her will." Specifically, some jurisdictions may apply the strict definition of carnal knowledge as "sexual intercourse" (i.e., penile-vaginal intercourse), whereas others may consider a fuller range of sexual acts and offensive touches. Also, when there is no apparent resistance on the part of the victim, some jurisdictions may count the act as "consensual" and, thereby, not against the woman's will. Contrary to the instructions provided in the UCR forms, local reporting agencies may also vary in their inclusion of male victims and female offenders in their counts of forcible rape. There is also likely to be considerable variation across local jurisdictions in the inclusion and counting of forcible rapes that occur within the context of marital partners and intimates.

Sources of diversity in the classification of robberies are related to the distinction between "strong-arm" robberies and types of larceny from the person (e.g., purse snatchings). Under the UCR classifications, a purse snatching is classified as a strong-arm robbery when force or threat of force is used to overcome the active resistance of the victim. This force is also considered more than is necessary to snatch a purse from the grasp of the person. However, is it reasonable to assume that all local law enforcement agencies and, for that matter, individual police officers share the same interpretation of "more than necessary" force? Likewise, if the victim falls to the ground when a bag or purse is yanked from her shoulder, would this offense be classified uniformly as robbery or as larceny-theft? Does the classification change if the victim was "pushed" rather than fell or stumbled to the ground? In addition, jurisdictional differences are likely in the counting of robberies with multiple victims in the same behavioral incident. The UCR rule is to ignore the number of victims and count "one offense for each distinct operation," but can we be certain that this rule is uniformly applied? How is this rule actually applied across jurisdictions in cases of "spree robberies" that may be interpreted as a continuation of the original incident?

Definitional and classification problems with aggravated assault concern the interpretation of the provision that it is not necessary that physical injury results from an aggravated assault. Threats and assaults in the context of domestic violence are also subject to various interpretations. When assault situations occur in private places with no witnesses besides the victim, the absence of physical injuries makes it especially difficult to ascertain on a consistent basis whether an "aggravated" threat or attempt with a dangerous weapon actually occurred. The mere brandishing of a dangerous weapon may also be interpreted by some, but not by other local agencies, as an aggravated assault. Domestic assault situations are especially problematic in their classification across jurisdictions. Physical injuries to victims of domestic violence are often treated under state codes as gross or simple misdemeanors rather than felonies such as "aggravated assault." Whether a threat with a dangerous weapon was involved (or a weapon was merely brandished) is also difficult to uncover in this particular context. Even under the best conditions of training and definitional clarity, local agencies will vacillate widely in their UCR classification of offenses with threats or no physical injury as aggravated or simple assault.

The major obstacles to uniformity in classifying and scoring the crime of burglary are the demonstration of intent beyond unlawful entry, the inclusion of attempts, the types of persons who qualify as being involved in an unlawful entry, and more general definitional misunderstandings. For example, burglary is a trespass with intent to commit a felony or theft, but how is this intent consistently determined when the alleged burglary is only attempted and not completed? Could the incomplete act be just a trespass, the destruction of property, or a type of vandalism? Does the apprehension of a suspect after breaking a window count as an attempted burglary or simply vandalism? Concerning the difference between lawful and unlawful entry, are acts of theft without forcible entry by previous intimates (e.g., ex-spouses, separated but not divorced parties, ex-roommates) counted as burglaries or larcenies? This determination will vary depending on the interpretation of particular parties as having the necessary legal status to define their behavior as lawful entry.

McCleary, Nienstedt, and Erven (1982) examined some additional problems in the classification of burglary. In an interview with a UCR coding clerk in a particular police department, they were informed that "a burglary has the element of breaking and entering a *building*. In a lot of cases, the thief breaks through a fence and steals something. That's not a burglary, but a lot of officers don't know that" (p. 362) and would still classify such an incident as a burglary.

Another issue with respect to the classification of burglary stems from what is known as the hotel rule. Under this rule, "If a number of units under a single manager are burglarized and the offenses are most likely to be reported to the police by the manager rather than the individual tenants/renters, the burglary should be reported as a single incident" (FBI 1999:6). Examples would include burglaries of a number of hotel rooms or storage units in commercial self-storage buildings.[1] Note that under this rule, even though a number of separate burglaries may have occurred, only one would be recorded in official data.

The major problem with the classification of larceny-theft stems more from the differential likelihood across jurisdictions of reporting particular types of thefts than from definitional ambiguity. Specifically, police underreporting and undercounting of particular thefts, such as shoplifting and stolen motor vehicle parts or accessories, is especially likely when these offenses involve minor financial losses and occur in large metropolitan areas. These frequently occurring offenses, however, may be more accurately reported to the FBI in smaller local areas.

Another perhaps more obvious problem with the larceny-theft category is related to the estimate of the dollar value of the item(s) stolen. The dividing line for UCR reporting was $50, and larceny more than $50 was the index offense that increased the most over the early history of the UCR—an increase of more than 550 percent between 1933 and 1967. However, because the purchasing power of the dollar in 1967 was only 40 percent of what it was in 1933, many thefts that would have been under $50 in 1933 were more than $50 in 1967 (President's Commission on Law Enforcement, 1968).

Differences across local areas in the UCR counting and scoring of motor vehicle theft may derive from the lack of internal consistency in the coding of motor vehicle thefts and thefts of accessories and parts. Although the UCR manuals clearly specify the different categories, it is possible that some agencies may assume that the theft of motor vehicle accessories and parts falls into the category of motor vehicle theft rather than larceny-theft. The theft of boats and bicycles may also be improperly classified as motor vehicle theft by some local jurisdictions.

The differential interpretation of "willful" or "malicious" burnings and how suspicious fires are classified are the major problems associated with the UCR category of arson. The UCR handbook clearly notes that suspicious fires of unknown causes should not be counted as arson. However, local areas are likely to vary widely in their investigative expertise in these crimes and their subsequent reporting of fires as arson.

The FBI has gone to considerable lengths in an attempt to monitor the accuracy of classifying and scoring crimes in the UCR. Starting in 1997, the FBI developed a voluntary Quality Assurance Review (QAR) for the UCR program that assesses the validity of crime statistics through an on-site review of local case reports. The review program also extends to the collection and compilation of crime statistics by the state repositories. Upon completion of the review, the QAR assessment team sends the agency a written evaluation of its performance in reporting methods, submission requirements, and overreporting or underreporting of incidents. The FBI (1998) has conducted quality assurance reviews at 74 agencies.

The Hierarchy Rule and Counting Multiple-Offense Incidents

The UCR's hierarchy rule applies to the classification and scoring of crimes when multiple offenses are committed at the same time by a person or group of persons. When the hierarchy rule is applied in a multiple-offense situation, only the most serious offense in the series is reported, and all others are ignored.[2] For example, if an individual breaks into a house, steals items from the house, kills the owner of the house, and makes a getaway in a stolen car, only the murder would be recorded in official statistics. Similarly, if, during the commission of a robbery, the offender strikes the teller with the butt of a handgun, runs from the bank, and steals an automobile at curbside, it would appear that three Part I offenses (robbery, aggravated assault, and motor vehicle theft) have occurred. However, because robbery is the most serious of the three offenses, only it would be counted, with the other two offenses ignored (FBI 2000). The hierarchy rule, in theory, involves the application of a rather simple two-step process. First, the reporting agency classifies each of the separate offenses and determines which of them are Part I crimes. Second, the ranking of Part I crimes under the UCR system is used to identify the most serious offense, and that offense is recorded in the data. The decision to apply the hierarchy rule becomes more complicated when it is unclear whether there was a separation of time and place between the commission of several crimes.

The major methodological concern regarding the hierarchy rule is how to determine compliance with it and what adjustments, if any, should be used to correct for potential classification errors. Greater oversight by the state or federal UCR program is an obvious way of determining compliance, but such coding decisions are usually of low visibility and detectability because the summary counts provided in monthly UCR data do not include the information necessary to make independent judgments of coder reliability. Perhaps ironically, the most direct solution to the problem of selective application of the hierarchy rule is its elimination through the greater utilization of the National Incident-Based Reporting System,[3] as discussed below.

National Incident-Based Reporting System

A recent enhancement to the UCR program is the development of an incident-based reporting system for reporting offenses and arrests, known as the National Incident-Based Reporting System (NIBRS). It has been described as "a new approach to measuring crime, one that is simultaneously ambitious, revolutionary, cumbersome, little known, and disappointingly slow to be adopted" (Maxfield 1999:120).

Implementation of the NIBRS program requires (a) a revision of the definitions of certain index offenses, (b) the identification of additional significant offenses to be reported, and (c) the development of incident details for all UCR offenses (see UCR 1998; FBI 1997). It is believed that, when fully implemented, NIBRS data will be better able to measure the true volume of crime than standard UCR data, because the former does not rely on the hierarchy rule and other practices that restrict the counting of crime incidents.

In contrast to the traditional UCR, which uses a summary or aggregate reporting approach, NIBRS categorizes each incident and arrest in one of 22 basic crime categories (see Exhibit 3.2) that span 46 separate offenses. A total of 53 data elements about the victim, property, and offender are collected under NIBRS.

The NIBRS was intended to be implemented as a phase-in program, and it has largely developed at that pace. The FBI has been able to accept NIBRS data from local agencies as of January 1989, and over the first 10 years a total of 19 state-level programs have been certified by the FBI for participation in NIBRS. An additional 14 state programs, several local law enforcement agencies, and five federal agencies have submitted test data to the FBI on their incident-based systems. Several other agencies remain in various stages of planning and development.

Although NIBRS data have been used in federally published reports on crime, it is too early to determine the overall effectiveness of this redesigned UCR program. As of 1999, approximately 6 percent of the U.S. population was represented by NIBRS contributing agencies. Participation in

Exhibit 3.2. Offense Categories and Data Elements Under the National Incident-Based Reporting System (NIBRS)

The NIBRS Group A Offenses

Arson
Assault Offenses
  Aggravated Assault
  Simple Assault
  Intimidation
Bribery
Burglary/Breaking and Entering
Counterfeiting/Forgery
Destruction/Damage/Vandalism of Property
Drug/Narcotic Offenses
Drug/Narcotic Violations
Embezzlement
Fraud Offenses
  False Pretenses/Swindle/Confidence Game
  Credit Card/ATM Fraud
  Impersonation
  Welfare Fraud
  Wire Fraud
Gambling Offenses
  Betting/Wagering
  Operating/Promoting/Assisting Gambling
  Gambling Equipment Violations
  Sports Tampering
Homicide Offenses
  Murder/Nonnegligent Manslaughter

Negligent Manslaughter
Justifiable Homicide
Kidnapping/Abduction
Larceny/Theft Offenses
  Pocket Picking
  Purse Snatching
  Shoplifting
  Theft from Building
  Theft from Coin-Operated Machines
  Theft from Motor Vehicle
  Theft of Motor Vehicle Parts/Accessories
  All Other Larceny
Motor Vehicle Theft
Pornography/Obscene Material
Prostitution Offenses
  Prostitution
  Assisting or Promoting Prostitution
Robbery
Sex Offenses, Forcible
  Forcible Rape
  Forcible Sodomy
  Sexual Assault with an Object
  Forcible Fondling
Sex Offenses, Nonforcible
Stolen Property Offenses
Weapon Law Violations

The NIBRS Group B Offenses

Bad Checks
Curfew/Loitering/Vagrancy
Disorderly Conduct
Driving under the Influence

Drunkenness
Liquor Law Violations
Nonviolent Family Offenses
Peeping Tom

Runaway
Trespassing
All Other Offenses

Administrative Segment:

1 ORI Number
2 Incident Number
3 Incident Date/Hour
4 Exceptional Clearance Indicator
5 Exceptional Clearance Date

Offense Segment:
6 UCR Offense Code
7 Attempted/Completed Code
8 Alcohol/Drug Use by Offender
9 Type of Location
10 Number of Premises Entered
11 Method of Entry
12 Type of Criminal Activity
13 Type of Weapon/Force Used
14 Bias Crime Code

Property Segment:
15 Type of Property Loss
16 Property Description

17 Property Value
18 Recovery Date
19 Number of Stolen Motor Vehicles
20 Number of Recovered Motor Vehicles
21 Suspected Drug Type
22 Estimated Drug Quantity
23 Drug Measurement Unit

Victim Segment:
24 Victim Number
25 Victim UCR Offense Code
26 Type of Victim
27 Age of Victim
28 Sex of Victim
29 Race of Victim
30 Ethnicity of Victim
31 Resident Status of Victim

(continued)

Exhibit 3.2. (continued)

32 Homicide/Assault Circumstances	*Arrestee Segment:*
33 Justifiable Homicide Circumstances	41 Arrestee Number
34 Type of Injury	42 Transaction Number
35 Related Offender Number	43 Arrest Date
36 Relationship of Victim to Offender	44 Type of Arrest
	45 Multiple Clearance Indicator
Offender Segment:	46 UCR Arrest Offense Code
37 Offender Number	47 Arrestee Armed Indicator
38 Age of Offender	48 Age of Arrestee
39 Sex of Offender	49 Sex of Arrestee
40 Race of Offender	50 Race of Arrestee
	51 Ethnicity of Arrestee
	52 Resident Status of Arrestee
	53 Disposition of Arrestee under 18

SOURCE: National Incident-Based Reporting System.

the program has been greatest in small- and medium-sized law enforcement agencies. Austin, Texas, is the only law enforcement jurisdiction covering a population of more than one half million that has reported NIBRS data to the FBI.

Despite its promise in terms of improving the accuracy of crime measurement, several potential problems exist with NIBRS data. Most obvious is the incredible complexity of the coding schemes: the coding specifications are documented in four volumes published by the FBI. As Maxfield (1999) suggests, few police officials are researchers, and diligence in paperwork is not among the skills most valued by police officers. As a result, missing data may become an even greater problem under the NIBRS because of the larger number of categories for which data are collected and the complexity of definitions within each of these categories. Furthermore, as Roberts (1997) notes, the incentives for law enforcement agencies to participate in NIBRS data collection are few. These agencies may feel that NIBRS data are of far more value to researchers than to themselves, and there is concern that the detailed, incident-level reporting required for NIBRS will require police officers to spend additional time filling out reports instead of responding to the needs of the public. A widespread perception also exists that NIBRS participation will result in an increase in reported crime because the UCR's hierarchy rule will be eliminated. This presents a potential public relations disaster for agencies who are, to at least some extent, evaluated on the basis of crime rates in their jurisdiction.

Official Crime Trends and Patterns Based on Uniform Crime Reports[4]

One of the primary purposes for the establishment of uniform crime reporting practices across jurisdictions was to provide a national barometer of crime and its distribution. The methods of classifying and counting offenses have remained relatively stable over time, allowing for estimation of national crime trends. Aggregate characteristics of particular types of offenses and some demographic characteristics of arrested persons are also presented in these national statistics.

Based on UCR data, the crime rate in the United States has vacillated over time and exhibits some variation by type of crime. Participation in the UCR program was sufficient to estimate national crime trends beginning in the 1960s. Starting then, the total index crime rate per 100,000 inhabitants increased steadily until the mid-1970s, decreased somewhat, and then peaked again in the early 1980s. It generally rose steadily from the mid-1980s to the early 1990s and has dropped since that time (see Exhibit 3.3).

Although the number of reported index crimes exceeded 11.5 million in 1999, the crime rate of 4,267 per 100,000 is at the lowest point since 1973; the index crime rate has declined by more than 20 percent over the last 10 years (1990 to 1999). Declining crime rates are found in each region of the country. Southern and western states have continued to experience the highest rates of reported crime, and lower rates are found in the Northeast and Midwest.

The FBI's report of *Crime in the United States, 1999* indicates that violent crime (i.e., murder, rape, robbery, and aggravated assault) accounts for about 12 percent of the total offenses in the crime index reported to law enforcement, whereas the remaining 88 percent were property crimes. This ratio of violent to property crimes in national data has been quite stable over time. Throughout the history of UCR reporting, larceny-theft represents, by far, the most common offense in these national data, whereas murders are the least common offense. Aggravated assaults account for nearly two thirds of all violent crimes.

Homicide

Among the violent index crimes, the most comprehensive police data are collected on murders and manslaughters. This is the case because (a) as the most serious UCR offense, this crime is never undercounted by the hierar-

Exhibit 3.3. Crime Rates, UCR 1960-1999

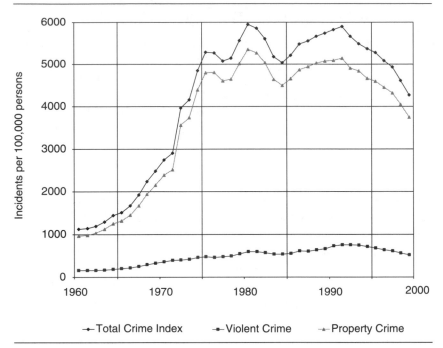

chy rule, (b) murder has the highest clearance rate of all index crimes (i.e., 69 percent of murders known to the police in 1999 were cleared or "solved" by an arrest), and (c) additional police data are collected on each homicide through the Supplemental Homicide Reports (SHR).

Both the number of homicides and rates per 100,000 population have followed a similar pattern to the trend for all index crimes combined. Homicide rates increased throughout the 1960s until the mid-1970s, dropped somewhat in the late 1970s before the peak appeared in 1980, stayed relatively high until the early 1990s, and have decreased steadily since that time. In 1999, 15,533 homicides were known to the police, representing a 39 percent decline from 1990 figures. The homicide rate of 5.7 per 100,000 population in 1999 was the lowest recorded in the United States since 1966.

Homicide rates based on UCR data vary across geographical areas. The homicide rate in southern states is higher than in any other region of the country, at more than double the rate for states in the Northeast. However, each region has experienced a declining homicide rate over the last five years. Metropolitan areas had a 1999 murder rate of 6 per 100,000, compared to rates of 4 per 100,000 in rural counties and suburban areas. Homicide rates in particular U.S. cities over time, however, exhibit fairly unique patterns. Some cities have homicide rates that have fluctuated considerably over the last 30 years (e.g., Houston), some cities have stable rates over this period (e.g., Baltimore, Phoenix, Seattle), and others have experienced general increases with dramatic upward swings in a particular decade (e.g., Detroit, New Orleans, Washington, D.C.).

Analysis of SHR data for 1999, based on 12,658 of the total 15,533 murders, indicates several dominant patterns in the characteristics of homicide victims and offenders (see Exhibit 3.4). More than three fourths of homicide victims are males, and nearly 9 out of every 10 victims are aged 18 years or older. Almost half of all homicide victims are black. Black males have the greatest risk of being homicide victims of all sex-race combinations. Concerning offender characteristics, approximately 90 percent of homicides for which complete information was available are comprised of male offenders, and the vast majority of homicide offenders are persons aged 18 years or older. In 1999, 50 percent of homicide offenders were black, and the vast majority of homicides are intraracial killings for both white and black offenders. Males are most often murdered by male offenders, and about 90 percent of female victims are killed by males.

Although these data are useful in terms of examining the characteristics of homicide offenders and victims, there are problems with the SHR data as well. Maltz (1999) points out that Washington, D.C., rarely records drug involvement in homicide incidents, whereas in Detroit, virtually every homicide is recorded in these reports as drug involved. The truth is likely somewhere between these two extremes.

Based on police reports of known offenses, homicides also exhibit wide variation in their offense characteristics and situational contexts (see Exhibit 3.5). The majority of victims know their assailants, and most of these incidents involve killings by acquaintances or friends. The killer is a stranger in approximately one in five murders in which information about the victim-offender relationship is known. Arguments and disputes are the most prevalent circumstances under which homicides take place, and a sizable minority of killings occur in the course of the commission of another felony offense (especially robberies). A firearm was the most common lethal weapon used in homicide incidents; 65 percent of homicides in the SHR data involved the use of a firearm, whereas approximately 13 percent involved knives or other cutting instruments. The proportion of homicides involving the use of firearms has changed very little over the last 30 years.

Exhibit 3.4. Characteristics of Homicide Victims and Offenders Based on UCR Supplemental Homicide Reports, 1999[a]

	Attribute	Victim Characteristics	Offender Characteristics
Sex:			
	Female	24%	10%
	Male	76%	90%
Age:			
	< 18	12%	10%
	≥ 18	88%	90%
Race:			
	White	50%	47%
	Black	47%	50%
	Other	3%	3%

SOURCE: Uniform Crime Reports.
a. Includes only cases in which victim and offender characteristics are known.

Forcible Rape

Based on UCR data, rape rates in the United States increased steadily and more than tripled between the early 1960s and the early 1980s, remained high and fairly stable across the 1980s, and have decreased throughout the 1990s. An estimated 89,107 rapes were known to the police in 1999, representing a rate of about 32.7 per 100,000 inhabitants.

Rape rates also vary by location. States in the South have slightly higher rape rates than other regions of the country. Western states have experienced the largest decrease in rape rates in the years 1990-99. Forcible rape rates in metropolitan and suburban areas are more than 20 percent higher than those in rural areas. Metropolitan areas have experienced a decline in rape rates over the years 1990-99, whereas these rates have increased over the same time period in cities outside metropolitan areas and in rural counties (see FBI 1999).

Several other factors are associated with rape in the UCR data. Most rapes known to the police involve completed offenses by force (89 percent), whereas the remaining cases involve attempts. The highest proportion of rapes occur in the late spring and summer months rather than other times of the year. According to UCR arrest data, almost half of those arrested for forcible rape in 1999 were under the age of 25, and compared to their distribution in the population, black males are overrepresented as persons arrested for forcible rape.

Exhibit 3.5. Offenses and Situational Characteristics of Homicides Based on UCR Supplemental Homicide Reports, 1999[a]

Victim-Offender Relationship	
Family Member/Relative	23%
Acquaintance/Friend/Neighbor	57%
Stranger	20%
Motive of Circumstance	
Arguments/Brawls	52%
Felonious Activity	25%
Other Reasons	23%
Weapon Use	
Firearm	65%
Knives or Cutting Instruments	13%
Blunt Objects (Clubs, Hammers)	5%
Personal Weapons (Hands, Fists, Feet)	7%
Other Weapon or Weapon Not Stated	10%

SOURECE: Uniform Crime Reports.
a. Includes only cases in which information on the offense is known.

Robbery

Robbery rates in the United States have vacillated widely over the last 40 years. These rates more than quadrupled from 1960 to 1980, then dropped in the early 1980s, rose dramatically in the late 1980s until 1991, and have decreased appreciably throughout the 1990s. More than 400,000 robberies were known to the police in 1999, representing a rate of 150 per 100,000 inhabitants. Compared to 1990 figures, 1999 UCR data indicate that the estimated number of robberies in the United States has decreased by approximately 36 percent.

Similar to other violent crimes, robbery incidents vary by geographical location (see Exhibit 3.6). Northeastern states have the highest robbery rates of all regions, and the Midwest has the lowest rate. Although nearly half of all robberies in the United States are street muggings, a far higher proportion than the national average for muggings is found in the Northeast. Convenience store robberies account for the highest proportion of robberies in the South. Although when the general public thinks about robberies they most likely envision bank robberies, these are rare in all geographical areas. Robbery rates are highest in the largest metropolitan areas, and street muggings account for a large proportion of robberies in such jurisdictions compared to other areas.

Several other characteristics of robbery are revealed in UCR data. For example, the average monetary loss from a robbery is approximately $1,100, which ranges from $620 taken in robberies of gas or service stations

Exhibit 3.6. Characteristics of Robbery Based on UCR Data, 1999

Region

Northeast	170 per 100,000
Midwest	129 per 100,000
South	156 per 100,000
West	146 per 100,000

Location

Metropolitan Area	180 per 100,000
City outside Metropolitan Area	59 per 100,000
Rural Counties	17 per 100,000

Type of Robbery Target

Street/Highway Mugging	48%
Commercial House	14%
Gas or Service Station	2%
Convenience Store	6%
Residence	12%
Bank	2%
Miscellaneous	16%

Weapon Used

Firearm	40%
Strong-Arm Tactics	42%
Knife/Cutting Instrument	8%
Other Dangerous Weapons	10%

Offender's Sex

Male	90%
Female	10%

Offender's Age

<25	62%
≥25	38%

Offender's Race

White	44%
Black	54%
Other	1%

SOURCE: Uniform Crime Reports.

to $4,552 per bank robbery. With respect to the type of weapon used in robberies, strong-arm tactics are the most common, followed closely by firearms. Males accounted for about 9 out of every 10 robbery arrestees, and nearly two thirds of persons arrested for this crime were under 25 years of age. More than half of arrested robbers are black.

Compared to the UCR data from 1972, there has been both change and stability in the factors associated with robbery over time. Robbery rates across this time frame have remained higher in major metropolitan areas and northeastern states, and similar proportions of robberies are found to involve strong-arm tactics over time. Based on arrest data, a similar proportion of robberies across time periods involve males, but the prevalence of robbery arrests among both persons under 25 years old and blacks has decreased somewhat over time.

Aggravated Assault

Aggravated assault rates increased in almost every year from 1960 to the early 1990s, before decreasing over successive years in the 1990s. More than 900,000 aggravated assaults were recorded in UCR data for 1999. The estimated rate of 336 aggravated assaults per 100,000 population is the lowest recorded since 1988. Southern and western states have the highest rates for this offense, and rates of aggravated assault are more than twice as high in large metropolitan areas as in rural counties.

Concerning offense and offender characteristics, the most common weapons used in aggravated assaults are blunt objects (35 percent) and personal weapons such as hands, fists, and feet (29 percent). Knives or cutting instruments and firearms each accounted for 18 percent of weapons used in aggravated assaults. Males account for about 80 percent of those arrested for aggravated assaults, and approximately 40 percent of these offenders were under the age of 25; the proportion of these arrests involving both males and adults has exhibited little change over time. Although 63 percent of aggravated assault arrestees are white, black offenders represented a higher proportion of persons arrested for aggravated assault in the early 1970s.

Property Crime

Property crimes account for about 88 percent of the known offenses in the UCR crime index, so overall crime rates in the United States primarily represent trends in property crime. As a group, property crime rates have exhibited a steady decline over the 1990s. More than 10 million of these offenses were known to the police in 1999, and the property crime rate of 3,742 per 100,000 in 1999 represented the lowest rate since 1973. Both property crime rates and incidents are highest in southern states and lowest in the Northeast (see Exhibit 3.7).[5] Urban areas have rates of property crime that are about two and one half times higher than rates in rural areas.

Burglary rates in the United States more than doubled between 1960 and 1980 and have generally declined over successive years since the early 1980s. More than 2 million burglaries were known to the police in 1999. The burglary rate in southern states is almost double the rate in the north-

Exhibit 3.7. Characteristics of Property Crimes Based on UCR Data, 1998

	% of All Property Crimes	% of All Burglaries	% of All Larcenies	% of All Motor Vehicle Thefts
Region				
Northeast	14	13	14	16
Midwest	22	21	23	20
South	41	43	40	36
West	23	23	23	28
Location				
Metropolitan Area	86	83	85	93
City outside Metropolitan Area	9	8	10	4
Rural Counties	5	9	5	3
Offender's Sex				
Male	71	88	65	84
Female	29	12	35	16
Offender's Age				
≤ 18	33	35	32	36
18 or over	67	65	68	64
Offender's Race				
White	65	68	65	58
Black	32	29	32	39
Other	3	3	3	3

SOURCE: Uniform Crime Reports.

eastern states. The data also indicate that urban areas have far higher rates than rural counties. The vast majority of burglaries involve forcible entry, and residential break-ins account for about two thirds of all burglaries. The majority of burglaries occur during the daytime hours, whereas almost two thirds of nonresidential burglaries happen at night. Males, persons under 18 years of age, and blacks are overrepresented among burglary arrestees.

Larceny-thefts are the most common crime in the UCR data, involving an estimated 6,957,412 offenses in 1999. Rates of larceny have remained more stable since the early 1970s than other UCR Part I offenses. Southern and northeastern states have the highest and lowest larceny rates, respectively. Larceny-theft rates are about three times higher in urban areas than rural counties.

The average value of property loss due to larceny in 1999 was $678. The average take from pocket picking was $451, and losses from purse snatching were approximately $392, compared to $165 for shoplifting and $1,015 for thefts from buildings. Thefts from motor vehicles are the most common type of larceny-theft, accounting for about 36 percent of these crimes. Only about 1 percent of larceny-thefts involve either pocket picking or purse snatching. Nearly half of the arrestees for this offense are under 21 years old, and 31 percent are black. Females were arrested for this offense more often than for any other Part I offense, comprising 36 percent of larceny-theft arrestees.

Motor vehicle theft rates based on UCR data increased throughout the 1960s, hovered between 400 and 500 per 100,000 in the early 1970s to the mid-1980s, and similar to the trend with other crimes, decreased over the 1990s. An estimated 1,147,305 auto thefts were known to the police in 1999, and the rates were substantially higher in western states compared to other regions. Large urban areas have offense rates that are far higher than smaller cities and rural areas. The average value of the stolen vehicle was approximately $6,104. Seventy-five percent of stolen vehicles were automobiles, 19 percent were trucks or buses, and the remainder were other types of vehicles. Arrestees for motor vehicle theft are disproportionately male (84 percent), under 18 years old (19 percent), and black (42 percent).

Although only about two thirds of the U.S. population is covered in UCR estimates for arson for 1999, several patterns are revealed in these data: (1) estimated arson rates are highest in the western states and lowest in the Northeast, (2) cities with a population of more than 1 million have arson rates nearly twice the national arson rate of 37 per 100,000 inhabitants, (3) nearly half of all reported arsons are directed at structures, with single occupancy residential units being the most common target in this category, (4) the monetary value of property damaged in reported arson cases averaged nearly $11,000, and (5) arrested arsonists are disproportionately male (86 percent), juveniles under 18 years old (54 percent), and black (24 percent).

Hate Crimes

Hate crimes were added to the UCR in 1990 with the passage of the Hate Crime Statistics Act. Hate crimes, also known as bias crimes, are defined as offenses committed against a person, property, or society that is motivated, in whole or in part, by the offender's bias against a race, religion, disability, sexual orientation, or ethnicity/national origin (FBI 1999). There is considerable doubt regarding the reliability of hate crime statistics (Center for Criminal Justice Policy Research 2000). In fact, nearly 83 percent of the agencies that participate in the UCR hate crime reporting program reported no such crimes in 1998. State comparisons of hate crime statistics are also instructive. For example, in 1998, 5 percent of law enforcement agencies participating in hate crime reporting were located in New Jersey; these agencies were responsible for recording nearly 10 percent of the total hate crimes in the United States. On the other hand, Pennsylvania comprised 10.5 percent of the participating agencies but recorded only 2 percent of all hate crime incidents. "Clearly, it would be negligent to assume from this information that New Jersey has five times more hate crime than Pennsylvania" (Center for Criminal Justice Policy Research 2000:11). There is also skepticism in the fact that although 29 percent of the nation's index crimes were reported in the South in 1997, only 6 percent of the hate crime incidents were reported there.

Clearance Rates

One measure of the effectiveness of local law enforcement agencies in apprehending criminals is the clearance rate. Crimes are "cleared" by either an arrest of a suspect or by exceptional means when some element beyond the control of law enforcement (e.g., the death of a suspect, international flight) precludes them from making formal charges against the offender (FBI 1999). As is often illustrated by the arrest of serial killers, the arrest of one person may clear several crimes. Alternatively, several people may be arrested in the clearance of one crime. Clearance rates represent the proportion of crimes known to the police that lead to arrest.

Clearance rates as reported in UCR data have varied over time, region of the country, and across the various types of Part I offenses (see Exhibit 3.8). According to the most recent UCR data, only 21 percent of crime index offenses were cleared in 1999. Clearance rates were higher for crimes against persons (50 percent) than for property crimes (18 percent). Murders had the highest clearance rate and robbery the lowest, among the violent offenses. Larceny-theft had the highest clearance rate among property crimes (19 percent) and the lowest rates were for burglary (14 percent). The Northeast had the highest clearance rates for all regions of the country for both violent and property offenses.

When examined over time, clearance rates for some crimes have decreased more rapidly than others. There has been more than a 20-percentage-point decline in clearance rates between 1960 and 1999 for murder and forcible rape in the United States. Wellford and Cronin (2000) note that a number of factors affect clearance rates for homicide. For example, the probability of clearance increases significantly when the first police officer on the scene quickly notifies the homicide unit, medical examiners, and the crime laboratory and attempts to immediately locate witnesses and secure the area.

Smaller decreases over time are found in clearance rates for aggravated assault, burglary, motor vehicle theft, and robbery. The clearance rate for larceny-theft has remained at about 20 percent across this period.

Exhibit 3.8. Clearance Rates for Each Index Crime over Time (Percentage)

	1960	1999	Differences
Total Index Crimes	31[a]	21	−10
Violent Crimes	62[a]	50	−11
Murder	92	69	−23
Forcible Rape	72	50	−22
Robbery	38	29	− 9
Aggregated Assaults	76	59	−17
Property Crime	26[a]	18	− 9
Burglary	30	14	−16
Larceny/Theft	20	19	− 1
Motor Vehicle Theft	26	15	−11

a. Estimated rate from hand calculations.

A careful consideration of clearance rates also serves to clarify distortions associated with the contribution of juveniles to crime rates. As Snyder (1999) notes, after the FBI released the 1997 *Crime in the United States* report, newspapers across the country reported that 30 percent of all persons arrested for robbery were juveniles, and many concluded that juveniles were responsible for 30 percent of all robberies committed in the United States. However, a substantial discrepancy exists between juvenile arrest proportions and juvenile clearance proportions. For example, although it is true that in 1997 juveniles constituted 30 percent of those arrested for robbery, they were responsible for only 17 percent of robberies that were cleared by arrest. This discrepancy is largely explained by the fact that, compared to adults, juveniles are more likely to commit crimes in groups. In short, simply accepting arrest statistics at face value can lead to dubious conclusions regarding trends in crime and the correlates of crime.

Problems with Police Data on Crime

Police reports are often considered to be the best official measure of the nature and extent of crime. Compared to prosecutorial, judicial, and correctional data, police reports are more comprehensive in their coverage of types of criminal offenses and include information on criminal incidents even when the offender has not been identified. However, as a measure of the true extent of crime in a jurisdiction, police statistics are inadequate for several fundamental reasons. The major problems with police data involve variation in citizen reporting and police recording practices, possible race and social class biases in the structure of policing, limited coverage of crime types under UCR data, conceptual and methodological factors that affect the classification of crime incidents and estimates of national crime rates, and political manipulation and fabrication of these data by police departments and other reporting agencies.

Variation in Citizen Reporting and Police Recording Practices

As discussed earlier, the term *dark figures* has been widely used by criminologists to represent the gap between the true extent of crime and the amount of crime known to the police. The major sources of this gap are the inability of police to observe all criminal activity, the reluctance of crime victims and witnesses to report crime to the police, and variation in the recording of "known" crime incidents due to police discretion.

Contrary to the image portrayed in crime dramas and media depictions of police work, the vast majority of crime becomes known to the police through citizen complaints or calls for service. In other words, police mobilization toward crime and its detection is largely because of a citizen complaint. If a member of the public fails to contact the police about a criminal incident they have experienced or witnessed, it will remain undetected in most cases. The magnitude of unreported crime vastly exceeds crime reported to the police.

The reasons victims and other citizens do not report most crimes to the police are wide and varied. Some victims lack trust in the police or have severe reservations about the ability of law enforcement officials to solve crimes. Some fear retaliation and reprisals from offenders for reporting crimes; others think it is not worth their while to report offenses because, for example, the property is uninsured and probably will not be recovered. The victims in some crime situations may also be involved in criminal activities themselves (e.g., drug sellers or prostitutes who are victims of robbery), which decreases their likelihood of reporting. Others may believe the incident was a "private matter," "nothing could be done," or was "not important enough." Public apathy and the desire to "not get involved" may underlie some witnesses' reluctance to report offenses they observe. Regardless of the particular reasons for underreporting of crime by citizens, this reporting gap raises serious questions about the accuracy of police data as a valid measure of the prevalence of crime.

Even if a crime incident is reported by citizens or directly observed by the police, there is no guarantee that such an offense will be recorded in police data. In fact, police discretion both across and within jurisdictions in recording an incident as crime is a major source of inconsistency in official counts of crime. In this context, the role of the police dispatcher can be crucial. Pepinsky (1976) found that the decision of patrol officers' about whether to report offenses was determined by the nature of the calls they received from the dispatcher. Apparently, if the dispatcher named no offense in the call or dispatched the officer to check a victimless or attempted offense, the chances were practically zero that the officer would report an offense.

In his classic study of police-citizen encounters, Donald Black (1970) identified the following factors that determine whether an incident reported by citizens is formally recorded as a crime by the police:

Legal Seriousness of the Crime. Police are more likely to write up a crime report when the crime is more serious. Approximately 72 percent of the felonies but only 53 percent of the misdemeanors in Black's study were written up as reports. This means that the police officially disregarded about one fourth of the felonies they handled.

The Complainant's Preferences. When called to a crime scene, police often follow the wishes of the complainant. They almost always agree with the complainant's preference for informal action (as opposed to arrest) in minor cases. When the complainant requested official police action, the police complied in the majority of both felony (84 percent) and misdemeanor (64 percent) situations.

The Relational Distance. Police are more likely to file an official report in cases involving strangers than friends or family members. Black (1970) asserts that the victim-offender relationship is more important than the legal seriousness of the crime in terms of whether an incident is officially recorded.

The Complainant's Deference. The more deference or respect shown to the police by the complainant, the more likely it is that the police will file an official crime report. This pattern was found for both felony and misdemeanor situations.

The Complainant's Status. Police are more likely to file an official report when the complainant is of higher social status. The effect of the race of the complainant on recording practices in Black's study was unclear.

Differences in citizen reporting and police recording practices are also likely to vary by region of the country and by rural and urban jurisdictions. Under these conditions, statistics on crime incidents are highly suspect for comparisons across jurisdictions.

Race and Social Class Biases in Policing

There is considerable evidence of racial and social class biases in street-level policing, which dates back to the earliest studies of police in the United States (see, e.g., Chicago Commission on Race Relations 1922; Myrdal 1944; Sellin 1928). Irwin (1985) argues that a tendency on the part of police to characterize lower-class persons and blacks as disreputable and dangerous may lead them to watch and arrest such individuals more frequently than is warranted on the basis of their actual criminal involvement. Although focusing more explicitly on socioeconomic status as opposed to race, Sampson (1986) provides further evidence of police bias in arrest decisions. In a study examining the police processing of juveniles in the Seattle, Washington, area, Sampson found that for the bulk of offenses committed by juveniles, official police records, and referrals to court were structured not simply by the act itself but by the socioeconomic and situational contexts of such acts. In addition, law enforcement officials apparently perceive lower-class neighborhoods as being characterized by a disproportionate amount of criminal behavior and accordingly concentrate their patrol resources in those "offensible space" (Hagan 1994) areas. As Smith (1986) suggests:

> Based on a set of internalized expectations derived from past experience, police divide the population and physical territory they must patrol into readily understandable categories. The result is a process of ecological contamination in which all persons encountered in bad neighborhoods are viewed as possessing the moral liability of the area itself. (P. 316)

Under these conditions, it is possible that at least some of the difference between minority and white crime rates is the product of a differential police focus on minority groups (Mosher 2001).

Limited Coverage of Different Crime Types

Police statistics on crime such as those developed under the UCR system are restricted to only a small class of criminal offenses. Most of these crimes involve street-level offenses that occur among individuals. UCR data do not measure federal crimes or political crimes, and severely undercount organizational and occupational crime. Corporate crimes such as price-fixing and environmental pollution are simply not covered by these data, and occupational crimes such as thefts and frauds by employees are underrepresented in UCR data. Beirne and Messerschmidt (2000:38) contend that there are at least three reasons why the FBI focuses on crimes committed by the powerless: (1) the FBI recognizes the fact that crimes typically or exclusively committed by the powerful are difficult to detect, often covered up, and seldom reported to the police, (2) the FBI is insensitive to the plight of the powerless, and (3) the FBI is politically biased in favor of the powerful.

Conceptual and Methodological Problems

Police data on crime in the United States are also problematic as valid and reliable measures of crime prevalence because of several conceptual and methodological problems. As described in detail earlier in this chapter, the major conceptual problems involve the definition of certain crimes under the UCR and the classification of a particular offense under one of the included crime categories. Even with extensive coding and classification rules, counting and scoring decisions in practice are subject to multiple interpretations and potentially large inconsistencies both within and across jurisdictions. Basic methodological problems involve estimating population figures in order to calculate crime rates in noncensus years, sampling error, imputation and estimation procedures, and the application of the hierarchy rule and other conventions in cases of multiple crime incidents.

Estimating Population
Figures to Calculate Crime Rates

The UCR calculates crime rates per 100,000 population; however, the most accurate counts of population are only available for census years. In noncensus years, estimates of the population are used to calculate crime rates, and if these estimates are inaccurate, then calculated crime rates will be similarly inaccurate. Bell (1967) noted that 1949 crime rates for California, which were based on 1940 population figures, were grossly inflated because the state's population increased by more than 3 million people over the decade. When the crime rate "automatically dropped . . . [in 1950] it was not due to sunspots or some other cyclical theory, but to a simple statistical pitfall" (p. 153). More recently, crime statistics for Illinois were questioned because the Illinois State Police used faulty population estimates in their calculations. The state police 1999 report underestimated the population of Chicago by tens of thousands of residents, which produced an inflated crime rate for the city. An Illinois sheriff whose county's crime rate was overstated claimed, "Hell, they never could add. You get those fellows off of chipped roads and they get confused" (as quoted in Berens and Lighty 2001).

Sampling Error and Participation Rates

Participation in the UCR is voluntary, and police departments are not under any legal obligation to report their crime data to the FBI. The reporting area covered by the UCR program has remained high since the late 1950s. For example, the national coverage rate was 93 percent in 1972, 97 percent in 1981, and 95 percent in 1999. Active participation in the UCR program is highest among law enforcement agencies representing large metropolitan areas (with more than 250,000 population) and lowest for rural areas.

Sampling error is a problem in any research when sample data are used to estimate and represent population values. Two general sources of sampling error and possible sampling bias are found in the UCR system. First, not all police agencies in the United States report crime data to the UCR program. If there are differences in the crime experiences of reporting and nonreporting agencies (as is suggested by the differences in crime rates and participation rates by urban and rural areas), this sampling error is actually sampling bias that may distort population estimates. Second, agencies that are defined as "participating" may not be providing complete crime data to the FBI. In fact, data from six states were excluded in the 1997 UCR because of erratic or nonreporting behavior. A study of reporting behavior covering the years 1992 to 1994 revealed that only 64 percent of law enforcement agencies reported crime for the entire 36 months; 17 percent were classified as partial reporting (i.e., 1 to 35 months of data) and 19 percent provided no reports (Maltz 1999). Under these conditions of incomplete reporting on the part of law enforcement agencies, claims that UCR data represent more than 90 percent of the U.S. population are misleading.

Incomplete reporting under the UCR program is due to a wide variety of reasons. Some of these include (a) natural disasters that prevent state agencies from submitting their data on time, or at all, (b) budgetary restrictions on police and the cutback on services, (c) changes in the personnel who prepare local UCR data and their replacement with persons with less training, experience, or commitment to the program, (d) new reporting systems or computerization of old systems that may cause delays or gaps in the crime reporting process, (e) small agencies with little crime that may feel it is unnecessary to file monthly reports, and (f) incompatibility in state and UCR definitions, resulting in data being submitted by states but not accepted by the FBI (Maltz 1999). Whatever the reason, incomplete reporting and nonreporting have obvious implications for the estimation of national trends in crime.

Problems with Imputation and Estimation

Problems related to sampling error and potential sampling bias are compounded when estimating arrest trends and the profile of persons arrested for crimes. As noted earlier, clearance rates vary widely according to the type of crime, hovering around 50 percent for violent crimes and only 17 percent for property crimes in 1999. Given that the majority of offenders are not counted in arrest data, inferences about the typical profile of particular types of offenders from UCR arrest data also represent a type of sampling bias, because some offenders (e.g., nonstrangers) are more easily identified by victims, and subsequently arrested, than others. Another problem with developing offender profiles from UCR arrest data is that arrests are a reflection of differential police priorities and enforcement practices, further contributing to the likelihood of qualitative differences between those arrested and not arrested for even the same type of offense.

Since 1958, the FBI has used two different methods of imputing crime data for police agencies that have incomplete data or that do not provide reports at all. If a particular agency reports for three or more months in a given year, the total annual crime for the jurisdiction is estimated by multiplying the reported number of crimes by 12, divided by the number of months reporting (Maltz 1999). This procedure implicitly assumes that the crime rate for nonreporting months is the same as for reporting months, which is a rather dubious assumption. If, on the other hand, an agency reports for less than three months, the number of crimes in that jurisdiction is essentially estimated from scratch. Such agencies are considered to be nonreporting agencies, and the FBI estimates data for these jurisdictions based on crime rates for the same year for similar agencies. These "similar agencies" are defined as those in the same population size category in the same state but that provide 12 months of data. If there are no comparable agencies in the state, the estimate is based on rates of crime in the jurisdiction's region.

Unfortunately, if the nonreporting agency is different from the "comparable" reporting agencies on crime-related correlates other than geographical location and size (e.g., income distribution, unemployment rates, population density, racial composition), the assignment of equal proportions of crime in each jurisdiction will distort the accuracy of these estimates. The fact that no two cities are alike in their economic opportunity, physical structure, history, and culture raises questions about this estimation approach. And although it is possible that inaccuracies in crime data that result from such estimation procedures may not be significant, the real problem is that there is currently no way of determining whether the estimation procedures produce major or minor discrepancies in crime data. As Maltz (1999) points out, such imputation can be especially problematic for crimes that vary according to season.

Alternative imputational methods have also been used with UCR data. For example, the process of conversion to the NIBRS program required the estimation of totals for some entire states. Unique estimation procedures are also required when yearly data for a particular jurisdiction are incomplete and in other situations (e.g., the inability of some state UCR programs to provide forcible rape figures in accordance with UCR guidelines). For these problems, the UCR program has used "known" data from other geographical areas in the same time period, regional data from the United States for that year (e.g., mountain states, west north-central division), or state totals from previous years to derive population estimates. Such extrapolations, however, are accurate only if trends in other jurisdictions or the same jurisdiction in previous years are representative of crime experiences in the nonreporting areas.

Although it is often overlooked by users of UCR data, the UCR program has relied extensively on extrapolations from other jurisdictions or other time frames for estimating national crime trends. The most recent UCR report (FBI 1999) provides the following examples of major nonreporting and estimation practices over the last 15 years.

1985 through 1994. State UCR programs were unable to provide forcible rape figures in accordance with UCR guidelines in Illinois (1985-94), Michigan (1993), and Minnesota (1993). Forcible rape totals were estimated for these states using national rates within eight population groups (e.g., cities with more than 250,000 population, cities with 100,000 to 249,999 population, suburban counties, rural counties) and then assigning counts of forcible rape proportional to each state's distribution in these population groups.

1988 and 1991. Reporting problems at the state level resulted in no usable data for Florida and Kentucky in 1988. NIBRS conversion required the estimation of state totals for Iowa in 1991.

1993 and 1994. NIBRS conversion efforts resulted in the estimation of state totals for Kansas and Illinois.

1994. Montana state totals were estimated by updating previous valid annual totals for individual jurisdictions in the state and subdividing them by population groups.

1996. Annual crime totals for the state of Kansas were extrapolated from state-level data for only the first six months. Valid state totals in 1994 and percent changes between 1995 and 1996 in their respective geographic regions were used to generate 1996 state totals for Kentucky and Montana. Aggregate state totals in Florida were derived from 94 individual agencies.

1998. State totals for Kentucky, Montana, New Hampshire, and Wisconsin were estimated using 1997 state figures and applying percentage changes from 1997 to 1998 in the geographic division in which each state is located. Total counts for Kansas in 1998 were estimated from 1997 state data and 1998 crime trends for the west north-central division. Forcible rape data in Delaware did not conform to UCR guidelines, so totals were estimated.

From these examples of imputation of UCR data, it is clear that cross-jurisdictional and over time comparisons must be made with considerable caution.

Political Manipulation and Fabrication

An additional limitation of official crime statistics involves their manipulation and fabrication for political purposes. For better or worse, police departments are evaluated to some extent on the basis of the volume of crime in their jurisdiction. The mass media, city and county commissions, local chambers of commerce that promote tourism in their "safe" city, elections for incumbent police chiefs and sheriffs, and the general public are sources of considerable pressure on police departments to provide a positive spin on the effectiveness of their crime fighting activities. Although Chambliss (1984) suggests that "other things being equal, it is in the interests of the police to prove an increase in crime [because] higher crime rates . . . mean increased budgets" (p. 176) in general, the image of a rising crime rate is not good news for local businesses and police departments who are held accountable for these crime trends. Favorable crime statistics apparently make everyone happy. In the early 1970s, for example, several large police departments in the United States downgraded their crime rates "to create the illusion that the country is a safer place to walk at night because President Nixon's anti-crime measures are working" (*Justice Magazine* 1972:1).

In another example of this manipulation, Seidman and Couzens (1974) identified a significant decrease in the number of larceny-thefts of $50 or more in one jurisdiction as a result of the installation of a new police chief, who threatened to replace police commanders who were unable to reduce the amount of crime in their precincts. The importance of the $50 criterion was that larcenies of less than $50 were not reported to the FBI. Thus, simply by estimating the value of stolen goods to be slightly less than $50, it was possible for the police to reduce the official crime rate. Similarly, McCleary et al. (1982) note that a significant decline in the number of burglaries in one jurisdiction was related to a change in police procedure whereby burglary complaints were investigated by detectives as opposed to uniformed police officers. When this experiment of using detectives was terminated 21 months later, the burglary rate in the jurisdiction increased again. In another example, a 72 percent increase in the number of major crimes in New York City from 1965 to 1966 was primarily due to a change in crime reporting; the actual increase was only 6.5 percent (Weinraub 1967). In a perhaps even more disturbing example, in 1973, Orange City, California, based the pay of its police officers on decreases in crime. At least partially as a result of this change, the reported crime rates for rape, robbery, auto theft, and burglary dropped by 19 percent in this jurisdiction over a one-year period (Holsendoph 1974).

Given that the police have exclusive control over the dissemination of crime data and there is little monitoring of the accuracy of their crime counts, one obvious way to demonstrate effective law enforcement is to distort, manipulate, and fabricate the number and nature of crime reports. The claim of "cooking the data" has long been alleged against law enforcement agencies, and numerous incidents of police misconduct over the last few decades have increasingly challenged the integrity of law enforcement and have led to growing suspicion about the pervasiveness of cooking data across the country.

When submitting crime data to the UCR program, there are various ways for local agencies to distort and undercount crime incidents. The most basic methods for "creative accounting" through falsifying crime reports include the following:

- Not reporting all crime incidents on monthly UCR submissions

- Combining separate events as if they occurred in multiple-offense incidents and falsely using the hierarchy rule to undercount the total number of crime reports

- Declaring large numbers of reported crimes as "unfounded" so they are not counted in UCR annual summaries

- "Downgrading" major Part I offenses to minor offenses so they are not tallied nationally in the UCR summaries

The particular reasons or motives for the police manipulation of crime statistics are wide and varied. Economic interests and political posturing are sometimes the underlying cause of the artificial inflation of crime statistics by law enforcement agencies, whereas these and other reasons may be the basis for the undercounting of crime. The following examples illustrate both the diversity of motives and the magnitude of distortion and manipulation of crime statistics by law enforcement officials.

Crime Reporting in Philadelphia, Pennsylvania

Some of the most serious allegations of fabrication of crime statistics involve practices in the Philadelphia Police Department. The distortion and manipulation of crime statistics in this jurisdiction has grown out of a "culture of statistical manipulation" that goes back for decades. In 1953, for example, Philadelphia reported 28,560 index crimes plus negligent manslaughter and larceny under $50, which represented an increase of more than 70 percent compared to 1951 figures. This tremendous increase in crime, however, was not due to an "invasion by criminals" (Bell 1967:152) but to the discovery by the new administration that earlier crime records had minimized the amount of crime in Philadelphia for a number of years. In fact, one district in the city had actually handled 5,000 more complaints than it had recorded (President's Commission 1968). This distortion of crime statistics apparently continued; in 1970, Philadelphia, which was the fourth largest city in the United States, reported fewer index crimes than any other city among the 10 largest. In fact, Baltimore, which had less than one half the population of Philadelphia, reported more than 60 percent more index crimes in 1970 (Seidman and Couzens 1974).

The two major forms of distortion that have been employed by the Philadelphia police in recent years are the excessive use of "unfounded" and "downgrading." It is estimated that literally thousands of sexual assault cases that occurred over the last two decades in Philadelphia have been buried by the sex-crime unit either by rejecting many of them as unfounded or by placing nearly one third of its caseload into noncriminal categories such as "investigation of person" and other "throwaway categories" (Faziollah, Matza, and McCoy 1999).When the high rates of unfounded sexual assault were scrutinized, the sex-crime unit reported low rates for the next year simply by shifting these cases to "investigation of persons," which are excluded in police summary data reported to the FBI.

A number of different types of downgrading have been used in Philadelphia to circumvent the counting of Part I index offenses. The city has consistently had one of the lowest rates of aggravated assault of any large city because many of these attacks are classified as "hospital cases" or downgraded to simple assaults, thereby being excluded from UCR data on serious crimes. Similarly, the index crime of burglary is often downgraded to "lost property," car thefts and break-ins are redefined as "vandalism," and street muggings without injury (categorized as robbery in the UCR) are downgraded to the minor offenses of "threats."

The manipulation of crime statistics in Philadelphia has been so notorious that dramatic actions have been taken to explore its source and curtail the practice. These procedures have included the auditing of police crime figures by the city controller's office, the assignment of 45 detectives to reinvestigate more than 2,000 sex offenses that were downgraded over a five-year period, the appointment of an academic panel to develop yearly auditing procedures, and a formal inquiry by former U.S. Attorney General Janet Reno. The new Philadelphia police commissioner has taken several measures to increase the accuracy of police data, including the dismissal of district captains who were in charge of crime data and the use of undercover investigators posing as crime victims to determine whether police are recording the incidents accurately.

Although these corrective actions should improve the accuracy of police statistics in this jurisdiction, the impact of these presumed improvements in reporting practices on actual crime rates in Philadelphia is debatable. In 1998, the Philadelphia police department failed to report an estimated 37,000 index crimes, but when these crimes were included, Philadelphia moved from the fifth to the second most dangerous city in the United States (*Time* 2000). Not surprisingly, police officials in Philadelphia attributed this major increase in crime rates to more accurate reporting rather than a surge in violent behavior. However, by blaming rising crime trends on better reporting procedures, officials in this jurisdiction may be engaging in other forms of manipulation and "creative writing" to deflect attention away from ineffective law enforcement practices. It is within this context that both accurate and inaccurate reporting of crime may be functional for local police departments.

Crime Reporting in Other U.S. Cities

In addition to the situation with the Philadelphia police force, there is also evidence that police officials in the city of Atlanta manipulated crime statistics through the use of the unfounded option. Slightly more than one rape report per week was written off by the Atlanta police as never having happened in 1996 (Martz 1999). These rape reports and nearly 500 robberies were quickly classified as unfounded and not counted in official crime reports.

By eliminating these serious crimes from official records, the Atlanta police department was able to make their city appear less violent than it actually was that year. City officials claimed that rapes had declined by 11 percent from 1995 (when including the unfounded rapes would have revealed a 2 percent increase), and that robbery rates had declined by 9 percent (instead of increasing by 1 percent when the unfounded robberies were included). The timing of this downgrading of violent crime was crucial because the Olympic games were held in Atlanta in late August of 1996 and a mayoral election was also held that year (Martz 1999).

As a result of a major public dispute between the Atlanta police chief and her deputy chief who managed the crime statistics section of the department, a joint state-federal FBI audit was conducted to assess the accuracy of crime reports in the city. The audit revealed that approximately 16 percent of the cases examined in the mid-1990s were improperly classified as unfounded, providing support for the deputy chief's allegation that the department was "manipulating crime reporting" (Martz 1999). Based on UCR policies, the reporting error rate for the most serious violent crimes was 26 percent in 1996.

As might be expected, the Atlanta police chief blamed the high error rate on confusion in the UCR classification rules for unfounded cases, rather than to the department's deliberate manipulation of the crime data. However, a former robbery detective was quoted as saying that detectives were encouraged in subtle ways by supervisors to record particular types of cases as unfounded (e.g., homeless people, both suspects and victims who were drug users). This detective noted that "the system was set up to cheat a little bit, not to cheat in big numbers" (as quoted in Martz 1999).

Substantial reductions in official crime rates in New York City from 1995 to 2000 have been attributed to aggressive and effective law enforcement practices by police officials, whereas critics have alleged that the reduction is due to distortion and manipulation through downgrading and unfounding cases. Downgrading in Boca Raton, Florida, resulted in an 11 percent decline in the felony crime rate in 1997. In that jurisdiction, a police captain downgraded crimes reported by investigating officers as burglaries and car thefts to vandalism and "suspicious incidents." In one particular case, the captain changed a burglary charge to vandalism when $5,000 worth of jewels were taken and $25,000 in damage was done (Rozsa 1998).

The use of categories such as "vandalism, trespassing or missing property" to downgrade residential burglaries has also occurred in smaller cities such as South Bend, Indiana (Sulok 1998). Alternative strategies include delaying the submission of crime data until after elections, as has occurred in some cities. Political opponents allege that these delays are used to conceal potentially damaging crime trends, whereas the incumbents claim the delays are due to such factors as computer problems that delay the timely release of the data.

Official data can also be distorted through the peculiar practices of individual police departments with respect to some crimes. For example, between 1996 and 2000, Detroit had arrested far more people in homicide cases than any other big-city police department, reporting an average of nearly three arrests per homicide. Most cities average roughly one arrest per homicide. As a result of these practices, Detroit, with less than 2 percent of the population of the United States, accounted for 1 in 13 homicide arrests in the United States in 1998 and 1999. When questioned about these statistics, officials in Detroit claimed that they were the result of computer glitches or the arrests of people at homicide scenes on unrelated charges (Belluck 2001).

The pattern of manipulation, distortion, and fabrication of official crime data is a serious problem that may be self-perpetuating. For example, the considerable media attention devoted to the declining crime rate in New York City has placed great pressure on other cities to report similar reductions in crime. If these data are generated through selective reporting practices, however, this may persuade other jurisdictions to use creative counting methods. Under these conditions, the continuing decrease in the number of UCR index crimes over the 1990-99 period may be more reflective of changes in police reporting and recording activities than changes in criminal activity in the larger society.

The Serial Killer Epidemic

During the early and mid-1980s, considerable media attention was focused on the apparent serial killer epidemic in the United States. Riveting television interviews with serial killers such as Ted Bundy and Henry Lee Lucas helped arouse public hysteria about these types of offenders. U.S. Justice Department officials, extrapolating from data in the UCR's Supplemental Homicide Reports, claimed that as many as 4,000 persons were murdered by serial killers in the United States each year.

Taking issue with these claims, Jenkins (1994) argued that Justice Department officials grossly inflated their estimates of the annual number of serial murders. This major counting error was the result of the dubious assumption that all or most of the Supplemental Homicide Report murders classified as "motiveless/offender unknown" were the work of serial killers. Jenkins concluded from his extensive analysis of serial killers that such offenders are responsible for no more than 350 to 400 murders in the United States each year.

The manipulation of official crime data to create the image of a serial killer "epidemic" served several organizational goals for the Justice Department. Specifically, this apparent epidemic provided an immediate justification for a new Violent Criminal Apprehension Program at a new center for the study of violent crime at the FBI Academy in Quantico, Virginia. The dramatic rise in the popularity of crime profiling was also initially based on this alleged serial killer epidemic.

Official Data on Juvenile Gang Crime

Official estimates of the number of youthful gang members and gang crime have skyrocketed in the United States over the last three decades. Agencies such as the National Youth Gang Center estimate from surveys of police departments that there are nearly 31,000 gangs and about 850,000 gang members currently in the United States (see Bilchik 1999). However, because there is no uniform procedure for removing files of inactive gang members, law enforcement agencies' estimates of the number and age range of gang members in their jurisdictions are very likely to be artificially inflated. In addition, political pressures to deny or minimize local gang problems, as well as the countervailing tendency to exaggerate them in order to secure monetary incentives to fight gangs, play a role in distorting the statistics on gang membership (Snyder and Sickmund 1999).

In a study of whether the law enforcement response to gangs in Nevada was commensurate with the magnitude of the gang problem, McCorkle and Miethe (2001) found that police statistics on gangs are seriously distorted. For example, contrary to the image of dangerous youthful offenders portrayed in the media and other sources, these researchers discovered that a large percentage of gang members included on police gang rosters were adults, and a large percentage were individuals who had not been charged with any criminal offense. Instead, they were persons who had been "field identified" as gang members because of their associates, style of dress, race, and geographical location.

The official image of gangs as violent hordes with guns and selling drugs is also inconsistent with the substantiated prosecutorial data collected in Nevada. Specifically, McCorkle and Miethe (2001) found that less than 10 percent of violent crimes and drug offenses filed in Las Vegas courts involved gang members as suspects. Although official police statistics in Las Vegas indicated a dramatic rise in gangs and gang members in the 1980s, this presumed rise in gang activity over time was not validated by a rise in gang prosecutions.

The results of this study of youth gangs are interpreted as representing a "moral panic." From this perspective, police used selective crime statistics and counting procedures to convey the notion of gang crime as a "clear and present danger" to the community. This presumed threat from youth gangs was more imaginary than real, but the police used their official statistics on gangs as part of a justification for additional financial resources to increase the size of the gang unit and to pass a special bond issue that provided for more police officers.

Summary and Conclusions

This chapter examined police statistics on the nature and prevalence of crime. We discussed the definitions of criminal conduct underlying the UCR classification system, the problems associated with classifying and scoring crimes under this system, the nature and prevalence of crime based on official measures, and the major limitations of police data as an accurate measure of crime.

Throughout the process of reporting and recording official instances of crime, criminal definitions are socially constructed. In other words, each official "count" of crime requires some amount of interpretation and negotiation. Under the widely regarded UCR system in the United States, a crime report becomes part of the official data only after surviving the following five decision points: (1) someone must perceive an event or behavior as a crime, (2) the crime must come to the attention of the police, (3) the police must agree that a crime has occurred, (4) the police must code the crime on the proper UCR form and submit it to the FBI, and (5) the FBI must include the crime in the UCR (Beirne and Messerschmidt 2000:39).

Of the many problems associated with police statistics on crime, charges of political manipulation and fabrication of these statistics are particularly insidious because they challenge the basic integrity of these data. Although more extensive auditing and monitoring may improve data quality, the processing of police crime data remains largely unavailable for public scrutiny and thus continues to be susceptible to creative accounting methods that may serve political ends. Under conditions of growing distrust of statistical data and numerous allegations about downgrading of offenses, UCR claims regarding declining national crime rates and the characteristics of offenders derived from these data may best be viewed as tentative estimates that are rooted on rather shaky grounds.

Notes

1. The hotel rule only applies to the offense of burglary, however. Thus, robbery of three individuals in three separate motel rooms would be scored as three separate offenses of robbery (UCR 1984).
2. The hierarchy rule does not apply to arson, which is always reported, even in multiple offense situations (FBI 2000).
3. It is not clear, however, that the implementation of NIBRS will eliminate the practice of using the hierarchy rule on the part of individual police departments. Roberts (1997) reports that only one third of law enforcement agencies using NIBRS collected information on all crimes involved in an incident, whereas the remainder continued to follow the hierarchy rule.
4. UCR data can be accessed through the following website: www.fbi.gov/ucr/ucr.htm
5. The data presented in Exhibit 3.7 are based on information from the 1998 UCR.

Chapter Four

Self-Report Studies

Respondents are a tricky bunch, and they do not always behave the way a researcher would wish or expect. In fact, surveys would be far more reliable without them.

Coleman and Moynihan (1996:77)

Self-report studies of crime were developed in the 1940s and 1950s, largely in response to concerns among criminologists that official measures of crime were systematically biased and provided a distorted picture of the nature and extent of crime and its correlates.

One of the primary advantages of self-report studies is that the information individuals provide regarding their behavior is not filtered through any official or judicial process. The criminal justice funnel—which illustrates how, at each stage of the system, fewer and fewer illegal behaviors are siphoned off for official crime counts—does not operate with respect to self-report data.

However, what individuals tell us about their behavior may or may not be a reliable and valid source for determining how involved they are in criminal activity. Memories of events—even of ones as dramatic as criminal episodes—may be fuzzy rather than clear, especially when it comes to recollecting the time period in which they occurred or the sequence of their occurrence. The questions that researchers ask may be phrased in ways that are different from the way people think of their behavior. For example, asking, "In the past six months, have you abused or aggressed against a family member?" may elicit a different response than "In the past six months, have you slapped, hit, or punched anyone in your house?" Even with "good" nonjudgmental questions, however, respondents may be reluctant to answer fully and truthfully—at least partially because of the fact that they are being asked to admit to behaviors that might result in their arrest if the actions became known to authorities.

Our purpose in this chapter is to make you a savvy consumer, as well as evaluator, of self-report measures of crime. Because of its importance to both self-report and victimization data, we begin with a brief discussion of survey methodology. We then review the methodology and findings of some of the more prominent self-report studies, including the National Youth Survey (NYS), the Monitoring the Future (MTF) survey, and the National Household Survey on Drug Abuse (NHSDA). This is followed by a review of a prominent and enduring debate in the discipline of criminology regarding the connection between social class and crime, a debate that led to further refinements and improvements in self-report methodology. We then discuss self-report data from known offenders, which have provided particular insights into the crime patterns of individuals who have been apprehended by the criminal justice system. The chapter concludes with an examination of studies focusing on the validity of self-reported data on drug use.

The Method behind the Measure

Self-report measures of crime are subject to the same constraints found in survey research more generally. Criticisms regarding the adequacy or accuracy of self-report as well as victimization data have as much, if not more, to do with *how* the data are collected as they do with *what* those data might tell us about crime and criminals. In order to anticipate and understand these criticisms, we briefly address the sources of error in survey research before discussing specific self-report studies.

Sources of Survey Error

At the core, evaluating any survey and the data derived from it revolves around two central issues (Phillips, Mosher, and Kabel 2000):

1. Were the right people asked the right questions?

2. Did they answer truthfully?

In survey research terminology, these two issues expand into the four sources of total survey error (see, e.g., Dillman 2000; Groves 1989; Groves 1996; Junger-Tas and Marshall 1999; Salant and Dillman 1994).

Coverage error means that researchers selected individuals from a list—a *sampling frame*—that did not include all the people they intended to study: the *target population*. To illustrate this principle, consider the following example. A researcher is interested in determining how welfare recipients feel about their encounters with social service and criminal justice agencies. They have access to a current list of welfare recipients in their state, from which they will select a sample. There are already two limits on coverage: only people receiving welfare as of a certain date who live in the state can be included in the survey and described by its results. There is an additional limitation imposed by the *survey mode* used to obtain information from the sample members. A telephone survey may be expedient, but a high percentage of welfare recipients may not have telephone service. A mail survey likely would include most, if not all, welfare recipients, but literacy may be a problem in enough cases to contribute to two other sources of error: nonresponse and measurement (see below). A face-to-face survey could address the deficiencies of either of the other two modes but at great cost in terms of time and money. As this example illustrates, coverage error can be relatively easy to identify but not easy to correct.

Sampling error is an automatic, unavoidable result of surveying a subset, rather than taking a census, of all the people in the target population. This is the source of survey error that is referred to when journalists report that a political exit poll or public opinion survey has a "margin of error of plus or minus five points." It means that it can be estimated, by using a well-established statistical formula, how closely the survey sample mirrors the target population. Although it is rarely reported by journalists, sampling error is estimated within a specified "confidence level" that indicates how sure we are about the estimate. For example, if the survey's sampling error is estimated as ± 5 percentage points at the 95 percent confidence level, we can be confident that 95 times out of 100 the percentage of sample members who gave a certain response will be within 5 percentage points either way of the "true" percentage in the target population who would give that response if asked. Unfortunately, confidence levels apply only to predictions in the long run (referred to as an infinite number of trials); any particular sampling outcome may fall within or outside the specific range of the 95 percent confidence level. Although sampling error cannot be eliminated from surveys, it can be reduced by increasing the sample size and obtaining responses from a larger proportion of people in the target population.

Nonresponse error affects survey data when *both* of the following are apparent: (a) too many people in the sample did not respond to the survey, either because they could not be contacted via the survey mode or they refused to participate and (b) the nonrespondents differ from respondents in ways that are important to the objectives of the survey. Why both conditions must hold is easily illustrated. Consider a survey in which researchers have completed interviews with 70 percent of their sample, a quite respectable response rate for social surveys. Most of the respondents have brown eyes, whereas most of the nonrespondents have hazel, green, or blue eyes. Is this survey plagued by nonresponse error? The answer to this question depends on the research questions. If the researcher is interested in the relative sun-sensitivity reported by people with different eye colors or their preferences for using contact lenses of different hues, then nonresponse likely is a problem. Even though there is a high response rate to the survey, respondents differ from nonrespondents on a variable of interest, eye color. If, on the other hand, the researcher is interested in attitudes toward capital punishment, nonresponse on the basis of eye color would not be a source of error, because eye color is not germane to this issue.

To return to the earlier example of surveying welfare recipients regarding their encounters with social service and criminal justice agencies, assume that the researcher obtains an 80 percent response rate. However, more than 60 percent of the respondents are female, and more than 70 percent of the nonrespondents are male. Nonresponse error is a serious problem in this case, because gender is a factor not only in the number but also in the character of contacts with social service and criminal justice agencies. It is possible for a survey with a 99 percent response rate to be subject to nonresponse error if the 1 percent who did not respond differ in predictably significant, substantive ways from the respondents. Likewise, a survey with a response rate of only 40 percent may be immune to nonresponse error if the nonrespondents are similar to respondents in ways that might make a difference in analyzing the data from the survey.

As mentioned in Chapter 1, the process of operationalization involves attaching meaning to abstract concepts and developing specific indicators and measures of those concepts. How researchers decide to measure these concepts, the nature and number of indicators that are used to identify them, and the specific wording used to define them are all sources of measurement error. In evaluating measures of any phenomenon, social scientists are concerned with issues of validity and reliability.

Validity and Reliability

Validity is the degree to which a measure captures what it is intended to measure: if a measure is valid, it is true and accurate. Some measures have prima facie (i.e., clear or self-evident, often called face) validity. Other measures possess validity only for specific cases and within strictly defined boundaries. Consider this example. Which of the following is more valid as a measure of the physical stature of human beings: (a) height and weight as recorded by physicians at routine physical exams and/or by coroners at an autopsy, (b) sizes of clothing most frequently purchased from the inventories of top- and/or bottom-tier manufacturers and department stores, (c) dimensions of seating and lavatory areas in commercial airlines, or (d) observations of, and conversations with, people at public events and/or on the streets at rush hour? The first option—height and weight as recorded by a medical practitioner—does seem to be prima facie valid for measuring physical stature, but the other three options have fairly obvious limitations when it comes to measuring what is intended. However, people who have routine physical exams or those whose deaths require an autopsy may not be representative of all human beings. Thus, even the validity of what appears to be the most accurate measurement can be compromised by an inadequate or biased sampling frame. We will return to these threats to validity after defining the second criterion for evaluating any measurement.

Reliability is the extent to which the same results are obtained each time the measure is used. If something is a reliable measurement, then it is a precise, consistent, and dependable one. A bathroom scale that showed an individual having three different weights on three different occasions over a 10-minute period would not be reliable. In the case of self-report studies of criminal and deviant behavior, reliability refers to the ability of the procedure used and the questions asked to generate consistent responses from the same respondents on repeated administrations. For example, if individuals are asked whether they have ever stolen something and they answer yes, then they should answer yes the next time they are asked the same question. But just as all squares are rectangles but not all rectangles are squares, all valid measures are reliable ones, but not all reliable measures are valid.

In survey research, threats to validity and reliability (i.e., measurement error) derive from any of four aspects of the study (see, e.g., Aquilino 1994;

Aquilino and Wright 1986; Dillman and Tarnai 1991; Dykema and Schaeffer 2000). The survey *mode*, whether it is telephone, mail, or face-to-face, may result in different answers to the same question, even when posed to the same types of respondents. For example, studies have found that respondents are more likely to report drug use on self-administered answer sheets than in face-to-face interviews (Harrison 1997). The survey *instrument* may include questions with response categories that are not mutually exclusive or with terms that are not interpreted in the same way by different respondents. The survey *interviewer* may unintentionally prompt a particular response by either attempting to clarify the meaning of a question (resulting in "leading" the respondent) or by giving the impression that a particular response is correct or expected (resulting in a "socially desirable" answer from the respondent). Finally, the survey *respondent* may misunderstand the question or may feel that the question is too nosy and prying or may just plain lie. All of these will result in mistakes in measurement.

To restate the sources of survey error in the context of the two key questions regarding survey research—were the right people asked the right questions and did they answer with the truth—if the *coverage* of the target population is inadequate or the *sampling* strategy is inappropriate or the *nonresponse* rate jeopardizes either of them, the right people have not been asked the right question. If the *measurement* strategy elicits responses that are imprecise or might be inaccurate or cannot be compared to others, then the data do not allow us to determine if the respondent is telling the truth.

Self-Reports on Crime and Delinquency

Chapter 2 documented that most of the early self-report measures of crime and its correlates were intended to discover, document, and describe the "true" dimensions—or dark figure—of crime. Some researchers believed that there was a great deal of illegal behavior that was not captured by official statistics. Rather than taking those statistics at face value, they attempted to learn about criminal activities directly from the individuals who were engaging in them, whether or not those activities were detected by law enforcement.

The work of James Short and Ivan Nye, briefly discussed in Chapter 2, serves as an instructive example of both the strengths and weaknesses of self-report data on illegal activities (see, e.g., Nye and Short 1957; Short 1955; Short 1957; Short and Nye 1957-58; Short and Nye 1958). "Non-institutionalized adolescents" was the targeted population, and, "because they seem likely to be more representative of the general population than are college or training school populations," Short and Nye (1958:297) drew their samples from public high schools, administering an anonymous questionnaire to these students. Exhibit 4.1 lists the items included on Short and Nye's questionnaire designed to measure the youths' involvement in delinquent and criminal activities. From responses to the questionnaire, Short and Nye (1958:301-2) drew the following conclusions, among others: (a) "delinquent conduct in the non-institutionalized population is extensive and variable," (b) self-reported delinquent conduct is similar to official delinquency and crime in that boys admit committing nearly all delinquencies more often than do girls, and the offenses for which boys and girls are most often arrested are the ones they admit to committing most often, (c) self-reported delinquent conduct differs from official statistics in that delinquency is distributed more evenly throughout the socioeconomic classes of noninstitutionalized populations, whereas official cases are concentrated in the lower economic strata.

There are, however, a number of questions that can be raised regarding Short and Nye's work. First, are students enrolled in high schools likely to be representative of the general youth population? What about dropouts and other young people who might have been absent for one reason or another on the day(s) the questionnaire was administered? Second, many of the behaviors listed in the questionnaire are not described in legalistic, "criminal" terms. One of the many challenges of obtaining valid and reliable self-reports and comparing these to official data is translating the reported behaviors into categories consistent with those in sources such as the Uniform Crime Reports (UCR). Third, and in a similar vein, many of the items contained on the Short and Nye questionnaire are oriented toward the less serious end of the crime scale. The fact that many self-report instruments focus on relatively "trivial" behaviors such as skipping school and defying parents' authority has become an enduring criticism of self-report studies.

Despite these shortcomings, Short and Nye's work was important in the sense that it revealed that a considerable amount of crime and delinquency was not officially recorded. And much of this hidden delinquency was apparently committed by young people from relatively privileged backgrounds; Short and Nye found few social class distinctions in either the range or frequency of involvement in self-reported illegal activities. As a result, "Short and Nye's work stimulated much interest in both the use of self-report methodology and the substantive issue concerning the relationship between some measure of social status (socioeconomic status, ethnicity, race) and delinquent behavior" (Thornberry and Krohn 2000:37).

Exhibit 4.1. Questionnaire Items on Self-Reported Delinquency and Crime

"Have you ever . . . ?" Have you . . . more than once or twice?"

Driven a car without a driver's license or permit
Skipped school
Had a fist fight with one person
Run away from home
[Been on] school probation or expulsion
Defied parents' authority
Driven too fast or recklessly
Taken little things (worth less than $2) that did not belong to you
Taken things of medium value ($2-$50)
Taken things of large value ($50)
Taken a car for a ride without the owner's knowledge
Bought or drank beer, wine, or liquor (including drinking at home)
Bought or drank beer, wine, or liquor (outside your home)
Drank beer, wine, or liquor in your own home
[Caused] deliberate property damage
Used or sold narcotic drugs
Had sex relations with another person of the same sex (not masturbation)
Had sex relations with a person of the opposite sex
Gone hunting or fishing without a license (or violated other game laws)
Taken things you didn't want
Beat up on kids who hadn't done anything to you
Hurt someone to see them squirm

SOURCE: Short and Nye (1958, from table 1, p. 297). Reprinted with special permission of Northwestern University School of Law, *Journal of Criminal Law and Criminology.*

Hundreds of self-report surveys that have been conducted in the past 50 years largely confirm the findings from the earliest self-report studies of crime. However, as we will discuss in more detail below, several more recent studies, using more sophisticated methods, instruments, and analyses, have challenged the conclusions regarding little or no association between social class variables and criminal behavior. In the following section, we describe three surveys, each of them national in scope, that arguably are standard bearers for collecting and analyzing self-report data. Not only do these provide self-report data on illicit activities, but they also form the basis for research on and debates about techniques for improving the quality of self-report data. The three surveys selected here for special consideration are presented in reverse chronological order in terms of when they were first conducted. The first of them, the NYS, is the only one that measures criminal and delinquent behavior in addition to use of controlled substances and alcohol.

National Youth Survey

First conducted in 1977, the NYS was designed specifically to provide both prevalence and incidence estimates of the commission of delinquent activities by youth. It is a longitudinal survey that uses a national-probability-based sample of young people who were 11 to 17 years old at the time of the first interview (Elliott, Huizinga, and Morse 1986). Participants in this study were interviewed in their homes at one-year intervals through 1981 and at two- to three-year intervals at least through 1995. More than 90 percent of the original 1,725 participants have remained in the survey over time. Exhibit 4.2 provides a list of some of the questions used in the NYS.

Confidential, face-to-face interviews solicit information on the number of times the respondent has engaged in a specific delinquent or criminal activity within the past calendar year, with two different response sets used. If an individual's response to an open-ended question indicates they have engaged in the activity more than 10 times, the interviewers ask the youth to select one of the following responses: (a) once a month, (b) once every 2 to 3 weeks, (c) once a week, (d) 2 to 3 times a week, (e) once a day, or (f) 2 to 3 times a day. Although described in nonlegalistic terms, the 47 activities asked about directly parallel offenses listed in the FBI's UCR. Of the Part I offenses, only homicide is excluded; about 75 percent of Part II offenses are included, along with a wide range of misdemeanors and status offenses.

Exhibit 4.3 presents data on prevalence and incidence rates of self-reported offending for the first five waves of the NYS. Because the NYS is a longitudinal survey, the panel of respondents reporting on their behavior for 1976 is the same group of people reporting for 1980, and this is why the age range is different for each of the five years. With respect to prevalence rates (i.e., the percentage of respondents who report having engaged in certain types of crime) for felony assault and theft, both whites and blacks report lower involvement for 1980 than for 1976, and their self-reported rates of involvement in these offenses are nearly identical. For general delinquency, whites report a slightly lower involvement, whereas blacks report a slightly higher involvement for 1980 than for 1976.

Turning to incidence rates (i.e., the average number of offenses reported by each respondent who admitted having committed a crime), the picture is more mixed. For general delinquency, both whites and blacks report a higher average number of offenses for 1980 than for 1976. For index offenses and felony assault, whites report a higher frequency, whereas blacks report a lower frequency for 1980 than for 1976. For felony theft, the two racial groups switch positions, with blacks reporting higher and whites reporting lower incidence for 1980 than for 1976.

Exhibit 4.2. Selected Deviance Items from the National Youth Survey

(Preface) This section deals with your own behavior. I'd like to remind you that all your answers are confidential. I'll read a series of behaviors to you. Please give me your best estimate of the EXACT NUMBER of times you've done each thing during the last year from Christmas a year ago to the Christmas just past. (RECORD A SINGLE NUMBER, NOT A RANGE, AND "0" IF RESPONDENT NEVER ENGAGED IN A BEHAVIOR.

FOR ANY BEHAVIOR THAT THE RESPONDENT HAS ENGAGED IN 10 OR MORE TIMES IN THE LAST YEAR, ALSO RECORD RESPONSE IN THE SECOND COLUMN, SAYING:)
Please look at the responses on card number 8, the second ivory card, and select the one that best describes how often you were involved in this behavior.

How many times in the LAST YEAR have you:

	Once a month	*Once every 2-3 weeks*	*Once a week*	*2-3 times a week*	*Once a day*	*2-3 times a day*
217. purposely damaged or destroyed property belonging to your PARENTS or other FAMILY MEMBERS?						
(IF IN SCHOOL)						
218. purposely damaged or destroyed property belonging to a SCHOOL, COLLEGE, or UNIVERSITY?						
221. stolen or tried to steal a MOTOR VEHICLE such as a car or motorcycle?						
224. purposely set fire to a building, a car, or other property or tried to do so?						
225. carried a hidden weapon other than a plain pocket knife?						
227. attacked someone with the idea of seriously hurting or killing him or her?						
228. been paid for having sexual relations with someone?						
230. been involved in gang fights?						
231. used checks illegally or used phony money to pay for something? (INCLUDES INTENTIONAL OVERDRAFTS)						
232. sold marijuana or hashish ("POT," "GRASS, "HASH")?						
233. hitchhiked where it was illegal to do so?						

SOURCE: Adapted from Elliott (1983).

Exhibit 4.3. National Youth Survey Prevalence and Incidence Rates of Self-Reported Offending As Percentage of Respondent Age and Racial Group, 1976-80

	11-17 yrs 1976		12-18 yrs 1977		13-19 yrs 1978		14-20 yrs 1979		15-21 yrs 1980	
	White	Black	White	Black	White	Black	White	Black	White	Black
PREVALENCE: Percentage who report committing offense										
General delinquency[a]	67	70	64	67	64	70	65	73	65	72
Index offenses[b]	19	29	16	20	14	16	13	20	12	13
Felony assault[c]	15	23	12	17	10	11	10	16	9	9
Felony theft[d]	12	14	12	10	11	8	9	7	9	8
INCIDENCE: Average number of offenses per self-reported offender										
General delinquency[a]	28.6	35.8	25.0	32.2	27.2	30.4	32.2	33.3	33.0	38.0
Index offenses[b]	4.8	5.2	10.6	10.4	5.1	4.0	6.5	6.9	5.0	4.6
Felony assault[c]	2.7	4.6	4.9	5.6	3.0	2.1	4.3	4.2	3.4	2.2
Felony theft[d]	6.1	3.0	6.8	17.9	4.7	7.3	6.7	5.0	4.6	6.3

SOURCE: Huizinga and Elliott (1987, compiled from tables 1 and 3, pp. 211 and 216).
NOTES:
a. General delinquency = less serious offenses (e.g., minor theft, minor assault, property damage), status offenses, and serious offenses (e.g., felony theft, felony assault, robbery)
b. Index offenses = all UCR Part I offenses except homicide and minor larcenies
c. Felony assault = aggravated assaults, sexual assaults, and gang fights
d. Felony theft = grand theft, auto theft, burglary, and possession of stolen goods

The NYS has provided the database for a number of important substantive and methodological studies, many of which we will discuss in more detail in subsequent sections of this chapter. Here we just mention a few to provide a sense of the range of topics that can be addressed by NYS data. Several studies have focused on gender, race, and social class similarities and differences in self-reported offending (see, e.g., Ageton 1983; Huizinga and Elliott 1987; Smith, Visher, and Jarjoura 1991; Zhang and Messner 2000). Some researchers have focused on the relationship between drug use and involvement in predatory crime or on juvenile involvement in violent crime (see, e.g., Chaiken and Chaiken 1990; Elliott, Huizinga, and Morse 1986). Still others have used NYS data to test explanatory theories of delinquent and criminal behavior (see, e.g., Heimer and Matsueda 1994; Jang 1999a, 1999b; Jang and Johnson 2001; Lauritsen 1999).

Monitoring the Future: A Continuing Study of U.S. Youth

Since 1975, the MTF study[1] has served as a primary source of information about illicit drug, alcohol, and tobacco use by young people in the United States (Johnston, O'Malley, and Bachman 1999). Each year, published reports based on MTF data reveal the extent of use of a variety of substances. The study also examines attitudes among 8th-, 10th-, and 12th-grade students but does not address involvement in criminal and delinquent activities.

MTF is an extraordinarily ambitious and costly project—between 15,000 and 20,000 students in each of three grades, in addition to between 9,000 and 16,000 college students and young adults, complete an MTF questionnaire each year. The data from any given MTF survey year are virtually directly comparable to those from previous years, largely because sampling techniques and questionnaire formats are consistent from one year to the next.

MTF began with a cross-sectional survey of a representative sample of all seniors in public and private high schools in the coterminous United States (Johnston et al. 1999) but quickly became a longitudinal survey. With the exception of the first graduating class, follow-up questionnaires are mailed to a representative sample, consisting of approximately 2,400 individuals, of the members of each senior class who participated in the MTF. These follow-ups occur on seven occasions between the year of high school graduation and the year that the cohort reaches a modal age of 32, and constitute the college student and young adult samples for each MTF survey year.

The MTF survey instrument has been modified over the years to accommodate the use of different types of drugs as well as corollary attitudes and behaviors. For example, a question on crack cocaine was first added to the instrument in 1986, and more detailed questions about all forms of cocaine were included in the 1987 version. Questions on crystal methamphetamine ("ice") have been included since 1990; 8th, 10th, and 12th graders have been asked questions about MDMA (ecstasy) since 1996. In addition to typical questions about licit and illicit drugs, such as age or grade at first use, frequency and quantity of use, and perceived availability of drugs, the MTF also queries respondents regarding their attitudes and beliefs about involvement in risky behaviors as well as their perceptions of the attitudes, beliefs, and behaviors of others with whom they associate.

Exhibit 4.4 shows the percentages of each MTF sample group who report having used various illicit drugs, alcohol, and tobacco at any time in the

30 days prior to completing the questionnaire in 1997 and in 1998. Four out of the six most notable changes indicate a reduction in past 30-day use of the substance over the 1997 and 1998 period. The two notable increases are found among 12th graders in their reported recent use of barbiturates (from 2.1 percent in 1997 to 2.6 percent in 1998) and of tranquilizers (from 1.8 percent in 1997 to 2.4 percent in 1998). Examining more generally the direction of changes over the two years, it is clear that a smaller number of 8th, 10th, and 12th graders report using any illicit drug, drinking any alcohol, or smoking any cigarettes in 1998 than in 1997. The situation is reversed for college students: a larger percentage report using any illicit drug, drinking any alcohol, or smoking any cigarettes in 1998 than in 1997. The

Exhibit 4.4. MTF 30-Day Use of Illicit Drugs, Alcohol, and Tobacco as Percentage of Respondent Group, 1997 and 1998

	8th grade 1997 1998		10th grade 1997 1998		12th grade 1997 1998		College 1997 1998		19-28 yrs 1997 1998	
Approximate Nos.	18,600	18,100	15,500	15,000	15,400	15,200	1,480	1,440	6.400	6.200
Any Illicit Drug[a]	**12.9**	**12.1**	**23.0**	**21.5**	**26.2**	**25.6**	**19.2**	**19.7**	**16.4**	**16.1**
marijuana	10.2	9.7	20.5	18.7	23.7	22.8	17.7	18.6	15.0	14.9
cocaine	1.1	1.4	2.0	2.1	2.3	2.4	1.6	1.6	1.6	1.7
crack	0.7	0.9	0.9	1.1	0.9	1.0	0.2	0.2	0.3	0.3
inhalants	5.6	4.8	3.0	2.9	2.5	2.3	0.8	0.6	0.5	0.7
hallucinogens	1.8	1.4	3.3	3.2	3.9	3.8	2.1	2.1	1.5	1.4
PCP	–[b]	–	–	–	0.7	1.0	–	–	0.1	0.2
LSD	1.5	1.1	2.8	2.7	3.1	3.2	1.1	1.5	0.9	1.0
heroin	0.6	0.6	0.6	0.7	0.5	0.5	0.2	0.1	0.1	0.1
other narcotics	–	–	–	–	2.3	2.4	1.3	1.1	0.9	0.9
amphetamines	3.8	3.3	5.1	5.1	4.8	4.6	2.1	1.7	1.7	1.7
crystal meth "ice"	–	–	–	–	0.8	1.2	0.2	0.3	0.2	0.3
barbiturates	–	–	–	–	2.1	2.6	1.2	1.1	0.9	0.9
tranquilizers	1.2	1.2	2.2	2.2	1.8	2.4	1.2	1.3	1.1	1.2
Any not marijuana	6.0	5.5	8.8	8.6	10.7	10.7	6.8	6.1	5.5	5.5
Alcohol	**24.5**	**23.0**	**40.1**	**38.8**	**52.7**	**52.0**	**65.8**	**68.1**	**67.5**	**66.9**
been drunk	8.2	8.4	22.4	21.1	34.2	32.9	–	–	–	–
Cigarettes	**19.4**	**19.1**	**29.8**	**27.6**	**36.5**	**35.1**	**28.3**	**30.0**	**29.9**	**30.9**
Smokeless	**5.5**	**4.8**	**8.9**	**7.5**	**9.7**	**8.8**	–	–	–	–

SOURCE: Adapted from Johnston et al. (1999, table 2-2, Vol. I, Chapter 2, pp. 34-7).
NOTES:
    a. Any Illicit Drug = use at least once of any of the listed substances, not under a doctor's order.
    b. Dashes indicate question not asked of that group that survey year.

picture is more mixed for young adults (ages 19-28), with a smaller percentage of them reporting using any illicit drug or drinking any alcohol, whereas a larger percentage report smoking cigarettes in 1998 than in 1997.

MTF surveys also collect measures of regular or daily use of particular substances. Measuring regular use is important, because a large proportion of people who report having used a substance in the past month may be first-time and possibly only-time users. The more regularly a substance is used in a 30-day period, the greater the risk for any negative consequences associated with long-term use of the substance. In addition, some substances are viewed as gateway drugs, whose regular use by young people may lead to more hard-core substance abuse and addiction (Johnston et al. 1999: I:25).

Exhibit 4.5 shows the percentages of the MTF sample groups reporting daily use (i.e., on at least 20 occasions in the past 30 days) of the so-called gateway drugs: marijuana, alcohol, and tobacco. The percentages are considerably lower than those in Exhibit 4.4: for marijuana and alcohol, they are as low as one tenth and never as high as one fourth of the percentages reporting use at least once in the past month. For cigarettes, the percentages in the two tables are closer: about one half to two thirds as many past-month users report being daily smokers. There is also the same relative decrease in daily smokers as in past-month smokers among 12th graders as well as the same relative increase in daily smokers as in past-month smokers among college students.

Exhibit 4.5. MTF 30-Day Prevalence of *Daily* Use of Marijuana, Alcohol, and Tobacco as Percentage of Respondent Group, 1997 and 1998

	8th grade 1997 1998		10th grade 1997 1998		12th grade 1997 1998		College 1997 1998		19-28 yrs 1997 1998	
Approximate Nos.	18,600	18,100	15,500	15,000	15,400	15,200	1,480	1,440	6.400	6.200
Marijuana[a]	**1.1**	**1.1**	**3.7**	**3.6**	**5.8**	**5.6**	**3.7**	**4.0**	**3.8**	**3.71**
Alcohol[a]	**0.8**	0.9	1.7	1.9	**3.9**	3.9	**4.5**	3.9	**4.6**	4.0
Been drunk	0.2	0.3	0.6	0.6	2.0	1.5	–[d]	–	–	–
5+ drinks/2 wks[b]	14.5	13.7	25.1	24.3	31.3	31.5	40.7	38.9	34.4	34.1
Cigarettes[a]	**9.8**	8.8	**18.0**	15.8	24.6	22.4	15.2	18.0	20.6	21.9
½+ pack/day[c]	3.5	3.6	8.6	7.9	14.3	12.6	9.1	11.3[a]	14.6	15.6
Smokeless[a]	**1.0**	1.0	**2.2**	**2.2**	4.40	**3.2**	–	–	–	–

SOURCE: Adapted from Johnston et al. (1999, table 2-3, Vol. I, Chapter 2, p. 38)
NOTES:
  a. Daily use = use on 20 or more occasions in the past 30 days.
  b. 5+ drinks/2 wks = 5 or more drinks on single occasion in last 2 weeks.
  c. ½+ pack/day = ½ pack or more of cigarettes per day in last 30 days.
  d. Dashes indicate question not asked of that group that survey year.

Although the data do not appear in the tables in this chapter, the 1988 MTF found that 2.3 percent of both 8th- and 10th-grade students reported heroin use, compared to 2.0 percent of seniors. These higher rates of heroin use by younger students may be an artifact of the MTF sampling strategy, as heroin users may be more likely than other students to drop out of school before their senior year (Snyder and Sickmund 1999).

MTF surveys have provided valuable panel data on substance use patterns among young people over time. Perhaps more important in terms of this chapter, they have provided essential data for evaluating the validity of self-report measures of illicit behaviors (see, e.g., Caulkins 2000; Harrison 1997; Johnston and O'Malley 1997).

National Household Survey on Drug Abuse

First conducted in 1971, the NHSDA[2] is an enduring source of information about illicit drug, alcohol, and tobacco use in the United States (Substance Abuse and Mental Health Services Administration [SAMHSA] 2000). Like the MTF, each year the NHSDA reveals the prevalence as well as incidence of drug use. Unlike the MTF survey, however, the NHSDA is administered each year to a different sample of noninstitutionalized civilians who are 12 years or older.

Like the MTF study, the NHSDA is ambitious and costly, involving face-to-face interviews across the United States with nearly 18,000 individuals in 1995 and almost 67,000 in 1999. The survey is cross-sectional as opposed to longitudinal, and some groups in the target population are oversampled to ensure that there is a sufficient number of interviews to calculate reasonable estimates of drug use by those groups that either may not show up in adequate numbers in a random sample of the population or may be of particular interest. For example, the NHSDA has traditionally oversampled people under age 35, and blacks and Hispanics have been oversampled since 1985. In certain years, residents from rural areas have been oversampled, whereas in other years, residents from urban areas or low socioeconomic status residents within those urban areas have been oversampled.

Similar to the survey used for MTF, the NHSDA survey instrument has been modified over the years to accommodate the use of different types of drugs as well as correlates of drug-using behaviors. Some of these modifications have been implemented for only one or two survey years. For example, the 1979 and 1982 surveys asked respondents not only about their own but also about their friends' use of heroin in order to obtain a better sense of the prevalence of heroin use in the United States. The 1982 survey also included a special section on medical as well as nonmedical use of stimulants, sedatives, tranquilizers, and analgesics. In 1995, respondents were asked about their need for drug or alcohol treatment and their criminal record. Other changes to the questionnaire have become standard features of the NHSDA since they were first introduced. For example, since 1985, there have been questions on (a) the use of cigarettes and related products such as smokeless tobacco, (b) perceived consequences of using various drugs, and (c) the various ways in which cocaine is administered. In 1988, other questions about crack cocaine and sharing needles for drug injection were added to the survey. Questions about health insurance and total annual family income were introduced in 1990, about employment and drug testing in the workplace in 1991, and about mental health and access to health care in 1994.

Although the questions on the NHSDA survey have varied over the years, its mode of administration remained unchanged until 1999. For nearly three decades, the NHSDA was a face-to-face, paper and pencil interview (PAPI) that took approximately one hour to complete. Trained interviewers read aloud the survey items to respondents, who recorded their answers to questions deemed sensitive (such as those on substance use) on separate sheets so that interviewers could not see their responses. Interviewers recorded respondents' answers to nonsensitive questions (such as those on occupational status and household composition) directly on the survey booklet.

The 1999 NHSDA heralded a major shift in the mode of administration. Rather than a PAPI, it was a combination of computer-assisted personal interview (CAPI) and a computer-assisted self-interview (CASI). The CAPI portion corresponds to the questions for which interviewers recorded respondents' answers on the booklet, whereas the CASI portion allows respondents to enter their own answers to sensitive questions. The use of computer-assisted interviewing (CAI) is expected not only to improve the efficiency of data collection and processing but also to increase respondents' honesty in reporting illicit drug use and related behaviors. Whether the latter expectation was met by the CAI on its first use in 1999 is not yet known. It is known, however, that the efficiency of data collection was not improved. Response rates early on in the 1999 survey were so low compared to previous years that additional, complicated subsampling and weighting techniques had to be applied. Furthermore, because the mode of administration has been shown to affect both response rates and the content of responses, "the NHSDA also included a supplemental sample using the paper and pencil interviewing mode for the purposes of measuring trends with estimates comparable to 1998 and prior years" (SAMHSA 2000, app. A:1).

Another complicating, although ultimately highly beneficial, change in the 1999 NHSDA was the introduction of state-based probability sampling. Through 1998, with the exception of those survey periods when particular regions were oversampled, the NHSDA sampling design was based on national figures. Estimates regarding illicit drug use by certain groups could be applied only to the United States as a whole, not to individual states. (Drawing inferences about drug use by region of the country was somewhat less risky, although still questionable.) To make it possible to calculate substance use estimates separately for states, as well as to allow for more detailed analyses of national patterns, the 1999 NHSDA drew "an independent, multi-stage area probability sample for each of the 50 states and the District of Columbia" (SAMHSA 2000, intro:1). California, Florida, Illinois, Michigan, New York, Ohio, Pennsylvania, and Texas—eight states that together account for 48 percent of the U.S. population age 12 and older—were oversampled. Also oversampled were youths and young adults, so that each state's sample was approximately equally distributed among three major age groups: 12 to 17 years, 18 to 25 years, and 26 years and older.

Exhibit 4.6 shows the percentages of respondents to the NHSDA who report current use (at least once in the month prior to the interview) of illicit drugs, alcohol, and tobacco for the NHSDA survey years of 1994 and 1999.[3] With respect to the correlates of involvement in these types of behaviors, the data are largely consistent with other measures of illegal or deviant behavior or both. For example, the 18- to 25-year-old age group has the highest percentage reporting "any illicit drug" use in the past month for both survey years. Of the specific illicit drugs listed, marijuana/hashish is far and away reported as used in the past month by the highest percentage of respondents of every age group for both survey years. In addition, the 18- to 25-year-old group shows a notable increase in current marijuana use from 1994 (12.1 percent) to 1999 (16.4 percent).

A few other things are worth noting about these data. One is the near doubling in the percentage of 18- to 25-year-olds reporting current use of hallucinogens (1.8 percent in 1994 to 3.5 percent in 1999). Other than PCP and LSD, both of which are listed separately, it is not clear what substances are included in the category of hallucinogens. Methamphetamine, a popular substance, particularly in the northwestern region of the United States, is not listed among the NHSDA illicit drugs. Is it possible that methamphetamine use is counted as current use of hallucinogens?

Exhibit 4.6. NHSDA Current/Past Month Use of Illicit Drugs, Alcohol, and Tobacco as Percentage of Respondent Age Group, 1994 and 1999 PAPI

	12 yrs + 1994	12 yrs + 1999	12-17 yrs 1994	12-17 yrs 1999	18-25 yrs 1994	18-25 yrs 1999	26-34 yrs 1994	26-34 yrs 1999	35 yrs + 1994	35 yrs + 1999
Any Illicit Drug[a]	**6.0**	**7.0**	**8.2**	**9.0**	**13.3**	**18.8**	**8.5**	**8.8**	**3.2**	**3.6**
marijuana	4.8	5.4	6.0	7.0	12.1	16.4	6.9	6.4	2.3	2.5
cocaine	0.7	0.8	0.3	0.7	1.2	1.9	1.3	1.0	0.4	0.6
crack	0.2	0.2	0.1	0.3	0.3	0.4	0.6	0.3	0.2	0.1
inhalants	0.4	0.3	1.6	0.9	0.8	0.6	0.4	0.4	0.1	0.1
hallucinogens	0.5	0.7	1.1	1.6	1.8	3.5	0.4	0.5	0.1	0.0
PCP	0.0	0.0	0.1	0.2	0.0	0.0	0.0	–	–	–
LSD	0.2	0.2	0.5	0.8	1.0	1.0	0.0	0.1	0.0	–
heroin	0.1	0.1	0.1	0.1	0.0	0.1	0.1	0.1	0.0	0.1
Any nonmedical[b]	1.2	1.5	1.7	2.4	1.6	3.5	1.8	1.8	0.9	0.8
stimulants	0.3	0.3	0.5	0.5	0.5	0.7	0.4	0.6	0.2	0.2
sedatives	0.1	0.1	0.1	0.3	0.1	0.0	0.1	0.1	0.1	0.0
tranquilizers	0.5	0.4	0.2	1.0	0.4	1.4	0.6	0.6	0.5	0.1
analgesics	0.7	1.0	0.3	0.8	1.2	2.3	1.0	1.0	0.4	0.5
Any not marijuana[a]	2.3	2.9	3.7	4.4	4.4	7.5	3.4	3.6	1.3	1.5
Alcohol	**53.9**	**52.0**	**21.6**	**19.0**	**63.1**	**60.2**	**65.3**	**61.9**	**54.1**	**53.4**
binge[c]	16.5	15.1	8.3	7.8	33.6	31.1	24.0	21.9	11.8	1.3
heavy[c]	6.2	5.7	2.5	3.6	13.2	13.0	8.0	6.9	4.8	4.3
Cigarettes	**28.6**	**29.7**	**18.9**	**15.9**	**34.6**	**41.0**	**32.4**	**34.4**	**27.9**	**28.5**
Smokeless	**3.3**	**2.2**	**2.8**	**1.2**	**6.2**	**3.7**	**4.9**	**3.8**	**2.2**	**1.6**

SOURCE: SAMHSA (2000, compiled from tables 4.1, 4.2, 4.3, 4.4, 4.5, 4.6, Chapter 4, pp. 5-16).
NOTES:
a. Any Illicit Drug = use at least once of any of the listed substances. Any Not Marijuana = use at least once of any of the other listed drugs; marijuana/hashish users who also have used any of the other listed drugs are included.
b. Any Nonmedical = use of any prescription-type substances listed; does not include over-the-counter drugs.
c. Binge = five or more drinks on the same occasion at least 1 day in the past 30 days. Heavy = five or more drinks on the same occasion 5 or more days in the past 30 days; all Heavy alcohol users are also Binge alcohol users.

Although one must be cautious in making direct comparisons between the MTF data shown in Exhibit 4.4 and the NHSDA data presented in Exhibit 4.6,[4] it is instructive to examine differences in what the two surveys reveal regarding substance use. Limiting the comparison to the 12- to 17-year-olds and 18- to 25-year-olds in Exhibit 4.6 and the 8th, 10th, 12th graders, and college students in Exhibit 4.4, MTF data show substantially higher percentages of illicit drug, alcohol, and tobacco use overall than do the NHSDA data. This could be due to the survey mode. Despite all best efforts to maintain privacy and ensure confidentiality, when questions about substance use are posed out loud, in person, and in one's home, as is the case with the NHSDA, there may be a tendency to underreport one's consumption of those substances. Alternatively, filling out a questionnaire anonymously, as is the case with the MTF survey, may allow a certain amount of bragging about, or of overreporting, one's use of illicit drugs, alcohol, and tobacco.

Similar to the NYS and MTF, the NHSDA has provided important data for substantive as well as methodological studies. Of particular value are studies addressing measurement issues such as response bias and nonresponse error as well as the general validity of self-reported drug use (see, e.g., Biemer and Witt 1997; Caulkins 2000; Gfoerer, Lessler, and Parsley 1997; Harrell 1997; Harrison 1997; Miller 1997; Turner, Lessler, and Gfoerer 1992; Wright, Gfoerer, and Epstein 1997).

Social Correlates of Self-Reported Offending

Since their inception in the 1940s, self-report measures have consistently revealed dimensions of crime and its correlates that either were at odds with, or could not be addressed by, official statistics. For example, girls and women reported being just as delinquent and criminal, though less frequently and intensely, as did boys and men. Whites likewise admitted to a range and number of delinquent and criminal acts closely paralleling that of blacks. Middle- and upper-class youth self-reported similar levels of involvement in delinquent activities as lower-class youth. Their consistency notwithstanding, such findings were not uniformly accepted as valid among researchers and practitioners. Indeed, debate over "the myth of social class and criminality" and the relationship between race/ethnicity and crime was, and continues to be, so essential to understanding the role of self-report measures that it warrants special attention here.[5]

Tittle, Villemez, and Smith (1978) standardized data from 35 studies, with publication dates spanning four decades, on the relationship between social class and criminality. Their conclusions were highly controversial and launched one of the more enduring and, at times, heated debates in criminology. In essence, their analyses indicated that the negative association between social class and criminality as revealed in official data not only was much more marked than the slight one observed from self-report data but also had been declining substantially and steadily over the decades while remaining fairly stable in self-report studies. They found no support for the notion that people of lower social status were more involved in delinquency and crime. "In short, class and criminality are not now, and probably never were related, at least not during the recent past" (p. 652).

Hindelang, Hirschi, and Weis (1979) took issue with the findings of Tittle et al., arguing that misinterpretation of self-report findings "create the illusion of discrepancy between the correlates of official and self-reported delinquency, when, in general, no such discrepancy has been demonstrated" (p. 996). Their main contention was that besides covering exclusively or primarily trivial offenses, self-report measures do not "tap the same domain of 'chargeable offenses' as do official statistics" (p. 997). This domain should include a full range of types of offenses (i.e., "behavioral content") as well as "seriousness, both within (e.g., amount of theft) and across (e.g., school versus violent) offense types" (p. 997). Their analyses showed that if type of offense and seriousness are taken into account, then self-report data look much like official statistics in terms of a disproportionate involvement by males and by blacks in more serious offenses. They contended that neither self-report data nor official statistics were adequate to make any comparisons between social classes with regard to specific illegal behavior. Hindelang et al. (1979) concluded:

> This evidence suggests to us that: (1) official measures of criminality provide valid indications of the demographic distribution of criminal behavior; (2) self-report instruments typically tap a domain of behavior virtually outside the domain of official data; (3) within the domain they tap, self-report measures provide reliable and valid indicators of offending behavior; (4) the self-report *method* is capable of dealing with behavior within the domain of official data; and (5) in practice, self-report samples have been inadequate for confident conclusions concerning the correlates of offending behavior comparable in seriousness to that represented in official data. (P. 1009)

Elliott and Ageton (1980) similarly contended that self-report data and official statistics do not measure the same things. They noted that "self-report measures of delinquency provide a different picture of the incidence and distribution of delinquent behavior than do official arrest records" (p. 95). Using data from the first year of the NYS, they constructed a measure of criminal behavior that was directly comparable to UCR data both in Hindelang et al.'s (1979) "behavioral content" (i.e., type of offense) and in time frame (i.e., the period during which the offenses occurred). They found "significant race differences for total [self-reported] delinquency and for predatory crimes against persons" (Elliott and Ageton 1980:102). In addition, Elliott and Ageton found that blacks and lower-class youth were found disproportionately among high-frequency offenders. In other words, these overall race and social class differences were largely the result of blacks and lower-class youth reporting the commission of so many, and so many more serious, offenses. Elliott and Ageton (1980) surmised that because "the more frequent and serious offenders are more likely to be arrested," their NYS "data are more consistent with official arrest data than are data from most prior self-report studies" (p. 107). Calling particular attention to the tendency in self-report studies to truncate measures of the frequency of commission of offenses while simultaneously paying little attention to the seriousness of offenses, Elliott and Ageton concluded:

> The most significant difference may not be between the nonoffender and the one-time offender, or even between the one-time and multiple-time offender. Equal or greater significance may be found between those reporting over (or under) 25 nonserious offenses, or between those reporting over (or under) 5 serious offenses. (P. 108)

Clelland and Carter (1980) began their critique of Tittle et al. by asserting that "the proposition of no relationship is the *new* myth of class and crime" and noting that "for Tittle et al., criminologists play the role of 900-pound intellectual gorillas—they define 'crime' any way they please." They argued that self-report studies are "nearly worthless" for examining the class-crime relationship, primarily because of the fact that they focused on minor acts of delinquency, such as "skipping school and throwing eggs" (pp. 320-4).

Braithwaite (1981) also took issue with those who denied an association between social class and criminality and noted that "if [a total of 35 works for Tittle et al.'s secondary analysis] is all that could be found, then they did not look very hard. . . . Perhaps Tittle et al. take their own findings seriously and adopt no extra precautions when moving about in the slums of the world's great cities than they do when walking in the middle class areas of such cities" (p. 37).

Braithwaite (1981) examined the findings of 143 studies that could address the relationship between social class and crime, 97 of which were based on official statistics and 46 on self-report measures. Nearly 93 percent of the official-record studies showed higher crime rates among lower-class as opposed to middle-class people; on the other hand, about 53 percent of self-report studies showed significantly, or at least notably, higher levels of delinquency by lower-class adolescents. Citing Elliott and Ageton's (1980) finding that differences in self-reported delinquency result entirely from the contrast "between the lower class group and the rest of the sample" (p. 42), Braithwaite went on to assert that "the nature of the class distribution of crime depends entirely on what form of crime one is talking about" (p. 47).

The debate continued with Kleck (1982) arguing that the finding of no relationship between social class and crime was largely due to the fact that lower-class youth had a greater tendency to underreport their involvement in delinquency. He used the following example. Suppose that in a given sample, lower-class respondents had committed an average of six delinquent acts, whereas middle-class youth had committed an average of four. If the middle-class group reported 90 percent of their delinquent acts but lower-class juveniles only reported 60 percent, both groups would show an identical mean number of reported acts, at 3.6. Kleck (1982) also noted that several self-report studies had drawn samples from a single school or cluster of schools in relatively class-homogeneous areas, resulting in a truncated range on the social class variable. This sampling strategy thus omitted the theoretically relevant underclass, who, he argued, were more likely to be involved in delinquency. Tittle, Villemez, and Smith (1982), in response to Kleck, suggested that "Kleck (and others) for example, believes that poor people are not only more criminal than those of other classes but bigger liars as well" (p. 437).

Researchers have continued to attempt to specify the conditions under which socioeconomic status is associated with self-reported delinquency and crime. They have also devoted considerable effort toward documenting, if not necessarily improving, the reliability and validity of self-report measures of key variables. But as Tittle and Meier (1990) observed, "Regardless of the conceptual and methodological reasons, criminologists seem no closer to identifying the nature of the relationship [between social class and criminality] than 50 years ago" (p. 271). "Sometimes SES does appear to predict delinquency; most of the time it does not" (p. 294). A decade later, Dunaway, Cullen, Burton, and Evans (2000) drew much the same conclusion about adult criminality. Results from their mail questionnaire survey of a random sample of adults in a midwestern city "largely reject the notion that social class has a strong main effect on adult criminality in the general population, and thus, they tend to support Tittle and Meier's (1990) more recent evaluation of the class-crime debate" (p. 617).

Reliability and Validity of Self-Report Data

Debate over whether, and under what conditions, indicators of social class and race/ethnicity are associated with self-report measures of delinquency prompted a flurry of studies aimed at establishing the reliability and validity of self-report data on crime (see, e.g., Elliott and Ageton 1980; Fendrich and Vaughn 1994; Hindelang, Hirschi, and Weis 1979; 1981; Huizinga and Elliott 1986; Mensch and Kandel 1988; Thornberry and Krohn 2000). Perhaps most important on the list of requirements for obtaining representative self-report data—as well as the one least likely to be met—is to have a sample that is large enough to include sufficient numbers of relatively rare individuals, that is, "high-rate, serious offenders most likely to come to the attention of authorities" (Thornberry and Krohn 2000:40).

Among the elements necessary for reliable and valid self-report survey instruments, four are particularly germane to measures of delinquency and crime (Thornberry and Krohn 2000:41): (1) a wide range and variety of behaviors must be included, (2) serious offenses must be covered if comparisons are to be made to other kinds of data, (3) respondents must be asked to report on the *actual*, not relative, *number* of times they engaged in a particular behavior so that people who committed robbery four times are not lumped together with those who committed it 60 times in the past year, and (4) follow-up questions often are required to distinguish chargeable offenses from others; for example, some respondents may initially indicate that they have committed theft, when what they actually have done is hidden someone's books between classes (Thornberry and Krohn 2000:43).

Panel studies have generally shown that self-reported delinquency measures yield stable and consistent results from one time period to another, that is, they are fairly reliable. Similarly, most tests find that self-reports measure what they set out to measure, that is, they are reasonably valid. However, there is evidence that some groups, some crimes, and some survey modes yield noticeably higher rates of underreporting. For example, "lower class youths tend to score higher on 'lie' scales within self-report measures"[6] (Braithwaite 1981:47). Similarly, African American males substantially underreport their involvement in delinquency (Thornberry and Krohn 2000). There is also some indication that girls my be more honest in reporting their involvement in delinquent behavior than boys (Kim, Fendrich, and Wislar 2000). At least for one type of criminal behavior—the use of illegal drugs—rates of underreporting are higher for the more serious offenses and for telephone interviews compared to self-administered questionnaires (see Aquilino 1994; Turner, Lessler, and Gfoerer 1992).

As Thornberry and Krohn (2000) observed, a conclusion drawn two decades ago may still be the most logical:

> The self-report method appears to behave reasonably well when judged by standard criteria available to social scientists. By these criteria, the difficulties in self-report instruments currently in use would appear to be surmountable; the method of self-reports does not appear from these studies to be fundamentally flawed. Reliability measures are impressive and the majority of studies produce validity coefficients in the moderate to strong range. (Hindelang, Hirschi, and Weis 1981:114, as cited in Thornberry and Krohn 2000:59)

Self-Reports from "Known" Criminals and Delinquents

Early researchers believed that official statistics might be just the tip of the iceberg—not only in terms of *who* engaged in *what* kinds of crimes but also in terms of *how much* crime those official criminals might account for. These researchers determined to get information directly from the source by surveying "known"—that is, arrested or incarcerated—criminals. Two prominent studies in this genre are the RAND inmate surveys and the ADAM program.

The RAND Inmate Survey(s)

What is commonly referred to as *the* RAND inmate survey is actually two surveys conducted at different times and with different samples. The objectives of both of these surveys were the same, however, and their findings parallel each other. Primary among those objectives was to learn from the source about the illegal behavior of convicted criminals, that is, "to gather information on individual patterns of criminal behavior—types of crime committed, degree of specialization in crime types, and changes in criminal patterns over time" (Visher 1986:166).

RAND researchers first completed exploratory interviews with 49 California prison inmates who were convicted of robbery (see Petersilia, Greenwood, and Lavin 1977, in Visher 1986). Using those interview data to construct a self-administered survey instrument, the first inmate survey was conducted in 1976 (Peterson and Braiker 1981, in Visher 1986; Tremblay and Morselli 2000). A total of 624 inmates (representing only a 47 percent response rate) from five California prisons completed the anonymous questionnaire. The results from the exploratory study and those from the inmate survey were similar: "Most inmates committed few crimes per year. . . . A small group reported much higher frequencies of offending" (Visher 1986:164). RAND researchers were not satisfied that the measurement and sampling were sufficient for broader generalization; thus, a more rigorous, more representative inmate survey was designed and conducted.

The second inmate survey, conducted in 1978, drew samples from both jail and prison populations in California, Michigan, and Texas (Tremblay and Morselli 2000; Visher 1986). Attempts were made to ensure that the samples were representative of a "typical" cohort of inmates for those states and that the offenses for which they were convicted covered a broad range in terms of seriousness. A total of 2,190 inmates from the three states completed the confidential questionnaire.[7] By making the survey confidential rather than anonymous, researchers were able to compare inmates' official records with their self-reported information.

The survey instrument included detailed questions about inmates' illegal activities as juveniles, their adult criminal behavior in the two years prior to the arrest that resulted in their incarceration, and past as well as recent use of drugs and alcohol. Inmates' attitudes on specific issues, their employment history, and demographic data were also solicited. Inmates were asked to estimate the number of times in the previous two years they had committed each of 10 crimes, including burglary, business robbery, personal robbery, assault during robbery, other assaults, theft, auto theft, forgery/credit card swindles/bad checks, fraud, and drug dealing.

Exhibit 4.7 summarizes some of the findings from RAND's second inmate survey. It presents both the median number of crimes per year (i.e., the maximum number of crimes 50 percent of the inmates report having committed) and the number of crimes per year at the 90th percentile (i.e., the minimum number of crimes 10 percent of the inmates reported having committed). Half of the active robbers reported committing the crime no more than 5 times per year, whereas 10 percent of them reported robbing a person no less often than 87 times a year. The difference between the number of crimes per year reported by low-rate and by high-rate offenders is even more dramatic for the other property offenses. These data led to the conclusion that most people who engage in illegal behavior, even convicted criminals, do so infrequently, but some individuals are involved in crime with such regularity that they can be labeled career criminals.

Exhibit 4.7. Median Number of Crimes Committed per Year as Self-Reported by California Inmates in RAND Second Inmate Survey

Crime Type	Median Number[a]	Minimum Number for "Worst" 10%[b]
Burglary	5.45	232
Robbery	5.00	87
Assault	2.40	13
Theft	8.59	425
Forgery and credit cards	4.50	206
Fraud	5.05	258
All except drug dealing	14.77	605

SOURCE: Adapted from Chaiken and Chaiken (1982, p. 44, as shown in Visher, 1986, p. 167).
NOTES:
a. A reminder: The median is the "center" value for a sample; 50 percent are above it, and 50 percent are below it. For example, in this table, half of the inmates who are active burglars report committing burglary not more than just over five times per year; the other half report committing it more than five times per year.
b. This is the number of crimes that the inmates at the low end (or beginning) of the 90th percentile report committing per year. In other words, 10 percent of inmates report committing at least that many of that type of crime per year.

The RAND inmate surveys provided the database for constructing offender typologies, that is, a classification of offenders according to the types of crime they commit (Chaiken and Chaiken 1984). One of the more important findings from the surveys was that criminals do not necessarily "specialize" in a single illegal enterprise but instead combine activities to accomplish a particular end. Researchers have also used RAND survey data to explore whether or not inmates were motivated by the expectation that "crime pays" and how much they claim to have earned through engaging in criminal behavior (see, e.g., Tremblay and Morselli 2000; Wilson and Abrahamse 1992). Others have used these data to examine the relationship between substance use and other types of illicit activity (see, e.g., Chaiken and Chaiken 1990). In many ways, and on the basis of attempts to replicate them, the RAND surveys persist as the standard for obtaining as well as analyzing self-report data from inmates (see, e.g., Auerhahn 1999).

Arrestee Drug Abuse Monitoring[8]

Another example of obtaining self-reported information from known offenders is the Arrestee Drug Abuse Monitoring (ADAM) program, a program established by the National Institute of Justice to monitor drug use among arrestees in urban jurisdictions in the United States (Taylor and Bennett 1999). The forerunner of ADAM, the Drug Use Forecasting (DUF) program, was initiated in 1987 and demonstrated the feasibility of urinalysis as a means of measuring drug use by arrestees. By focusing on arrestees, a group that is more likely than other populations to be involved in drug use, ADAM presents a different picture of drug use than general household surveys such as NHSDA. DUF and ADAM have been used extensively to provide information for the purposes of criminal justice policies, and the studies represent a major resource for criminologists analyzing the association between drug use and criminal activity (ADAM 2000).

At each ADAM collection site, trained interviewers conduct voluntary and confidential interviews with arrestees who have been in a jail or booking facility for less than 48 hours. In addition, voluntary urine samples are taken from the arrestees. These urine samples are tested for the presence of (at least) five common drugs: marijuana, cocaine (including crack), opiates (including heroin), methamphetamine, and PCP. In 1999, the ADAM program collected data from more than 30,000 adult male arrestees at 34 sites

Exhibit 4.8. Percentage Positive for Drugs, by ADAM Offense Category: Adult Males and Females, Seattle, Washington, 1999

	Cocaine		Marijuana		Methamph		Any Drug		N by sex	
	M	F	M	F	M	F	M	F	M	F
	SEATTLE									
Violent Offense	**28.3**	16.7	**41.7**	**30.6**	10.6	2.8	59.4	**44.4**	180	36
Robbery	0.0	–	0.0	–	0.0	–	0.0	–	1	0
Assault	28.7	12.9	42.6	29.0	8.1	3.2	57.4	41.9	136	31
Weapons	41.2	–	47.1	–	23.5	–	76.5	–	17	0
Other Violent	28.9	40.0	34.2	40.0	10.5	0.0	60.5	60.0	38	5
Property Offense	40.1	55.2	**37.0**	27.6	**10.4**	5.7	74.0	**71.3**	192	87
Larceny/Theft	42.0	54.7	34.8	24.5	7.1	1.9	74.1	71.7	112	53
Burglary	36.4	66.7	54.5	33.3	0.0	0.0	81.8	66.7	11	3
Stolen Vehicle	25.0	50.0	58.3	25.0	25.0	0.0	75.0	50.0	12	4
Other Property	36.1	54.8	37.5	38.7	16.7	16.1	72.2	77.4	72	31
Drug Offense	48.0	65.9	**49.6**	34.1	15.4	24.4	**85.4**	**95.1**	123	**41**
Drug Sales	100.0	–	0.0	–	0.0	–	100.0	–	1	0
Drug Possession	47.5	65.9	50.0	34.1	15.6	24.4	85.2	95.1	122	41
Prostitution	37.5	**72.4**	12.5	**20.7**	0.0	3.4	**62.5**	**82.8**	**8**	**29**
Other Offense	30.7	**48.7**	37.2	**29.5**	**9.3**	**14.1**	63.5	**70.5**	430	**78**

SOURCE: Adapted from ADAM (2000).

Exhibit 4.9. Percentage Positive for Drugs, by ADAM Offense Category: Adult Males and Females, Spokane, Washington, 1999

	Cocaine		Marijuana		Methamph		Any Drug		N by sex	
	M	F	M	F	M	F	M	F	M	F
SPOKANE										
Violent Offense	**13.1**	20.0	**43.6**	**30.9**	9.7	16.4	54.4	**52.7**	25.9	55
Robbery	50.0	66.7	60.0	33.3	20.0	33.3	90.0	100.0	10	3
Assault	10.8	19.6	42.1	32.6	7.7	15.2	51.3	52.2	195	46
Weapons	30.0	33.3	65.0	0.0	20.0	33.3	85.0	66.7	20	3
Other Violent	6.7	0.0	42.2	25.0	8.9	0.0	51.1	25.0	45	4
Property Offense	26.4	31.8	**42.9**	29.5	**26.4**	40.9	66.4	**79.5**	140	44
Larceny/Theft	23.4	26.9	42.2	30.8	20.3	34.6	64.1	73.1	64	26
Burglary	44.4	20.0	47.2	0.0	25.0	40.0	72.2	60.0	36	5
Stolen Vehicle	28.6	40.0	42.9	0.0	28.6	100.0	85.7	100.0	7	2
Other Property	18.0	47.1	42.0	41.2	30.0	47.1	64.0	94.1	50	17
Drug Offense	32.2	43.9	**58.4**	36.8	45.0	47.4	**91.9**	**94.7**	149	**57**
Drug Sales	29.2.	50.0	58.3	41.7	41.7	33.3	100.0	91.7	24	12
Drug Possession	32.5	39.6	57.9	37.5	46.0	52.1	90.5	95.8	126	48
Prostitution	–	66.7	–	**0.0**	–	0.0	–	66.7	0	3
Other Offense	15.6	**30.0**	42.2	**33.3**	**18.4**	**28.3**	**60.3**	**73.3**	365	**60**

SOURCE: Adapted from ADAM (2000).

and from more than 10,000 adult female arrestees in 32 sites. In addition, data were collected from more than 2,500 juvenile male detainees at 9 sites and more than 400 juvenile female detainees at 6 sites (ADAM 2000).

We focus here on 1999 ADAM data from Spokane and Seattle in the state of Washington[9] and from New York City. The ADAM project in Washington enjoys a 70 percent plus cooperation rate (percentage of eligible arrestees who agree to be interviewed) and a 90 percent plus completion rate (percentage of interviewed arrestees who provide a urine specimen) at both sites.[10] Exhibits 4.8, 4.9, and 4.10 show the percentages of interviewed arrestees in Seattle, Spokane, and New York, organized according to the most serious offense charge that brought them into jail, who tested positive for certain drugs.

Looking first at the "Any Drug" column and the broad offense categories (violent, property, drug, prostitution, other), of the arrestees who completed an interview and provided a urine specimen in Seattle, between about 59 percent (violent offenses) and 85 percent (drug offenses) of the males and between about 44 percent (violent offenses) and 95 percent (drug

Exhibit 4.10 Percentage Positive for Drugs, by ADAM Offense Category: Adult Males and Females, New York, New York, 1999

	Cocaine		Marijuana		Methamph		Any Drug		N by sex	
	M	F	M	F	M	F	M	F	M	F
NEW YORK										
Violent Offense	30.7	39.3	**40.6**	**33.5**	0.0	0.0	60.7	**65.5**	456	206
Robbery	25.9	51.4	61.7	27.0	0.0	0.0	76.5	81.1	81	37
Assault	32.5	37.6	37.3	36.1	0.0	0.0	58.3	64.7	271	133
Weapons	28.9	33.3	46.1	33.3	0.0	0.0	64.5	64.1	76	39
Other Violent	33.1	31.0	33.1	29.6	0.0	0.0	57.4	53.5	169	71
Property Offense	48.3	65.9	**33.6**	19.3	**0.0**	0.0	72.8	**78.8**	602	311
Larceny/Theft	47.2	52.5	32.4	10.8	0.0	0.0	72.7	63.3	176	120
Burglary	44.4	57.1	24.4	28.6	0.0	0.0	66.7	85.7	45	14
Stolen Vehicle	50.0	37.5	41.7	37.5	0.0	0.0	83.3	75.0	24	8
Other Property	48.5	64.9	33.5	19.8	0.0	0.0	73.2	77.9	493	262
Drug Offense	52.6	80.8	**48.8**	25.0	0.0	0.0	**88.8**	92.9	848	**505**
Drug Sales	55.9.	81.4	42.3	21.7	0.0	0.0	87.9	88.2	272	161
Drug Possession	53.7	80.0	49.4	26.1	0.0	0.0	89.6	93.9	684	410
Prostitution	**43.6**	66.7	35.9	**31.9**	0.0	0.0	61.5	**88.6**	39	185
Other Offense	38.0	**51.4**	35.9	**24.5**	**0.0**	**0.0**	**66.1**	**67.8**	608	**208**

SOURCE: Adapted from ADAM (2000).

offenses) of the females tested positive for recent use of some controlled substance. In Spokane, the range was between about 54 percent (violent offenses) and 92 percent (drug offenses) of the males and between about 53 percent (violent offenses) and 95 percent (drug offenses) of the females. In New York, the range was between about 61 percent (violent offenses) and 89 percent (drug offenses) of the males and between about 66 percent (violent offenses) and 93 percent (drug offenses) of the females. Thus, over half of all interviewed arrestees brought into jail for the commission of violent offenses in Seattle, Spokane, and New York have used drugs recently, whereas approximately nine tenths of those charged with a drug offense have done so.

More suggestive patterns are revealed through an examination of positive tests for the three specific drugs by gender of the arrestee. In Seattle, marijuana shows up more often than the other two drugs in the urine of both males and females arrested for violent offenses. Cocaine is present more often for males and females alike among those arrested for property offenses and prostitution. For drug offenses and all other offenses, marijuana shows up more often for males, but cocaine is present more often for females. In Spokane, the picture is somewhat different, with marijuana showing up more often than the other two drugs in the urine of both males and females arrested for violent offenses and for all other offenses. Marijuana also shows up more often for males arrested for property and drug offenses. Cocaine is present in the urine more often for females arrested for property offenses, but among those females arrested for drug offenses, methamphetamine is most common. This points to one of the most interesting differences between the two Washington ADAM sites and New York. Although urinalyses indicate that marijuana is the most commonly used substance by arrestees in all three locations, cocaine use is much higher among arrestees in New York. In addition, methamphetamine appears to be used at nearly twice the rate in Spokane as it is in Seattle, with the relative rates nearly the reverse for cocaine. In contrast, no arrestees in New York tested positive for methamphetamine in 1999.

In addition to providing useful information regarding patterns of drug use by arrestees, the ADAM project offers a rare opportunity to assess the validity of self-report data—that is, to determine to what extent people tell the truth when responding to a survey. Through comparisons of the self-reported drug use information to urinalysis results, researchers can analyze under- and overreporting of drug use.

Verifying the Validity of Self-Reported Drug Use

Research has shown that there is often a discrepancy between self-reporting of drug use and the results of urinalysis tests. For example, a study comparing self-reports and urinalysis results that relied on 1999 ADAM data from five U.S. cities (New York-Manhattan, Fort Lauderdale, Miami, Washington, D.C., and Birmingham, Alabama) found that 7.8 percent of arrestees underreported drug use, compared with 1.9 percent who overreported (that is, they reported using drugs but their urinalysis results were negative) (Taylor and Bennett 1999).

Studies have also indicated that underreporting varies according to the type of drug. There is generally a higher concordance rate for marijuana use, but for harder drugs such as cocaine and heroin, underreporting is much more common. For example, on the basis of 1988 DUF data, 47 percent of arrestees in New York City reported cocaine use, whereas 75 percent had positive urinalyses for the substance. In the same year, 41 percent of Philadelphia arrestees self-reported cocaine use, but 72 percent tested positive. However, 28 percent of the arrestees in New York City self-reported marijuana use, and 30 percent tested positive. Similarly, in Philadelphia, 28 percent reported using marijuana, and 32 percent tested positive (Thornberry and Krohn 2000).

Magura et al. (1987, as cited in Magura and Kang 1997) compared self-reports of drug use with urinalysis results for patients who were receiving methadone treatment in four clinics in New York City. Among subjects who tested positive for each drug, 65 percent did not report opiate use, 39 percent did not report benzodiazepine use, and 15 percent did not report cocaine use. Magura and Kang (1997) also found that African Americans were more likely than other groups to underreport drug use.

The findings of differential honesty in reporting by type of substance are consistent with social desirability theory (Edwards 1957), which suggests that the distortion of self-reports, by underreporting or overreporting, occurs as a function of the perceived acceptability of the behavior in question. Because the use of marijuana is less stigmatized than the use of hard drugs in U.S. society, subjects may be more likely to truthfully report using the substance (Harrison 1997).

Summary and Conclusions

Thornberry and Krohn (2000) suggest that "the self-report method of collecting data on delinquent and criminal behavior is one of the most important innovations in criminological research in the 20th century" (p. 34). Considerable improvements in survey methodology, as well as research efforts focused on enhancing the validity of self-reports over the years, have yielded greater confidence in the data that are collected in this manner.

Self-report data, however, are by no means without their weaknesses. Self-report measures of crime and its correlates continue to be constrained by the same elements that affect self-reports of all types of behaviors. Concerns over sampling, representativeness, generalizability (i.e., did we ask the right people?) along with instrument design, question wording and order (i.e., did we ask the right question?) plague survey researchers generally and can be especially troublesome with respect to surveys on crime. Concerns over the validity of responses (i.e., did respondents answer with the truth?) likewise are not unique to self-report measures of crime.

At the same time, self-report data have unique strengths; for all their problems, self-report measures of crime provide valuable information that is not available through other measures. This is especially true if researchers are interested in etiological issues such as explanatory variables and models (theory testing) for delinquency and crime, circumstances surrounding illegal behavior, age at beginning as well as ending criminal activity, patterns of offending over the life course, and related issues. To maximize the value of self-report data, proper care should be taken to approximate as much as possible the "ideal" in methods, sampling, and instruments.

As a simple indicator of the discipline of criminology's reliance on self-report data, it is worth considering recent issues of the discipline's flagship journal, *Criminology*. In the August 2000 issue, for example, eight of the nine articles utilized self-report data. In the February 2001 issue, four of five articles utilized self-report data. Similar heavy reliance on, if not dominance of, self-reports can be witnessed in articles published in other professional criminological journals. Given that victimization data likewise are a form of self-report measure, as will be discussed in the next chapter, it is impossible to overstate their importance to our understanding of crime and its correlates.

Notes

1. Updates to and recent press releases on MTF surveys can be accessed through the following Web site:www. monitoringthefuture.org
2. Data collected by NHSDA belong to the public domain and can be accessed through the following Web site: www.samhsa.gov
3. The 1999 data are taken from the PAPI subsample, rather than from the full CAI sample, so they were collected under arguably the same conditions as the 1994 data.
4. The two surveys cover different years and the respondents are grouped differently. In addition, the MTF survey is a self-administered questionnaire, whereas the NHSDA involves face-to-face interviews.
5. Before discussing this debate, it is important to note that self-report and official data are not directly comparable with respect to what they reveal regarding the relationship between social class and crime. This is due to the fact that UCRs do not collect individual-level information on the social class of those arrested. Studies using official data to examine the class-crime relationship typically rely on aggregate data that are compared with indicators of social class of particular areas derived from the census or other sources. In contrast, self-report studies collect individual-level information on the social class of respondents.

6. As noted by Braithwaite (1981) and others, this may be perfectly understandable in that "when confronted by unfamiliar white middle-class researchers with their probing questions, lower class respondents are more suspicious and defensive than their middle class counterparts" (p. 47).

7. Response rates for California and Michigan were 49 percent for prison inmates and 66 and 72 percent, respectively, for jail inmates (Chaiken and Chaiken 1982). "More than 2,500 inmates actually completed the questionnaire, but jail respondents in Texas were excluded from the analysis because, unlike jail inmates in other states, they were predominantly sentenced offenders awaiting transfer to prison" (Visher 1986:164).

8. ADAM reports and press releases can be accessed through the following Web site: www.ojp.usdoj.gov/nij

9. We chose these two sites for three reasons. First, we have a more than superficial knowledge of the ADAM program in Washington because two of us have worked on the project, with one being site coordinator. Second, western and particularly northwestern ADAM sites reveal different patterns of drug use and abuse among arrestees than do (the more commonly studied) northeastern ADAM sites. Third, Washington ADAM data reveal how, even in the same state, arrestees may exhibit drug preferences specific to their geographical area.

10. These cooperation and completion rates are slightly lower than those for other sites. "In most sites, more than 80 percent of the individuals approached agree to the interview, and, of those, more than 80 percent agree to give the urine specimen" (ADAM 2000:6)

Chapter Five

Victimization Surveys

Homicide victims are notoriously poor respondents to Census Bureau interviewers.

Benjamin Renshaw*

Another method of studying crime that arose in response to concerns about the limitations of official data was the victim survey. Instead of asking criminal justice system officials or offenders about criminal behavior, this approach asked people about their experiences as victims of crime. The first large-scale victimization survey appeared in the late 1960s. Since that time, they have been widely used to measure the frequency and characteristics of particular types of crime and the demographic profiles of victims, both in the United States and other countries. By eliciting information about both crimes that citizens report to the police and those they do not, victimization surveys provide us with further information regarding the dark figures of crime. These surveys have also had a profound effect on theories of crime causation. Routine activity, opportunity, and even rational choice theory have flourished in the discipline of criminology in recent years in part because of the availability of victim survey data

---

*1990:226, former acting director of the Bureau of Justice Statistics, recounting a conversation with Attorney General William Smith in which the Attorney General asked about the failure to measure homicide in victimization surveys

(Cantor and Lynch 2000). However, as we will see in this chapter, similar to other measures of crime, victimization surveys have their own unique strengths and limitations.

Victimization surveys differ from other methods of measuring crime in their nature, scope, and type of information collected. As implied by the basic definition, these surveys involve self-reports of victimization experiences by victims themselves, and, as such, they are subject to many of the same problems associated with any form of survey research. Victimization reports are usually elicited from random samples of the general public, and a variety of screening questions are utilized to identify different types of victims. A number of crimes addressed in other data sources, for example, prostitution and drug and alcohol use, are not covered in these surveys because they are considered to be victimless. In addition, in some crime situations, it is not possible to interview the victim; it is obviously not feasible to interview the victim of a homicide. Finally, some crimes, such as vandalism, are viewed as trivial and are not covered by these surveys; others, such as white-collar and corporate crime victimizations, are seen as difficult to accurately measure. This lack of coverage of certain types of crimes renders direct comparisons between victimization and official data problematic, an issue that will be addressed in more detail later in the chapter.

This chapter examines how victimization surveys have been used to measure crime. We begin with a review of the major victimization surveys used in the United States in the last four decades and proceed to describe the distribution of crime that emerges from a consideration of these surveys. We conclude with a discussion of the various problems associated with current efforts to accurately measure victimization experiences. While focusing on the findings from victimization surveys in the United States, where relevant, we will include research from international studies, including the British Crime Survey and the International Crime Victimization Surveys, which shed light on the methodological weaknesses of this method of counting crime.

U.S. National Crime Victimization Surveys

As discussed in Chapter 2, surveys of crime victims in the United States developed in the late 1960s out of a concern with the weaknesses of official data in measuring the extent and characteristics of crime.

Given the initial success in using survey methods to provide information on victimization experiences, a number of additional pilot studies were conducted to address several important methodological questions: How likely were people to report their victimization experiences to interviewers? What was the appropriate reference period for recalling victimization experiences? What particular forms of question wording would elicit the most accurate responses? These test studies to validate and improve the techniques used in victimization surveys were designed by the Law Enforcement Assistance Administration, in cooperation with the Census Bureau.

With insights derived from the earlier surveys, the National Crime Surveys (NCS) were initiated in 1972. The original NCS involved a national panel study of the victimization experiences of both households and individuals, as well as a number of surveys in particular cities. The initial NCS included samples of approximately 60,000 households (containing approximately 136,000 individuals) and about 15,000 businesses. The central-city surveys had samples of approximately 10,000 households in each of 26 cities; in addition, a probability sample of between 1,000 and 5,000 businesses was selected for each city. Both the national surveys of businesses and the city surveys of individuals were terminated in the mid-1970s, apparently due to their cost. However, the national victimization survey of households, although undergoing several modifications over time, continues as an annual series.

Compared to official reports of crime, national victimization surveys have several advantages. These surveys, for example, have been perceived to provide more accurate measures of the absolute rates of some serious crimes and are believed to be more reliable than official statistics in analyzing crime trends in the United States (see O'Brien 1985). It is also believed that victim surveys provide more detailed information about the situational factors surrounding criminal acts—for example, the physical location of crime events, the day and time of events, the type of weapon used, if any, the number of victims and offenders, and the relationship between the victim and offender. General characteristics of offenders, such as their race, gender, and age in direct-contact predatory crimes such as assaults and robberies, can also be identified in victim surveys.

Procedures in the National Crime Victimization Survey

The National Crime Victimization Survey (NCVS) is the most comprehensive and systematic survey of victims in the United States.[1] This survey has been designed and modified by the leading researchers and institutions in the country. The sampling procedure is supervised by the Census Bureau, the survey is conducted by well-trained staff and interviewers, and changes in the sampling design and format of questions are rigorously evaluated in terms of their effects on estimates of victimization experiences.

The basic procedures for selecting households to participate in victimization surveys have been essentially unchanged since the inception of the national survey. Recall that the goal is to obtain a nationally representative sample. The NCVS uses a complex, stratified, multistage cluster sample in which approximately 2,000 primary sampling units are initially identified by either standard metropolitan statistical areas (SMSAs), a county, or small groups of contiguous counties. These clusters are then stratified with respect to important demographic characteristics, and sample elements (in this case, households) are selected from each stratum in a manner that is proportionate to their representation in the larger population.

The NCVS uses what is known as a rotated panel design for the selection of households in successive waves of the survey. Thus, each household selected for inclusion is interviewed a total of seven times at six-month intervals. Note that the NCVS is a panel survey of *housing units* rather than *individuals*, meaning that the housing unit will remain in the sample even if the original residents of the household have moved during the three and one-half-year rotation period. The sample is subdivided into groups of about 10,000 households, and every six months one group is rotated out of the sample and replaced by a new group. Although all this certainly sounds complex, the rotation pattern is designed with the goal of ensuring the representativeness of the sample.

In the earliest surveys, approximately 50,000 households were selected, with more than 100,000 residents interviewed about their victimization experiences. In 2000, 86,800 households and 159,420 people age 12 or older were interviewed. The response rate for the survey was 93.4 percent of eligible households and 89.6 percent of eligible individuals (Rennison 2001).

The data collection instrument used in the NCVS consists of a "control card," a basic "screen" questionnaire, and crime incident reports. The control card provides the basic administrative record for each sampling unit, including information identifying the address of each sample unit and basic household data such as family income, whether the household unit is owned or rented, and the names, age, race, sex, marital status, and education of all individuals living there. The control card also serves as a record of visits, telephone calls, interviews, and information about noninterviews (see Biderman and Lynch 1991).

A "knowledgeable adult" provides answers to the basic questions on the control card, and this individual is interviewed about victimizations that may have occurred against the household (for example, burglaries, motor vehicle thefts, and household larcenies). This individual also serves as a proxy for household members who are less than 12 years of age and considered too young to answer the questions, for those too old or too ill to be interviewed, and for those who are temporarily away from the household.

The screen questions within the NCVS are designed to elicit information about whether particular types of victimizations either have occurred in the household or have been experienced by the particular respondent. The screen questions are then followed by more detailed questions about any victimization experiences identified by respondents. The NCVS uses these screen questions to elicit maximum recall of victimization experiences, primarily by reducing respondent fatigue that can result from answering a large number of questions. As illustrated in Exhibit 5.1 and discussed in more detail below, changes in the wording of these screen questions can affect respondent recall and alter subsequent estimates of victimization derived from the survey.

Incident reports in the NCVS involve a series of questions about the particular crime event, the offending parties, and the consequences of the crime. For each separate incident mentioned in the screen questions, respondents are asked whether the crime was reported to the police, whether the offense was completed or merely attempted, whether the offender was identified or known to the victim, the demographic (race, gender, age) characteristics of the offender, if known, whether there was a weapon used in the crime, whether the victim resisted, and the amount of monetary loss or physical injury or both resulting from the victimization.

The NCVS are rigorous in terms of data collection procedures and processes. NCVS interviewers receive extensive training prior to conducting interviews, with explicit and detailed instructions about how the questionnaire is to be administered, adherence to question wording, and the use of "probes" to elicit answers from respondents. Quality control is further enhanced by periodic monitoring of the interviewers by supervisors, office edits of completed work, and verification of the data through reinterviews of some individuals. The use and refinement of these procedures have served to enhance the reliability of the NCVS data collection activities.

The Redesign of the NCVS

Recall that one of the major reasons for the development of the NCVS was to provide an alternative measure to official data of the extent and nature of crime in the United States, a measure that would also allow for comparisons over time. Researchers and staff involved with the NCVS have been

Exhibit 5.1. Comparison of Screen Questions in the Old and Revised National Crime Victimization Survey (NCVS)

Old NCVS 1972-92	Revised NCVS 1992-2000
Did anyone take something directly from you by using force such as by a stickup, mugging, or threat? Did anyone TRY to rob you by using force or threatening to harm you? Did anyone beat you up, attack you, or hit you with something such as a rock or bottle? Were you knifed, shot at, or attacked with some other weapon by anyone at all? Did anyone THREATEN to beat you up or THREATEN you with a knife, gun, or some other weapon, NOT including telephone threats? Did anyone TRY to attack you in some other way?	Has anyone attacked or threatened you in any of these ways — With any weapon, for instance, a gun or knife– With anything like a baseball bat, frying pan, scissors, or stick– By something thrown such as a rock or bottle– Include any grabbing, punching, or choking– Any rape, attempted rape or other type of sexual assault– Any face-to-face threats– OR Any attack or threat or use of force by anyone at all? Incidents involving forced or unwanted sexual acts are often difficult to talk about. Have you been forced or coerced to engage in unwanted sexual activity by— Someone you didn't know before A casual acquaintance OR Someone you know well.
Was anything stolen from you while you were away from home, for instance, at work, in a theater or restaurant, or while traveling? Did you call the police to report something that happened to YOU that you thought was a crime? Did anything happen to YOU that you thought was a crime, but did NOT report to the police?	Were you attacked or threatened OR did you have something stolen from you— At home, including the porch or yard– At or near a friend's, relative's, or neighbor's home– At work or school– In a place such as a storage shed or laundry room, a shopping mall, restaurant, bank, or airport– While riding in any vehicle– On the street or in a parking lot– At such places as a party, theater, gym, picnic area, bowling lanes, or while fishing or hunting? OR Did anyone ATTEMPT to attack or attempt to steal anything belonging to you from any of these places? People often don't think of incidents committed by someone they know. Did you have something stolen from you OR were you attacked or threatened by – Someone at work or school– A neighbor or friend– A relative or family member– Any other person you've met or known? Did you call the police to report something that happened to YOU which you thought was a crime? Did anything happen to you which you thought was a crime, but did NOT report to the police?

SOURCE: Kindermann, Lynch, and Cantor (1997, p. 6).

reluctant to implement major changes in the design of the survey, fearing that this would compromise the over-time comparisons. However, as victimization surveys were subject to methodological critiques and as advances occurred in areas related to survey methodology more generally, it became increasingly clear that some changes were necessary in the procedures and practices underlying the NCVS. In the early 1980s, a consortium of experts in the fields of criminology, survey design, and statistics was organized to reexamine all aspects of the survey, including questionnaire design, sampling strategies, administration, errors, dissemination, and utilization of the NCVS data (see Biderman and Lynch 1991; Taylor 1989).

Three separate phases were identified in the possible redesign of the NCVS. The first phase was directed at immediate improvements that could be made in the survey. The second phase emphasized the development of so-called near-term changes that could improve the NCVS without incurring significant financial costs or disrupting the time series. The third phase involved more fundamental, long-term changes that could dramatically increase the quality of the data or reduce the costs of data collection or both.

As described by Biderman and Lynch (1991:19) the Crime Survey Redesign Consortium proposed the following set of recommendations for implementation in the near term:

Screening and Scope Changes. Include vandalism in the NCVS, and interview 12- and 13-year-olds directly instead of by proxy.

Expanding Incident Descriptions. (a) Revise place of occurrence codes so that there are consistent distinctions regarding the "publicness" of places or their exposure, (b) add codes to specifically identify crimes occurring in the respondent's town, (c) obtain information on victim-offender interactions, and (d) expand information on the outcomes of victimization incidents, such as the response of the criminal justice system and other agencies.

Expanding Explanatory Variables. (a) Place supplements in the survey that can be used to distinguish victims from non-victims, and (b) collect more information on the perceived motivation of offenders, including the role of substance use.

Changing Crime Classification and Reporting. (a) Use the current collection period for preliminary estimates that can be disseminated in a more timely fashion, (b) adjust annual estimate rates for the major sources of measurement error, and (c) increase the power of statistical tests used in the NCVS.

After various types of design work and field testing by the Census Bureau, most of these recommendations were accepted by the Bureau of Justice Statistics and were subsequently introduced into the NCVS design in 1986. However, the scope of crimes covered in the NCVS was not expanded to include vandalism, primarily because it was believed that such a change would disrupt the series and cause difficulties in comparing victimization data over time.

The Redesign Consortium also recommended various changes in the NCVS to be implemented over the long term. These recommendations focused on the design of the survey and carried substantial implications for survey costs and data quality.

Quality Enhancements. (a) Make the NCVS a longitudinal survey of individuals rather than housing units, (b) use a four-month instead of a six-month reference period to reduce the underreporting of victimization events, (c) use interview-to-interview recounting to simplify the recall task rather than recounting to the beginning of the month in which the interview is conducted, (d) employ more productive short-cue screen questions to encourage more complete reporting of victimizations, and (e) use centralized telephone interviews to enhance control over interviewers.

Cost Reducing Changes. (a) maximize the use of telephone interviewing, which is less expensive than in-person interviews, and (b) use data from "bounding" interviews for estimation purposes (bounding interviews are the first interviews conducted with a household in which questions about victimization experiences are asked, but there is no specific reference period to the previous interview).

Many of these suggested changes have been phased into the more recent versions of the NCVS. Centralized telephone interviewing was initiated at the same time as the use of the new survey instrument, and computer-assisted telephone interviewing (CATI) technology is now used in five of the seven waves of the NCVS interviews. However, due to cost considerations, the six-month reference period rather than the recommended four-month period is still used. The implementation of a longitudinal design using individuals as the unit of analysis has been delayed until further studies indicate the feasibility of this change.

Given the importance of maintaining continuity in the NCVS series, the redesign was structured in such a way as to assess the impact of the various changes in the survey instrument and procedures on inflating or deflating national estimates of victimization. Changes in the NCVS procedures that have had minimal effects on estimated victimization rates include modifications in the wording of several existing questions, expansion of the list of questions in the survey to include perceived drug and alcohol use by offenders, self-protective measures taken by victims, police actions, victim contact with the justice system, the location of the crime, and the victim's activity (see Bachman and Taylor 1994). Research comparing predesign and postredesign data indicates that changes in the nature and coverage of screen questions, changes in the definition of "series crime," the increased use of telephone interviewing, and changes in the classification of crimes have substantially altered the recall of victimizations. In fact, when changes in the NCVS were implemented in 1992, the number of crimes reported by survey respondents increased by 50 to 200 percent, depending on the type of crime (Cantor and Lynch 2000). Most of these changes have been viewed as positive improvements in that the enhanced screening questions are thought to better stimulate respondents' recall of victimizations. These questions serve to clarify crime victimization incidents and diminish the effects of respondents' subjective interpretation of survey items. In addition, the enhanced questions and inquiries about experiences of domestic violence, rape, and sexual attacks are believed to provide better estimates of these victimizations that are often difficult to measure. The new screen questions also expand cues that assist respondents in recalling an incident such as items that ask about being a victim of a violent crime committed by someone the victim knows, such as co-workers, neighbors, and family members, and questions for burglary regarding how the offender entered the structure. The following consequences have been observed in studies on the impact of these procedural changes (see Bureau of Justice Statistics Bulletin 1994; Kindermann, Lynch, and Cantor 1997).

CATI and Use of a Centralized Phone Facility. These procedures are believed to help standardize the interviewer-respondent interactions leading to the greater reporting of victimizations and more realistic crime rates. The use of CATI has increased the reporting of crimes of violence, crimes of theft, and household larceny by approximately 15 to 20 percent and burglary by about 20 percent. CATI's effect on the reporting of motor vehicle theft has been negligible.

Changing Definitions of "Series Crimes." Series crimes are similar but separate crimes that the victim is unable to recall individually or describe in detail to an interviewer. Older versions of the NCVS used three crimes as the minimum limit for a series, but the redesign changed the number to six similar offenses. Under this change, if a respondent reports three to five similar incidents to an interviewer, data on each incident are now collected. For most types of crime, it is estimated that this change in the definition of series crimes increases the rate of crime by only 1 to 5 percent. However, for assaults, especially situations of domestic abuse, and some types of theft, the increase in crime rates may be in the 10 to 15 percent range.

Reporting Crimes to the Police. A lower percentage of crimes identified in the redesigned NCVS are now being reported to the police than in previous versions. This change is attributed to expanded cuing of less serious crimes (which are less likely to be reported to the police) in the redesigned survey.

Changes in Crime Classification of Personal and Household Larceny. Under the older versions of the NCVS, larceny was defined according to the location in which it occurred, with household thefts involving stolen items on the grounds of the home and personal thefts involving items stolen someplace away from the home. Under the redesign, all thefts are classified as household thefts unless there was contact between the victim and offender. Accordingly, the number of household thefts increased and the number of personal thefts decreased as a consequence of the redesigned coding procedures.

Overall Effects on Victimization Estimates. Kindermann et al. (1997) indicate that the impact of the redesign varies by the type of crime. In particular, the redesigned NCVS yielded higher estimates of crime rates for the following offense types: personal crimes (increase of 44 percent), crimes of violence (increase of 49 percent), rapes (increase of 157 percent), assaults (increase of 57 percent), property crimes (increase of 23 percent), burglaries (increase of 20 percent), and thefts (increase of 27 percent). No substantial differences were observed for rates of robbery, personal theft, and motor vehicle theft.

Redesign Effects on Select Population Subgroups. The redesign procedures had different effects on the victimization rates for particular subgroups. For crimes of violence, the redesigned NCVS elicited more recounting of victimizations for whites than for blacks, for 33- to 44-year-olds than for other age groups, for persons with household incomes of $15,000 or more than for lower-income persons, and for suburban residents more than urban residents. Rates of household crimes were recounted more for suburban than rural residents through the use of the new procedures, and higher rates of burglary were elicited from black than white respondents in the redesign (see Kindermann et al. 1997).

These research findings indicate that the continuity of the NCVS series has been compromised by changes in the screening questions and classification procedures, which leads to difficulties in comparing victimization rates over time. As is done in many published reports using NCVS data, it is possible to make adjustments to the pre-redesign and post-redesign series to increase their comparability. However, it is also likely that a number of these changes have complex interaction effects that vary across particular combinations of offense, victim, and method attributes. If these interaction effects are not fully incorporated in the estimation procedures, current adjustments in the NCVS data may not necessarily enhance the comparability of the two data panels.

The Distribution of Victimization Rates and Risk Factors for Criminal Victimization

One basic indicator of crime prevalence used in the first 20 years of summary reports of NCVS trends was the proportion of households "touched by crime." From 1975 to 1992, the estimated proportion of U.S. households that experienced any type of victimization in the previous year decreased steadily from about 32 percent to approximately 23 percent (Zawitz et al. 1993). The estimated proportion of households experiencing burglary decreased from approximately 8 percent in 1975 to 4 percent in 1992, whereas the proportion of U.S. households experiencing a violent crime vacillated between 5 and 6 percent over this period. Unfortunately, this measure of victimization prevalence has not been computed or disseminated in published reports by the Bureau of Justice Statistics since 1992.

Examining the NCVS data from 1973 to 2000,[2] it is clear that rates of criminal victimization in the United States have exhibited patterns of stability and change over time (see Exhibit 5.2). Victimization rates for crimes of violence (e.g., assaults, robberies, and rapes) hovered around 50 per 1,000 persons age 12 or older in the late 1970s to the early 1980s, decreased somewhat during the mid- to late-1980s, increased until the mid-1990s, and steadily declined from 1994 to 2000.

Property crime rates based on the NCVS data have exhibited a steady decrease over the last 30 years (see Exhibit 5.3). The most common property crimes experienced in the United States are household thefts, followed by residential burglary and motor vehicle thefts. Property crime rates have decreased from 520 per 1,000 households in 1973 to 178 per 1,000 house-

Exhibit 5.2. Violent Crimes Victimization Rates in the United States, NCVS, 1973-2000

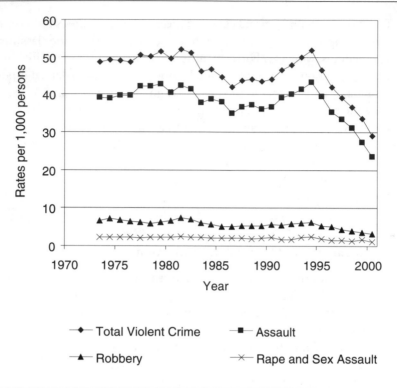

SOURCE: NCVS.

holds in 2000. Among specific property crimes, thefts from the household decreased more than twofold from 391 to 138 per 1,000 households between 1973 and 2000. Burglary rates in 2000 were nearly more than three times lower than their rate in 1973, and rates of motor vehicle theft are more than two times lower over this period.

National victimization surveys indicate that the risks of victimization are not uniform across different demographic subgroups (see Exhibit 5.4). Men have higher risks of victimization than women for all violent crimes combined and for the specific offenses of robbery and assault. Women have higher risks of sexual assault and slightly higher risks than men for personal thefts. On the basis of comparisons with NCVS data in the 1970s and 1980s, the magnitude of gender differences in the risk of violent victimization has exhibited little change over the last 30 years.

Exhibit 5.3. Property Victimization Rates in the United States, NCVS, 1973-2000

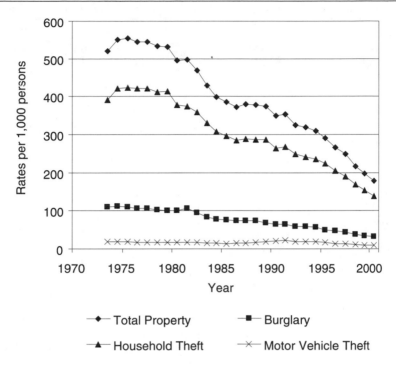

SOURCE: NCVS.

African Americans experience greater risks of violent victimization than whites for each type of crime. However, racial differences are not particularly large in absolute magnitude, and these racial differences in rates of violent victimization have diminished somewhat over time. Persons of Hispanic origin have slightly greater risks of robbery and personal theft, but non-Hispanic persons are more susceptible to rape and assaults.

The highest rates of violent victimization across age groups involve teenagers between the ages of 16 and 19, with the overall rate of violent victimization in this age group being three times higher than it is for all age groups over 35 years old. Rates of violent victimization for particular offenses (e.g., assault, robbery, and sexual assault) decrease quite dramatically for successive age groups over 25 years old. Risks of personal theft (e.g., pickpocketing, purse snatching), however, are more uniform across the different age groups.

Exhibit 5.4. Violent Crimes Victimization Rates per 1,000 Persons (NCVS 2000)

	Total Violence	Assault	Robbery	Rape and/or Sex Assault	Personal Theft
Gender:					
Male	32.9	28.3	4.5	0.1	1.0
Female	23.2	19.0	2.0	2.1	1.4
Race:					
White	27.1	23.3	2.7	1.1	1.1
Black	35.3	26.9	7.2	1.2	1.9
Other	20.7	16.7	2.8	1.1	1.8
Hispanic Origin:					
Hispanic	28.4	23.0	5.0	0.5	2.4
Non-Hispanic	27.7	23.5	3.0	1.2	1.1
Age:					
12-15	60.1	53.8	4.2	2.1	1.8
16-19	64.3	52.7	7.3	4.3	3.0
20-24	49.4	41.2	6.2	2.1	1.1
25-34	34.8	29.5	3.9	1.3	1.5
35-49	21.8	18.4	2.7	0.8	0.9
50-64	13.7	11.1	2.1	0.4	0.5
65+	3.7	2.9	0.7	0.1	1.2
Household Income:					
<$7,500	60.3	48.1	7.1	5.2	2.3
$7,500-$15,000	37.8	31.3	4.7	1.7	2.1
$15,000-$25,000	31.8	27.2	3.2	1.4	1.2
$25,000-$35,000	29.8	23.7	4.2	1.9	1.4
$35,000-$50,000	28.5	25.3	2.3	0.8	0.6
$50,000-$75,000	23.7	19.1	3.6	1.0	1.0
$75,000+	22.3	20.2	2.0	0.2	1.2
Marital Status:					
Never Married	51.4	43.0	5.7	2.6	2.3
Married	12.8	10.8	1.8	0.1	0.5
Divorce/Separated	42.2	36.2	3.8	2.3	1.3
Widowed	8.1	6.6	1.3	0.2	1.3
Region:					
Northeast	23.5	18.8	3.3	1.5	2.3
Northwest	30.4	26.3	3.1	1.1	1.2
South	24.9	21.0	3.0	0.9	0.6
West	33.9	28.8	3.6	1.4	1.3
Residence:					
Urban	35.1	27.6	6.0	1.5	2.3
Suburban	25.8	22.4	2.6	0.8	1.0
Rural	23.6	20.9	1.3	1.4	0.4

SOURCE: Rennison (2001).

Over the last 10 years, NCVS data indicate that rates of violent victimization for younger teenagers (aged 12-15) have increased more rapidly than for any other age group. As a group, teenage black males are especially vulnerable to violent victimization (see, e.g., Zawitz et al. 1993).

Risk of violent victimization also differs by household income, marital status, regional location, and residence in urban or rural areas. Risks are highest among the lowest income groups, and this pattern is consistent across each type of violent crime. Compared to those for married or widowed persons, rates of violent victimization are far higher among those who are never married, divorced, or separated. Robbery and assault rates are higher in the western region of the United States than in other regions of the country. For each type of violent victimization, risks are higher among urban residents than rural residents. Each of these demographic differences in risks of violent victimization have also been found in earlier years of the NCVS.

Major demographic differences in the risk of victimization are also revealed for property offenses (see Exhibit 5.5). Minority-headed households, compared to households headed by whites, are at greatest risk for burglary, household theft, and motor vehicle theft. Rates of motor vehicle theft are fairly uniform across different income groups. However, low-income households are the most prone to residential burglary, and the highest income groups have the greatest risk of experiencing theft from their homes. Regardless of the specific type, residents in the western states have the greatest risk, and persons in the Northeast have the lowest risk of experiencing property crime. Urban residents and persons who rent their homes also have greater risks of experiencing each type of property crime.

NCVS data provide the additional opportunity to examine particular characteristics of criminal offenses and those who commit them. As shown in Exhibit 5.6,[3] these offense and situational characteristics for violent crimes include whether the act is completed or merely attempted, the number of victims and offenders, the victim-offender relationship, the time of day, location of the crime and its distance from the victim's home, whether there was any physical injury to the victim, and the type of weapon used, if any. Offender attributes include the victims' perception of their attacker's sex, race, age, and drug or alcohol use.

The vast majority of violent offenses derived from the national victimization data involve attempted or threatened rather than completed offenses. This overall pattern is produced by the fact that simple assaults, the majority of which are classified as "attempts" because they do not involve

Exhibit 5.5. Property Victimization Rates per 1,000 Households (NCVS 2000)

	Total Property	Burglary	Household Theft	Motor Vehicle Theft
Race:				
White	173.3	29.4	136.0	7.9
Black	212.2	47.6	151.4	13.2
Other	171.3	32.4	128.6	10.4
Hispanic Origin:				
Hispanic	227.0	41.7	165.6	19.7
Non-Hispanic	173.4	31.0	134.7	7.6
Household Income:				
<$7,500	220.9	61.7	151.2	7.9
$7,500-$15,000	167.1	41.1	116.8	9.1
$15,000-$25,000	193.1	39.3	143.8	9.9
$25,000-$35,000	192.2	33.3	149.4	9.5
$35,000-$50,000	192.9	32.0	151.4	9.6
$50,000-$75,000	181.9	24.0	147.9	10.0
$75,000+	197.2	27.7	162.5	7.0
Region:				
Northeast	143.7	21.8	114.6	7.3
Northwest	181.9	31.4	141.2	9.3
South	167.8	33.2	127.8	6.9
West	223.4	39.1	172.0	12.3
Residence:				
Urban	222.1	40.9	168.1	13.1
Suburban	163.7	27.2	128.4	8.1
Rural	152.6	29.5	118.7	4.4
Home Ownership:				
Owned	153.4	26.2	120.6	6.7
Rented	228.3	43.2	172.5	12.6

SOURCE: Rennison (2001).

actual physical injury to the victim, are the most frequent crimes reported in victimization surveys (Rennison 2001). Most robberies and sexual assaults, however, involve completed rather than attempted offenses.

Both multiple victims and multiple offenders are the exception in violent incidents reported in the NCVS. More than 90 percent of violent incidents reported in the 1994 data involve a single victim, and this proportion was higher for rapes and sexual assaults (99 percent) and robberies (95 percent). Sole offenders were reported in more than three quarters of all violent incidents, but this rate was much higher for incidents of sexual assault (88 percent) and far lower for robberies (54 percent).

Exhibit 5.6. Offense and Offender Characteristics in Violent Crimes, 1994 and 1998 (Percentages)

	All Violent Crimes	Assault	Robbery	Rape/Sexual Assault
Crime Type, 1998				
Attempt/Threat	68	75	31	45
Complete	32	25	69	55
Multiple Victims, 1994				
No	92	92	95	99
Yes	08	08	05	01
Multiple Offender, 1994				
No	77	80	54	88
Yes	20	17	43	09
Don't Know	03	03	03	02
Victim-Offender Relationship, 1998				
Nonstranger	55	55	41	74
Intimates	12	11	12	18
Other Relatives	06	06	08	08
Friends/Acquaintances	37	38	21	48
Strangers	44	44	57	25
Unknown	01	01	02	02
Time of Day, 1994				
6 a.m.-6 p.m.	53	62	42	31
6 p.m.-Midnight	35	37	43	37
Midnight-6 a.m.	12	01	15	32
Location of Crime, 1994				
At/Near Victim's Home/Lodging	26	26	24	37
Friend/Relative/Neighbor's Home	07	07	04	21
Commercial Place	13	14	08	07
Parking Lot/Garage	08	07	12	06
School	13	15	04	03
Street Other than Near Victim's Home	20	18	37	08
Other	13	13	10	17
Distance from Victim's Home, 1994				
Inside Home/Lodging	05	14	14	34
Near Victim's Home	16	15	13	10
1 Mile or Less	24	21	29	12
5 Miles or Less	26	24	22	14
50 Miles or Less	24	22	19	23
More than 50 Miles Away	05	04	04	06
Physical Injury to Victim, 1994				
No	00	76	68	00
Yes	100	24	32	100

Exhibit 5.6. (continued)

	All Violent Crimes	Assault	Robbery	Rape/Sexual Assault
Weapon Use/Type, 1998				
No Weapons	68	69	49	87
Gun	08	07	21	04
Knife	06	05	10	03
Other Weapon	08	08	07	00
Unknown Weapon Type	02	02	01	02
Missing Data	09	08	13	04
Offender's Perceived Sex, 1994				
Male	83	82	86	99
Female	17	18	12	01
Don't Know	<1	<1	02	<1
Offender's Perceived Race, 1994				
White	64	67	35	68
Black	25	23	51	21
Other	09	09	10	09
Don't Know	02	01	04	02
Offender's Perceived Age, 1994				
< 30	60	60	66	46
>= 30	37	37	28	52
Don't Know	03	02	06	02
Perceived Drug or Alcohol Use by Offender, 1994				
No Drug or Alcohol	28	30	13	28
Drug or Alcohol	30	29	25	48
Don't Know or Not Ascertained	42	41	62	24

SOURCE: NCVS.

The most common interpersonal relationship between the victim and offender in violent crimes depends on the particular type of offense. For all violent offenses combined in the NCVS data, the majority of victims (55 percent) report that the offenders are nonstrangers, with "friends/acquaintances" being the most common in this category. Offenses committed by nonstrangers are most common in rapes and sexual assaults (74 percent), followed by assaults (55 percent) and robbery (41 percent). The proportion of violent victimizations that involves intimates (e.g., current and former spouses, girlfriends, boyfriends) ranged from 5 to 17 percent across these types of violent offenses.

The risk of experiencing violent victimization is not uniform over time of day or physical location. On the basis of the 1994 NCVS data, the peak six-hour time period for violent crime is the early evening (6 p.m. to midnight). More than 40 percent of personal robberies occur in the early evening, and this is also the riskiest time for other violent crimes. Approximately one in four violent crimes occur in or near the victim's home, and nearly half of them take place within a mile from the home. Rapes and sexual assaults are more likely to occur in the victim's home than are other violent offenses. Regardless of the type of violent crime, these offenses rarely occur more than 50 miles away from the victim's home.

The likelihood of physical injury and the type of weapon used are also important components of violent situations. Although violent offenses may involve serious psychological harm to victims, the clear majority of robberies and assault victimizations do not result in any physical injuries. Less than one third of robbery victims and less than one fourth of assault victims sustained physical injuries as the result of being attacked. More than two thirds of the violent victimizations did not involve the use of a weapon, and this was especially true of sexual assaults and assaults. Robbery was the only violent crime in which a large proportion of victimizations involved a gun as the weapon.

Victims of direct-contact crimes are sometimes able to provide a demographic profile of those who offend against them. Unless the suspect is thwarted in the attempt or subsequently apprehended, victims of property crime are typically unable to provide this type of information. According to 1994 NCVS data on single-offender incidents, the vast majority (83 percent) of violent offenders are identified as males by their victims; this rate for male offenders was highest for rape and sexual assault (99 percent) and lowest in cases of assault (82 percent). Most offenders are also judged by their victims to be white for all violent offenses except robbery, where black offenders are identified as the majority. Persons under 30 years old are more commonly identified as the offender than older persons for the majority of violent incidents. For rape and sexual assaults, however, the typical offender is judged to be over 30 years of age.

Although many victims are not able to report on this variable, the offender is perceived to be under the influence of either drugs or alcohol in approximately 3 out of every 10 violent incidents. Rates of perceived substance use are highest in rape and sexual assault (48 percent) and lowest in robbery incidents (25 percent). Of offenders viewed as "under the influence," the vast majority of these incidents involve alcohol rather than drug use.

As a measure of the dark figure underlying official data, victimization surveys reveal that most offenses are not reported to the police and that reporting rates vary by type of crime and characteristics of the victim (see Exhibit 5.7). An average of fewer than 4 out of 10 victimization incidents are reported to the police, with reporting rates higher for violent crimes (48 percent) than personal thefts (35 percent) and household crimes (36 percent). Robberies and aggravated assaults are the most frequently reported, and simple assaults the least reported, violent crimes. Motor vehicle thefts have the highest rate of reporting (80 percent) among all types of victimization. This is related to the fact that in order for victims to make insurance claims for stolen vehicles, a police report must be filed. When examined over time, overall reporting rates have remained relatively stable over the last three decades.

Reporting rates are far higher for the following groups of offense attributes: (a) completed acts versus attempted acts, (b) crimes involving injury versus those without injury, and (c) crimes committed by strangers versus non-strangers. Particular groups of people also have higher reporting rates than others. For example, females are more likely than males to report their victimization to the police for both violent and property crimes. Black victims have a slightly higher rate of reporting for both types of crimes than white victims. Households in southern states have higher reporting rates than other regions of the country. There are no major differences in reporting property crimes across urban, suburban, and rural households (Rennison 2001).

Reasons for not reporting crimes to the police vary according to the type of offense. The most commonly given reasons for not reporting violent offenses are that "the crime was a personal or private matter" and that "the offender was not successful." For property offenses, the most common reasons for not reporting were that "the object was recovered," "the offender was unsuccessful," "the police would not want to be bothered," and "lack of proof" (Zawitz et al. 1993).

Other Victimization Surveys

In addition to the national and international victimization surveys, research in the last four decades has included a diverse array of smaller-scale victimization studies, usually focused on particular types of crime within specific jurisdictions. Surveys of victims of domestic violence and sexual assault are widely recognized as an important measurement strategy due to the significant underreporting of these crimes in official data sources. College campus surveys, statewide surveys of quality of life, and local surveys of neighborhood revitalization and development also often include measures of victimization experiences. In addition, Gallup polls and national surveys such as the General Social Survey, conducted by the National

Exhibit 5.7. Crimes Reported to the Police for Selected Years (NCVS Data) (Percentages)

	1974	1984	1992	2000
All Victims	33	35	39	38
Violent Crime	47	47	50	48
Aggravated Assault	53	55	62	57
Simple Assault	39	40	44	44
Robbery	54	54	51	56
Rape/Sexual Assault	52	56	52	48
Personal Theft with Contact	34	31	31	35
Household Crime	37	38	42	36
Burglary	48	49	54	51
Theft	25	27	26	30
Motor Vehicle Theft	67	69	75	80

SOURCE: NCVS.

Opinion Research Center, also frequently include items on victimization. The National White-Collar Crime Center recently conducted a survey of individuals regarding their experiences as victims of white-collar crime (Rebovich et al. 2000).

Although useful for their particular purposes, these other victimization surveys are often less comprehensive than national surveys, and they are usually based on smaller samples. Low response rates and selective sampling frames also limit the generalizability of sample estimates from such studies.

Problems with Victimization Surveys

Large-scale public surveys of victims are widely regarded as an alternative measure of the true extent of crime in a jurisdiction because they provide estimates of both reported and unreported offenses in a particular time period. Similar to official data and self-reports of criminal behavior, however, victimization surveys are limited by basic restrictions on their scope and are susceptible to major conceptual and methodological problems that contribute to their mismeasurement of crime. Several of these issues are addressed below.

Limitations on the Scope of Crimes Covered

One immediate problem with victimization surveys as a measure of the distribution and nature of crime is that they can only capture criminal offenses involving victims. By definition, "victimless" crimes—such as drug and alcohol violations, prostitution, and gambling—are excluded from victimization surveys.[4] Other criminal offenses—such as illegal weapon possession, tax evasion, murder, and crimes in which a business or commercial establishment is the victim (e.g., nonresidential burglary, bank robbery, employee theft, corporate collusion, and industrial theft), consumer fraud, possession of stolen property, and a host of public order offenses (e.g., trespassing, disorderly conduct, breach of peace, curfew violations)—are also excluded from these surveys.

The restricted scope of crimes covered in victimization surveys becomes problematic because the included crimes represent only a small minority of all criminal offenses that may be of interest to criminologists and policy makers. For example, based on official data on crime in the United States, the most common arrests involve drug- and alcohol-related crimes (e.g., possession of a controlled substance, public drunkenness, liquor law violations, driving under the influence of alcohol), and a sizable proportion of robberies (27 percent), burglaries (37 percent), and larcenies (12 percent) are crimes committed against the property of businesses rather than individuals (Biderman and Lynch 1991). By excluding these major and frequently occurring forms of crime, existing public surveys of victims are limited to only a relatively small subset of crimes.[5]

Conceptual and Definitional Problems

Even among the subset of personal and property crimes included in victimization surveys, this measure of crime suffers from conceptual ambiguity regarding how crimes are defined by the researcher and the respondent. Differential perceptions of crime across individuals that derive from competing conceptualizations of criminal acts contribute to measurement error in the coding and counting of victimizations.

One serious problem in victim surveys that limits their comparability with official counts of crime involves the basic definition of crimes used in each data source. Specifically, victimization surveys use a potentially more inclusive definition of some types of crime than police reports, because victim surveys include incidents that may be legally justified (e.g., self-defense assaults) and incidents lacking the basic necessary elements for legal culpability (e.g., criminal intent, particular injuries, or monetary loss). By simply counting as violent crime "any attack or threat or use of force by anyone at all" without an examination of the context of the event, victimization surveys may provide us with a distorted image of the prevalence of particular types of crimes. The tendency for victimization surveys to include many "noncrimes" and trivial offenses is well documented (see Biderman and Lynch 1991; O'Brien 1985).

Different definitions of crime across cultures and social groups is another fundamental problem with victimization surveys. Although the magnitude of bias in these surveys from differential interpretations of questions has not been empirically assessed, there is undoubtedly much variation in the meaning of particular words and phrases to members of different demographic groups. For example, the new screening questions in the NCVS use words such as "attacked" or "threatened" to cue memories about victimization experiences, but the subjective meaning attached to these terms varies widely. Is the act of brandishing a firearm or knife a threat of violence? Is someone "attacked" when it is a situation of mutual combat? How do respondents in victimization surveys interpret situations of "grabbing," "punching," or "choking" done in the context of either male or sibling roughhousing or of physical banter among peers or spirited athletic contests (like football, hockey, and basketball)? Is it reasonable to assume that there are no major gender, age, race, social class, or cultural differences in the interpretation of what constitutes a threat or attack? Similarly, wording for the property offense questions such as burglary (e.g., has anyone "broken in," or "attempted to break in" your home?) and motor vehicle theft (e.g., has anyone "stolen" or "used without permission" your vehicle?) are also subject to differential interpretations. Under these conditions, estimates of the prevalence of violent or property crimes are likely to be distorted.[6]

By failing to include reference to the particular context in which "threats" or "attacks" take place, most victimization surveys further compound measurement error stemming from differential interpretation of questions on the part of respondents. The NCVS redesign has attempted to deal with this problem somewhat by including screening cues about the offender or place of the crime (e.g., attacked by someone at work or school, a neighbor or friend, a relative or family member, while riding in a car, on the street or in a parking lot). Unfortunately, these contextual cues are still unable to standardize across different groups the meaning that should be attached to words and phrases such as "attack," "threaten," "grab," "punch," "have something stolen from you," "break in," and "use without permission" that underlie questions about an individual's victimization experiences. Regardless of how refined the objective meaning is that researchers attach to these terms, they remain prone to varied subjective interpretations by respondents.

Methodological Problems

In addition to conceptual and definitional limitations, current victimization surveys suffer from numerous methodological problems that further call into question the accuracy of estimates of victimization rates, subgroup variation in these rates, and the measurement of the characteristics of offenders, victims, and crime incidents. These methodological problems involve both simple and complex issues of sampling (e.g., sampling error, sampling bias, characteristics of nonrespondents), survey research (e.g., interviewer effects, telephone versus personal interviews, social desirability, reference period), and technical procedures used in the calculation of rates (e.g., appropriate numerators and denominators, series incidents).

Sampling Issues

National victimization surveys use the responses of a sample of residents to estimate rates of victimization for the entire population. Unfortunately, whenever samples are used to represent populations, there is always the possibility of a discrepancy between the sample estimates and the true population parameters. When this discrepancy is due entirely to the properties of random sampling, it is referred to as sampling error. The discrepancy is referred to as sampling bias when it derives from sources other than random sampling. Both sampling error and sampling bias are characteristic of victim surveys.

Sampling error will result in fluctuations in estimates of national victimization rates. For example, the 2000 reported NCVS rate of violent victimization of 28 per 1,000 persons 12 years of age and older is our best single guess of the true rate for the United States. However, we cannot be certain of the accuracy of this estimate, because it is based on a sample, rather than the entire population. It is quite possible that another random sample of U.S. households for the same period would yield a different estimate of violent victimization.

As discussed in Chapter 4, as a strategy for correcting the effect of sampling error, statistical theory about probability sampling tells us that in the long run, these sample estimates will converge on the true value in the population. Information from the sample and estimates of sampling error can then be used to develop a range of values in which the true population parameter is likely to fall. Unfortunately, even with the construction of such confidence intervals, there is no guarantee that the estimates derived from a particular sample necessarily reflect the true population values.

All other things being equal, large samples are preferred over small samples, because sampling error will decrease as sample size increases. Given the relatively large size of NCVS samples (approximately 60,000 households), we have far greater confidence in their estimates than other victimization surveys.

Several sources of sampling bias have been identified in victimization surveys. For example, particular groups of people are less likely to participate in victimization surveys than others, and the excluded groups tend to be more prone to victimization. In the NCVS, homeless persons, young males, and members of minority groups are less likely to be included, and each group has higher risks of victimization than their older, female, and nonminority counterparts (see Skogan 1978). At the other extreme, the very wealthy are probably underrepresented in victimization surveys because of their ability to isolate themselves from interviewers (Garafalo 1990). Nonrandom differences in response rates in surveys across social groups (e.g., lower response rates among minority and inner-city residents compared to other groups) is another source of sampling bias in victimization research. The exclusion of victimization experienced by businesses and crimes against the government in household victimization surveys can also be interpreted as a source of sampling bias that dramatically lowers estimates of national victimization rates. Although adjustments for sampling bias are sometimes made in national estimates, there is no universally accepted method of adjusting for this source of error, and many of the correction factors that are used are based on rather dubious assumptions about the nature of the excluded cases.

Survey Research Issues

Survey research is an ideal data collection strategy for victimization studies because surveys are best designed to describe a characteristic in a population. Unfortunately, survey responses are affected by a wide variety of factors that alter the accuracy of estimates of victimization rates. These problems with survey research include differences across the mode of administration of surveys, question wording and reference periods, and the basic limitations of human judgments.

One basic issue in victimization surveys involves whether to collect data through a telephone or face-to-face interview. Telephone surveys have the advantage of being cheaper and quicker to implement. When the interviews are conducted by reading the survey questionnaire from the CATI and are monitored in a central facility, telephone surveys provide greater assurances of uniformity and standardization. Greater anonymity for respondents is also provided through telephone interviewing, which may generate more truthful answers to sensitive questions. In contrast, face-to-face interviews are believed to provide higher response quality because trained interviewers can maximize the use of various visual and nonverbal cues to ask more complicated questions and to determine whether the respondent understands the questions. Both telephone and face-to-face interviews have been used in national and international victimization surveys. For example, since 1996, the NCVS uses face-to-face interviews for only two of the seven contact periods; the remaining five interviews of each housing unit are conducted via telephone.

In terms of the accuracy of information and eliciting victimization incidents, several general statements can be supported from previous research comparing telephone and face-to-face interviews. First, there is no convincing evidence that telephone surveys provide less accurate information about crime victimization than personal interviews in the NCVS (Biderman and Lynch 1991). However, differences across methods in the NCVS projects are probably smaller than in other surveys because of the extensive training and monitoring that is done in the NCVS for both telephone and face-to-face interviewers. Second, the use of computer-assisted telephone interviewing from a centralized telephone facility has been found to increase the number of reported crimes for at least some offenses. As mentioned earlier, the use of CATI increases estimates of the rates of crimes of violence, crimes of theft, and household larceny by approximately 15 to 20 percent and burglary by about 10 percent, but it had only a marginal impact on reports of motor vehicle theft (see Bureau of Justice Statistics Bulletin 1994). CATI is presumed to yield higher and more realistic estimates of crime rates in victimization surveys by enhancing administrative control over the interview process. Under these conditions, differences across studies in the type of survey method utilized and changes over time in the increased use of telephone interviewing makes rather dubious many comparisons of the estimates of victimization rates over time.

Another major issue in survey research involves question wording and response formats. This issue has been raised most pointedly in victimization surveys within the context of the type and nature of screen questions as well as the reference period for the reporting of victimization experiences.

Both incident rates and subgroup variation in victimization risks are affected by the particular screen questions used to elicit reports of victimization experiences. Short screen questions may cue a respondent's recall of only a small subset of incidents that involve the most serious or frequent violations, whereas longer screens encourage the recounting of a fuller range of experiences across various contexts.

When compared to results using the "old" NCVS instrument, the redesigned survey (which includes new screens and enhanced questions) yields substantially higher estimates of victimization rates for particular crimes. Specifically, changes in the survey wording resulted in a dramatic increase in the estimated rates of personal crimes (which increased by 44 percent), crimes of violence (which increased by 49 percent), assaults (57 percent increase), and rapes (157 percent increase). However, the redesigned survey did not substantially affect estimated rates for robbery, personal theft, or motor vehicle theft (Kindermann et al. 1997). The new method also had a significant impact on estimates of crime committed by nonstrangers, attempted acts, and those offenses that were not reported to the police. As mentioned previously, the recalling of violent crimes in the redesigned survey was higher for the following groups: whites, mid-aged residents (35-44 years old), persons with higher incomes, and suburban residents.

Estimates of victimization rates are also affected by the length of the reference period used in the survey. Obviously, longer time periods (e.g., asking about victimization experiences in the previous five years) will elicit more incident reports than a shorter time period because of the greater time at risk for victimization. However, survey respondents who are asked retrospective questions may also report an incident as occurring earlier than it actually did. Although this telescoping of the reference period may be due to faulty memory or an unconscious effort to please interviewers, it is a serious problem in any survey that attempts to elicit information about past events.

Surveys that use a reference period of one year or more are susceptible to forward telescoping (i.e., remembering events as occurring more recently than they actually occurred). The six-month reference period used in the NCVS makes this survey prone to backward telescoping (i.e., remembering incidents as having occurred in a more distant past). However, both types of telescoping are minimized in the NCVS data through the process of the "bounding interview," in which the first interview of a household serves as a baseline for anchoring the recall period. When reinterviewed in six months, NCVS respondents are asked about incidents since the last interview, and repeated incidents can be filtered out. Incident reports from the first interview of a household in the NCVS panel are not used in the estimation of national rates because they are "unbounded" and susceptible to telescoping. Biderman and Cantor (1984) suggest that the failure to bound incidents in the NCVS would increase the number of estimated victimizations by almost 50 percent.

This bounding procedure may be a partial solution to the problem of telescoping, but it does not correct several other potential response effects often found in panel studies. For example, and unlike cross-sectional surveys, subjects in panel surveys are interviewed repeatedly. Their responses to survey items may be at least partially dependent on the previous interview experience (Lenhen and Reiss 1978).

Decisions regarding which reference period to use in victimization surveys are often based on balancing the issues of telescoping, sample size, and financial costs. Forward telescoping is minimized by a shorter recall period, but this choice also requires the use of larger and ultimately more expensive samples to uncover a sufficient number of individuals who have recently experienced a victimization. Unfortunately, the use of different recall periods and bounding procedures limit the ability to make over-time comparisons of large-scale victimization surveys such as the NCVS.

In addition, because victimization surveys rely only on the report of the victim, the data may be distorted by variations in how respondents define crime. In the 1976 survey, for example, persons with college degrees recalled three times as many assaults as those with only an elementary education (Gove, Hughes, and Geerken 1985). It is possible that persons with lower levels of education may see a certain act as a normal aspect of daily life, whereas individuals who have had very little experience with physically assaultive behavior may view the same act as one of criminal violence. Alternatively, these differences in reporting of victimization across educational levels could be due to differential respondent productivity, that is, people with higher levels of education may be better able to recall incidents of victimization.

Another issue is related to interviewer and interviewer-respondent interaction effects: different interviewers may elicit different accounts from the same individual because, for example, they prompt respondents more or less or appear more or less open to certain responses. Clarren and Schwarz (1976:129) (as cited in Gove et al. 1985) concluded that "the upper bound for the number of crimes that could be elicited is limited only by the persistence of the interviewer and the patience of the respondent" (p. 461). In the context of the British Crime Surveys, Coleman and Moynihan (1996) note that respondents, not wanting to disappoint the often persistent interviewers, may recall incidents experienced by friends or neighbors rather than themselves personally. It is also possible, they suggest, that with the crime problem so high on the media's agenda and thus ingrained in peoples' minds, respondents may fabricate incidents in the hope that this will somehow lead to policy changes.

Victimization surveys are also an imperfect measure of crime because of the inherent fallibility of human information processing and judgments. People experience lapses in memory, selectively perceive and misperceive particular actions, and interpret actions and events from their own perspectives. In the case of reports of victimization, people may overestimate or underestimate their experiences through outright deception, exaggeration, embarrassment, or misinterpretation. The not uncommon perceptions that lost items were stolen, that open doors and windows are evidence of attempted break-ins, as well as the misunderstanding of particular words and phrases such as "threats" and "fighting words" are simple examples of how victimization surveys may provide seriously distorted estimates of the "true" amount of crime.

The reliability of victimization data can be ascertained through comparisons of survey data with official records, but the results from the limited number of studies that have made such comparisons are not overly encouraging. For example, Turner (1972) found that only 63 percent of the cases of robbery, assault, and rape from police records were reported on victimization surveys, and there were important differences according to the relationship of the victim to the offender. When the offender was a stranger, 76 percent of the incidents were reported to the interviewer on the victimization survey; when the offender was known to the victim, 57 percent of the incidents were reported; and when the offender was a relative, only 22 percent of the incidents were reported. In a similar record check study in Baltimore, Murphy and Dodge (1981) found that only 37 percent of the assaults—compared to 75 percent of the larcenies, 76 percent of the robberies, and 86 percent of the burglaries—uncovered in police records were reported by respondents in victimization surveys.

A second type of record check involves "forward record checks" (O'Brien 1985), which involves examining crimes that respondents in victimization surveys claim to have reported to the police. Apparently, the only study of this type was conducted by Schneider (1977) in Portland, Oregon, who found that only 45 percent of the crimes that respondents claimed to have reported to the police were listed in police records.

Technical and Procedural Issues

A number of technical issues associated with victimization surveys also place limits on their utility as measures of crime. These issues focus on the numerator (i.e., the number and type of crimes) and the denominator (i.e., the relevant population base) used in the calculation of crime rates and trends. Changes in technical aspects of national surveys have further eroded the comparability of victimization estimates across jurisdictions and over time.

Changes in the definition of "series victimizations" and how they are treated is a major technical problem with current victimization surveys. A series involves multiple incidents that are very similar in detail but for which the respondent is unable to recall specific dates and details well enough to report the incidents separately. For example, many cases of spouse abuse involve repeated attacks on a number of occasions over the reference period, but the victim cannot recall the particular dates or details of each incident.

National surveys vary widely in their definition of series victimizations and how these are handled in estimation procedures. For example, the NCVS defined a series as involving "three or more criminal acts" prior to the redesign in 1992, and since that time has changed the crime threshold to six incidents. Although some special reports using NCVS data count series crimes as one victimization, series victimizations are excluded in the computation of incidence rates. It is estimated that this change in the definition of series crimes will result in only a small (1 to 5 percent) increase in the rates for most crimes, but the increase may be as large as 10 to 15 percent for rates of assault and some types of theft (Bureau of Justice Statistics Bulletin 1994). Aside from decreasing the overall estimated rates of victimization, the exclusion of series incidents also artificially deflates the victimization risks for women and other subgroups who are more susceptible to these crimes.

Another technical issue that affects the counting of incidents for rate calculation involves the incomplete bounding of interviews in the NCVS data. Specifically, NCVS procedures dictate that only the first rotation of a housing unit in the survey be treated as a bounding interview, excluding victimization data from that housing unit in the first contact period. However, when new persons move into an eligible housing unit or they were not successfully contacted in the first rotation, the data from their first interview are unbounded but still used for rate calculations. Thus, by bounding the housing unit but not the individuals within it, NCVS estimates remain highly susceptible to telescoping and overestimation of victimization risks. The seriousness of this problem is illustrated in a study by Biderman and Cantor (1984), who found that approximately 18 percent of the total interviews used to generate NCVS estimates in the 1970s were first unbounded interviews. The inclusion of these data increased the number of victimizations used for published estimates of national trends by almost 50 percent. The replacement of households that leave the panel because they move may also lead to lower estimates of victimization; individuals in such households generally have higher rates of victimization than people who remain at the same address.

As sample data used to estimate population values, national counts of victimizations are derived from various types of weighting procedures and imputations for missing data. Although based on sound statistical theory, these adjustments in practice involve making rather questionable assumptions about the behavior of nonrespondents and the homogeneity of classes or subgroups. For example, the weighting of the British Crime Survey data to adjust for oversampling of inner-city and minority respondents may be of limited value simply because it does not take into account the differential response rates across these subgroups and their differences in victimization risks. By making unrealistic assumptions that errors in measurement and sampling are random (rather than correlated with other factors), the complex weighting and adjustments used in the NCVS are also subject to debate.

When moving from a consideration of victimization incidents to victimization rates, other technical issues arise that may lead to a distortion in the interpretation of results. For example, Bureau of Justice Statistics' publications of NCVS data trends compute rates of victimizations per 1,000 persons or households by taking the total number of incidents and dividing by the respective number of persons or households. The resulting rate, however, does not translate into a proportion of persons or households, because multiple victimizations are included in the calculations. For instance, a burglary rate of 100 per 1,000 households does not mean that 10 percent of households experience a burglary, because it is possible that one household may report an enormous number of victimizations. Unfortunately, by spreading these multiple victimizations of a particular household across all households, a somewhat misleading image of risks is provided by the calculated rate. Under these conditions, a measure such as "proportion of households touched by crime," which was included in NCVS reports until 1992, may be a better barometer of victimization risks.

An assortment of other technical and procedural issues affect the number of victimizations estimated from these surveys. The following additional factors have been found to influence the counting of victimization incidents:

- Using one household respondent as a proxy to report victimizations of all members of households results in lower numbers of incidents being reported than when all household members report their own experiences. The NCVS used a proxy for all 12- or 13-year-old household members (until 1992), non-English or non-Spanish speakers, and those temporarily absent or unable to be interviewed.

- Response rates vary across national surveys, and those who refuse to participate or are undercounted in household enumerations (e.g., younger persons, the poor and homeless, ethnic minorities, and frequent movers) generally have higher victimization risks than survey respondents. Although the underrepresentation of these high-risk groups will obviously decrease estimates, the impact of differential response rates across subgroups may either inflate or deflate the number of recorded incidents, depending on whether groups with the highest response rates have high or low risks of victimization.

- Various types of violent behavior and thefts are seriously under-counted in victimization surveys. These include crimes committed by family members and intimates, homicides, robbery, and thefts from commercial establishments, rape and sexual assaults, and all crimes committed against tourists and other nonresidents.

- Changes in procedures utilized in the NCVS studies over time (e.g., more extensive screens, greater use of telephone interviews, changes in the definition of series incidents, decreased sample sizes) also influence the number of incidents recorded in yearly samples. All else being equal, reductions in the size of NCVS samples over time increase sampling error and the subsequent ac-curacy of the estimates of the numbers and rates of victimization.

- The number of reported victimizations decreases through succes-sive interviews in the NCVS rotation panels (Garafolo 1990). In other words, the number of recalled incidents decreases consis-tently between the first and seventh interview. Given that the pro-portion of persons in the NCVS who are being interviewed for all seven rotations has decreased over time (due to increased popula-tion mobility), there has been (a) an increase in the number of persons who receive a smaller number of interviews (e.g., one to three interviews) and (b) a subsequent increase in the apparent number of victimizations due to this time-in-sample problem. Changes in the average time-in-sample affects estimates of the number of incidents and the comparability of the NCVS victim-ization rates over time.

- Many of the incidents reported in victimization surveys are trivial and may not even qualify as a crime from a legal perspective. Most violent crimes in the NCVS involve simple assaults without injury to the victim or threats and attempted acts. The redesigned NCVS yields more incidents of violent crime, but the new method has a greater impact on estimates for violent offenses by nonstrangers, attempted crimes, and violent crimes not reported to the police.

The level of victimization risks in national surveys depends in large part on the denominator used in the calculation of estimated rates. Property victimization rates for each national survey are calculated as an incident rate per 1,000 households. Rates of violent victimization are often expressed as an incident rate per 1,000 population 12 years of age and older. The measurement of victimization risks, however, is in many cases better served by a different base for rate calculation, using for the denominator the entity most at risk for that particular victimization. For example, the calculation of motor vehicle theft per household is probably a less accurate measure of one's vulnerability to this crime than a motor vehicle theft rate expressed per 1,000 households with motor vehicles or thefts per 1,000 motor vehicles. Similarly, the calculation of rape rates per 1,000 persons ignores the fact that women are the victims of this crime in more than 90 percent of the cases. Under these conditions, computing rape rates per 1,000 females is a more meaningful barometer of victimization risks.

It is possible to compute victimization rates on a wider variety of population bases that correspond to risky groups and settings. These include, for example, (a) the rate of stranger assaults per 1,000 contacts with strangers, (b) mugging rates per 1,000 hours spent in public places, (c) home burglary rates per 1,000 households with burglary alarms, and (d) violent crime rates per 1,000 persons between 12 and 35 years old. Although numerical data for each of these particular base comparisons may not be readily available in all cases, the use of rate calculations that directly incorporate risk factors may be a better reflection of one's chances of particular types of victimization than measures of victimization rates that are not adjusted for differential exposure and vulnerability.

Summary and Conclusions

National victimization surveys have been widely used as an alternative measure of the prevalence and distribution of crime in the United States. The major advantage of these surveys is that they provide a profile of criminal incidents that are both reported and not reported to the police.

Who is better able to enumerate the nature and distribution of crime incidents and the consequences of crime than those who experience it?

Unfortunately, all victimization surveys have four inherent problems that limit their utility as accurate measures of criminal activity. First, victim surveys cover only a small range of criminal acts—excluding "victimless" and public order violations, homicides, commercial and business victimizations, and white-collar crimes against consumers—and seriously undercount incidents of domestic violence and other crimes among known parties. Second, victimization surveys are based on sample data and not population counts, making them subject to serious distortion because of sampling error and sampling bias. Third, these surveys are based entirely on victims' perceptions without independent confirmation that the offenses they claim to have experienced actually occurred or would qualify as a crime from a legal perspective. Just as the offenders described in Chapter 4, victims may either underreport or overreport their experiences because of factors such as forgetfulness, misinterpretations of events, embarrassment, fear of getting in trouble, trying to please interviewers by giving socially desirable answers, and deliberate distortion or manipulation. Fourth, the number of victimizations uncovered in surveys depends on how the questions are worded and numerous technical elements associated with the survey itself. The use of different procedures over time renders problematic any comparisons of estimated victimization rates from these surveys.

The problems with victimization surveys, however, are neither more nor less serious than the problems with official data and self-report measures of crime. In fact, problems of definitional ambiguity, limited coverage, reporting biases, and various sources of measurement error plague each method of counting crime. Nonetheless, a comparison of the results across these three primary methods of counting crime reveals several common themes about the prevalence of crime, its spatial distribution, and the correlates of crime. The common themes across these methods and some concluding thoughts about crime measurement are addressed in the final chapter.

Notes

1. The National Crime Survey of a panel of households (as of 1991) is now called the National Crime Victimization Survey. We use the label NCVS to avoid confusion.
2. NCVS data can be accessed through the following Web site: www.icpsr.umich.edu/NACJD/SDA/ncvs.html

3. In contrast to other victimization data presented in this chapter, the data in Exhibit 5.6 are taken from the 1994 and 1998 NCVS.

4. The term victimless crime is often viewed as inappropriate for these offenses because they often result in physical, economic, psychological, or moral harm to others, including family members and the larger society. For the purposes of this discussion, these offenses are victimless in the sense that they involve consensual acts between adults, and asking individuals whether they have been victimized by their own drug, alcohol, prostitution, or gambling behavior is problematic.

5. As a measure of crime in a particular jurisdiction, victimization surveys are also limited in that they exclude crimes against commuters, visitors, or tourists in the jurisdiction. These persons are excluded because victimization surveys sample households and so are given only to local residents.

6. This distortion becomes even more extreme if differential interpretations of questions vary across social groups and sampling designs are weighted by social groups. For example, the British Crime Victimization surveys, which use a design similar to the NCVS, oversample inner-city and minority residents. For computing national rates of victimization, this oversampling is corrected by giving more weight to noncity and nonminority residents. However, if inner-city and minority residents have a different view of what constitutes an "attack" or "threat" than noncity and nonminority residents, the standard weighting procedure would result in an inflated estimate of the prevalence of assaults in Britain. In other words, national rates will be inflated because (a) noncity and nonminority residents overestimate their victimization experiences and (b) these groups are given more weight in the calculation of national estimates from the sample data.

Chapter Six

Crime Patterns, Evaluating Crime Policies, and Criminological Theories

Any set of crime statistics, including those of survey research, involve some evaluative, institutional processing of people's reports. Concepts, definitions, quantitative models, and theories must be adjusted to the fact that the data are not some objectively observable universe of "criminal acts," but rather those events defined, captured, and processed as such by some institutional mechanism.

Biderman and Reiss (1967:1)

The basic assumption underlying this book has been that accurate crime measurement is essential for describing the social and spatial distribution of crime and for evaluating the effectiveness of various criminological theories and crime control policies. We began the book with a discussion of social measurement more generally, proceeded to a discussion of the history of measuring crime and other social phenomena, and addressed the three major methods of measuring crime. What has not been done in the previous chapters, however, is to synthesize the findings from the three approaches and examine how the reliability and validity of crime statistics relate to the evaluation of crime control theory and practice.

Three major issues about crime measurement are addressed in this final chapter. First, we summarize the collective wisdom about crime that derives from police reports, self-reports, and victimization surveys. This involves a description of crime trends and the characteristics of offenses, offenders, and victims. Second, the link between accurate crime statistics and public policy is examined by illustrating how dubious crime measurement has hampered the evaluation of the effectiveness of crime control programs as well as the validation and development of criminological theory. We then discuss an emerging and important issue in official crime data—the collection of race/ethnicity data by law enforcement officers. We conclude the chapter with a discussion and assessment of recent developments in measuring crime.

Crime Trends

Whatever their limitations and orientation, all three major methods of counting crime provide estimates of its extent and social distribution. Crime trends may exhibit similarities and differences across these different methods and over time. By examining the crime data that derive from these methods collectively, several general conclusions are supported about the prevalence and nature of criminal activity.

The Volume of Crime

By all indications, crime statistics reveal that there is a great deal of crime in industrial societies. Given the limitations in methods discussed in earlier chapters, however, the absolute volume of crime in a given jurisdiction is anyone's guess. But crime in the United States seems especially high when compared to other countries.

According to the most recent UCR data (UCR 2000), a serious property crime becomes known to the police every 3 seconds in the United States, with a larceny-theft reported every 5 seconds, a burglary every 15 seconds, and a motor vehicle theft every 27 seconds. Serious violent crimes are reported at a somewhat lower rate of every 21 seconds, with a reported aggravated assault every 34 seconds, a robbery every minute, a forcible rape every

6 minutes, and a murder every 34 minutes. An estimated total of about 11.6 million Part I offenses were known to the police in 1999 and recorded in the UCR program. Obviously, for reasons discussed in Chapter 3 (e.g., a majority of crimes are unknown to the police, many are unfounded or downgraded by the police departments that discover them, and the use of the hierarchy rule), these official counts of crime in the United States grossly underestimate the true volume. Even among serious violent and property crimes, UCR data represent only the tip of the proverbial iceberg.

The volume of crime in the United States based on self-reports of offending and national victimization surveys is equally staggering. Illegal drug and alcohol use is rampant, according to National Youth Surveys (NYS), and although they are not Part I offenses, these account for the highest number of arrests in official crime data. When self-report questions focus on more serious violent and property offenses, a large proportion of U.S. youth admit to engaging in these activities.

According to the most recent National Crime Victimization Survey (NCVS 2000), people in the United States aged 12 or older experienced approximately 25.9 million violent and property victimizations in 2000. If these victimizations were equally dispersed across all persons and households, it would mean that about 4 percent of U.S. residents experienced a violent crime and about 21 percent of U.S. households were victims of property crime in 2000. Given the biases in reporting both offending and victimization experiences, these "unofficial" measures of crime in the United States are also likely to severely underestimate the volume of crime.

Changes in Crime Rates over Time

Police statistics on known offenders and victimization surveys reveal different patterns with respect to changes in crime rates over time. Crime rates based on police data in the United States increased dramatically between 1960 and 1990, followed by a noticeable decline since the mid-1990s. These official crime trends are similar for both violent and property crimes. Victimization surveys in the United States, however, indicate crime trends that are qualitatively distinct from those based on police data. Specifically, violent victimization rates remained fairly stable between the early 1970s and mid-1990s, before declining in a fashion similar to the trend revealed in UCR data. Contrary to the pattern of a rise and fall in property crime exhibited in UCR data, victimization surveys indicate that property crime has exhibited a rather continuous decline since the mid-1970s.

The contradictions in crime trends based on UCR and NCVS data are explained in large part by differences across these methods in their coverage of crimes, rules for counting crime incidents, and the population base from which rates are computed. Unfortunately, the limitations that surround both these measures of crime make it difficult to have strong confidence in either of the apparent trends. Under these conditions, it is unclear whether, or in what way, crime rates in the United States have actually changed in the last four decades.

The Nature of Crime Offenses

The convergence in findings across methods is more pronounced in regard to the nature of criminal offenses. By all accounts, most crime in the United States involves relatively minor property offenses that occur with some frequency. Larceny-theft is by far the most frequently reported offense under the UCR classification, and thefts from in and around the household are the most common victimization experience in the NCVS data. Although these property offenses may generate fear and concern about the effectiveness of law enforcement and other crime control efforts, the direct objective harm to the victim from these property offenses is often minimal. Likewise, the vast majority of violent offenses in the United States are attempts or threats that involve little or no injury to the victim. These offenses are classified as either simple or common assaults under various jurisdictions. Although less than 5 percent of individuals responding to victimization surveys report being the victim of an assault in the previous six months, these offenses are grossly underreported in both victimization and police data, especially when they involve no physical injury, mutual combat and arguments among peers, and domestic violence situations.

Another common pattern with respect to the nature of crime involves the victim-offender relationship in violent offenses. Specifically, UCR data indicate that most homicides occur among known parties (especially acquaintances), and a similar pattern is found for assaults and rapes in NCVS data. The actual proportion of violent crimes occurring among known parties is probably even greater when one considers the underreporting of crimes among intimates in police data and the typical exclusion of violent crimes by intimates in victimization surveys.

Although it is certainly true that the majority of homicides committed in the United States involve the use of firearms, contrary to the popular image of the nature of violent crime, the vast majority of violent offenses do not involve the use of deadly weapons. No external instrument (e.g., gun, knife, club) was used in more than two thirds of assaults and rapes in NCVS data. In official data, robbery was the only offense other than homicide in which most of the incidents involved a lethal weapon. Almost 4 out of every 10 robberies identified in UCR data involve the use of a firearm, compared to only about 20 percent of the robberies reported in victimization surveys.

Several other characteristics are also associated with incidents of crime. For example, the majority of violent crimes involve situations of single victims and single offenders. More than 90 percent of violent crimes identified in victimization surveys involve an attack on a sole victim, and about three fourths of these offenses involve one offender. Multiple offenders are most prevalent in cases of robbery victimization. Contrary to popular images of interracial conflict, the vast majority of violent offenses involve victims and offenders who are of the same race.

Profile of Crime Offenders

Police arrest statistics, self-reports of criminal activity, and victims' reports on their attackers provide somewhat different perspectives on the profile of criminal offenders. Nonetheless, these data sources yield a comparable image of the sociodemographic characteristics of criminal offenders.

Across all three methods of counting crime, offenders are disproportionately young, male, and members of ethnic or racial minority groups. UCR data indicate that approximately 17 percent of the arrestees are under the age of 18, 83 percent are male, and about 40 percent are black. A higher proportion of arrests for property offenses in the UCR involves juveniles (33 percent), whereas the overrepresentation of both males (71 percent) and blacks (33 percent) in property offenses is less dramatic than is true for violent crime (UCR 1999).

Although the differences across some social groups are less pronounced, victims in the NCVS also perceive their assailants to be disproportionately young, male, and black. Smaller differences by age, sex, and race are found in studies of self-reported criminal behavior.

It is important to consider these demographic differences in offending in the context of the limitations of the particular data sources. Specifically, the largest differences are in police reports, but these official data are also the most vulnerable to selective reporting and recording practices. Self-report studies, in contrast, often measure involvement in less serious crimes and elicit the smallest differences across groups. Under these conditions, one of the most serious mistakes for criminological theory and crime control policy may be placing too much emphasis on these presumed differences by age, sex, and race. The safest strategy is to recognize these differential risks of involvement in criminal offending while at the same time acknowledging that criminal offending is a general problem that occurs across all social groups.

Profile of Crime Victims

The dominant conclusion from victimization surveys in the United States is that the risks of being a crime victim are not uniform across persons, places, or time. Persons who run the greatest risks of violent victimization are males, members of racial/ethnic minority groups, the young, the never married, the poor, and inner-city residents. Risks of property victimization are also highest for members of each of these groups. The most notable exceptions to these trends are the higher risks for women in the case of rape or sexual assault and the higher risks of property victimization among higher-income households.

Considering the most dangerous places and times for criminal acts, risks of violent victimization in the United States are substantially higher in urban areas (especially inner cities) and for residents of the western United States. The most common location for a violent crime is in or near the victim's home. Weekends and evening hours are the most frequent times for violent victimization. Property crime victimization rates are also higher in urban areas and western states.

Using Crime Data to Evaluate Crime Policies and Criminological Theory

Accurate measurement of crime has always been important as the basis for evaluating criminological theory and the effectiveness of various crime control policies. However, over the last three decades, a growing climate of accountability and validation has placed greater pressure on crime measurement to verify the empirical accuracy of competing crime theories and the success of various programs. Decisions about the success or failure of various crime policies and practices depend on the accuracy of crime measurement. The following examples illustrate this important connection.

Community-Oriented Policing

One of the major changes in the nature of policing over the last two decades has been the dramatic growth in community-oriented policing

(COP). Under this model of policing, law enforcement works closely with local neighborhoods to identify their problems, and the community helps shoulder the burden of crime detection by increasing community surveillance and monitoring. The implementation of COP programs has involved such activities as the development of bike patrol teams, block watch and neighborhood watch programs, property identification procedures, regular community meetings on crime prevention strategies, community support networks, and the sponsoring of social gatherings to enhance residents' sense of neighborhood solidarity (see Green and Mastrofski 1988; Oliver 2001).

The primary research design for evaluating COP programs involves the comparison of neighborhood crime rates and calls for police service before and after the implementation of COP. More rigorous designs also involve comparisons with a control neighborhood that is similar in population characteristics and criminal history but has not implemented a COP program. By examining changes over time in criminal activity in the control neighborhood, researchers are better able to determine whether changes over time in the COP neighborhood are due to changes that resulted from the program itself rather than simply changes in the level of crime that is occurring in the wider jurisdiction, which may be due to larger structural and unmeasured factors.

Contrary to expectations based on the presumed effectiveness of these programs, it is not uncommon in evaluations of COP to observe an increase in crime reports and calls for service after program implementation. Proponents of COP attribute such increases to the greater public sensitivity to the variety of suspicious activities and greater public awareness of criminal opportunities. However, it is just as probable that such an increase is due to the general ineffectiveness of COP in reducing neighborhood crime levels. Under these conditions, volatility in crime measurement that may derive from changes in crime reporting makes it impossible to isolate the true impact of COP on criminal activities in the targeted neighborhood.

Specific Deterrence and Mandatory
Arrest Policies in Domestic Violence Cases

After years of neglect and the questionable use of police discretion in domestic violence cases, mandatory arrest policies have been implemented in numerous states as the appropriate response to such cases. These mandatory arrest policies are based on the assumption that the temporary removal of the perpetrators of domestic violence through arrest will immediately defuse the domestic violence situation and serve as a specific deterrent by reducing the individual's subsequent abusive behavior.

Previous evaluations of the specific deterrent effect of mandatory arrest policies in Minneapolis and other jurisdictions have yielded mixed results (Berk and Newton 1985; Sherman and Cohn 1985). The original study found that mandatory arrest was more effective than other responses to domestic violence, but these results have not been replicated in other settings.

One of the major problems in evaluating mandatory arrest policy is how to best measure recidivism or rearrest. The private nature of much domestic violence places severe limitations on the accuracy of subsequent police reports of arrests as a satisfactory measure of reoffending behavior. Self-reports of abusive behavior are equally problematic because of the lack of any reason for such offenders to tell the truth. Surveying the victims of domestic violence after the initial arrest seems like a more defensible strategy, but such surveys are likely to involve sampling bias, in that those victims who participate in the survey will be qualitatively different from those who refuse to participate. For example, nonrespondents may be more prone to experience repeat victimization but refuse to cooperate in the survey because of fear of retaliation, whereas survey participants may provide a distorted "success" rate because this group may consist of a larger proportion of women who had fewer physical opportunities to be abused as a result of moving away from their partners. Unfortunately, the lack of a reliable and valid measure of reoffending behavior makes it difficult to ascertain the true effectiveness of these mandatory arrest policies.

Zero Tolerance Policies

The preceding paragraphs highlighted problems associated with policies based on questionable data. Similar hazards are encountered when policies are enacted without sufficient consideration of available data. One example is zero tolerance policies, enacted in the 1990s in response to a series of widely publicized school shootings. These policies have been passed in every state and the District of Columbia. A report from Harvard University (Civil Rights Project 2000) estimated that in 1998, more than 3.1 million students were suspended and another 87,000 were expelled from schools. These policies also appear to be disproportionately imposed against minority students: although African American children represent 17 percent of public school enrollment, they constitute 32 percent of school suspensions.

Examples of the "lunacy" (Taranto 2001) of zero tolerance policies abound. In Manalapan, New Jersey, a 10-year-old girl who stated, "I could kill her," after she wet her pants because a teacher refused to let her go to the bathroom was suspended for three days (Zernike 2001). Elementary students in Texas and Louisiana have been suspended for pointing pencils at each other and saying "Pow!" and for drawing pictures of soldiers (Lott 2001). A six-year-old boy in Pittsburgh, Pennsylvania, was suspended for carrying a plastic ax as part of a fireman's costume for Halloween (Leland 2001). More generally, under these policies, aspirin, Midol, cough drops, and Certs Mints have been treated as drugs, and paper clips, nail files, and scissors have been considered weapons (Civil Rights Project 2000).

Of even greater concern than the punishment meted out in schools is the tracking of youth into the juvenile justice system for incidents of minor misconduct in schools (Civil Rights Project 2000). In an incident in Mississippi, for example, five African American males were arrested for felony assault after one of the peanuts they were playfully throwing at each other accidentally hit their school bus driver. The sheriff responsible for making the arrest commented to a newspaper, "This time it was peanuts, but if we don't get a handle on it, the next time it could be bodies" (Civil Rights Project 2000).

Fear and concern over school shootings is legitimate, but a careful consideration of the available data on school violence might lead to a reconsideration of these particularly Draconian policies. School violence decreased by 30 percent from 1990 to 2000 (Zernike 2001). Between the fall of 1997 and June of 2001, 32 students and three teachers were shot to death at elementary or secondary schools in the United States, an annual rate of less than 1 death per 4 million students. In contrast, during the same period, 53 students died as a result of playing high school football (Lott 2001). A report by the Juvenile Law Center noted that students are three times as likely to be hit by lightning as to be killed by violence in school (Leland 2001). More generally, approximately 1 out of every 100 murders of school-age children takes place at schools (*USA Today* 2001b), and the number of deaths in the 1999-2000 school year was approximately one quarter the number that occurred in 1992-93 (*Secondary School Educators Newsletter* 2001).

As the Civil Rights Project (2000) concluded: "Efforts to address guns, drugs, and other truly dangerous school situations have spun totally out of control, sweeping up millions of schoolchildren who pose no threat to safety into a net of exclusion from educational opportunities and into criminal prosecutions" (p. 2).

Testing Criminological Theory

A wide variety of sociological, psychological, and biological theories have been proposed to explain the underlying causes of crime and its social, spatial, and temporal distribution. All of these theories are based on the assumption that crime is accurately measured. But when variation in crime patterns and characteristics is partially attributable to unreliability in the measurement of crime, it is impossible to empirically validate the accuracy of competing criminological theories.

One group of criminological theories that ultimately assume that crime is accurately measured are criminal opportunity theories of victimization (see, e.g., Cohen and Felson 1979; Miethe and Meier 1994). According to these theories, demographic differences in victimization risks are attributable to differences in individuals' lifestyles and routine activities that affect their exposure and proximity to motivated offenders, their attractiveness as crime targets, and the availability of suitable guardians to protect them from criminal victimization. For example, males are said to have higher risks of violent victimization than females because they are more involved in risky and dangerous public activities. In contrast, older adults are assumed to have lower risks of victimization than other age groups because they spend more time in the privacy of their home, use greater safety precautions against crime, and are less likely to be in contact with dangerous persons and places.

Criminal opportunity theories developed out of the findings of victimization surveys that showed that the risks of experiencing crime varied across social groups. If the measurement of victimization experiences is problematic, then it is unclear whether observed differences in victimization risks across social groups is real or a methodological artifact. Unfortunately, the serious problems with victimization surveys in terms of their underreporting of violence among intimates, selective perceptions of respondents, and telescoping issues raise some doubts about the empirical foundation that underlies these theories of criminal behavior.

According to "pure" biological theories, high rates of violent behavior by men are due to sex differences in biological and evolutionary traits. Sociobiological theories, in contrast, focus on the interplay between genetic and environmental factors that influence the differential propensities toward violence (see Ellis and Hoffman 1990). The accuracy of each of these types of biological theories depends on the nature and extent of gender differences in violent crime. If gender differences are not consistent across geographical areas or over time, a purely biological explanation would not be supported. If gender differences in violent offending are relatively constant across social settings, a sociobiological approach lacks empirical validity. Unfortunately, the variability in reporting of crime statistics across jurisdictions makes it impossible to evaluate the accuracy of these competing biological theories.

A similar situation characterizes sociological theories of crime. Social structural approaches (e.g., Merton's [1957] anomie theory, Shaw and McKay's [1942] social disorganization theory) are based on the assumption that crime is a lower-class phenomenon and offer explanations for these class differences. For example, anomie theory states that crime is the result of the disjunction between cultural goals and the institutional means of achieving them. According to this theory, lower-class people engage in street crime because they have accepted the cultural goal of material success but do not have access to, or have rejected, the legitimate means of achieving it. According to social disorganization theory, lower-class areas are "natural areas" for crime because they are characterized by various factors that impede social control and monitoring of youth (e.g., high population turnover, lack of economic opportunity, and high ethnic diversity).

As with the evaluation of biological theories, the utility of these social structure theories is tied directly to the accuracy of crime data. If police statistics on crime are seriously biased against lower-class persons (e.g., because of more intensive police activity in lower-class areas), these types of criminological theories are based on a dubious empirical foundation. The uncritical acceptance of police statistics as an accurate measure of crime has been a major criticism of many sociological theories.

One of the most popular and widely tested recent explanations in criminology is Gottfredson and Hirschi's (1990) self-control theory. They define crime as "acts of force or fraud undertaken in pursuit of self-interest" (p. 15) and assert that certain features are shared by all crimes: (a) they provide easy and immediate gratification of desires, (b) they are exciting, risky, and thrilling, (c) they offer few, if any, long-term benefits, and (d) they require very little skill, planning, or specialized knowledge. Individuals who engage in these acts are characterized by (a) low self-control, (b) they tend to be insensitive, (c) they are likely to take risks, and (d) they are short sighted. The source of low self-control, according to Gottfredson and Hirschi, is inadequate child-rearing.

Self-control theory has been critiqued on a number of grounds in the criminological literature (see, e.g., Akers 1997; Tittle 1995). But one of the most problematic aspects of this theory—in terms of the relationship between data sources and theories—is its reliance on official data as a source of information on white-collar crime. Gottfredson and Hirschi rely on UCR data to specify the types—in particular, the Part II offenses of embezzlement, fraud, and forgery—and incidences of offenses that constitute the category of white-collar crime. As Curran and Renzetti (1994) point out,

Gottfredson and Hirschi view white-collar crime as relatively uncommon in occurrence but sharing features of other, relatively common crimes. That is, for Gottfredson and Hirschi, white-collar crimes likewise are spontaneous and quick, require no specialized knowledge, and yield limited profits for offenders.

Their operationalization of white-collar crime, then, is especially problematic. The crimes they have chosen do fit with their general definition of crime but do not encompass the full range of offenses that constitute white-collar crime. Embezzlement, fraud, and forgery often *may* be spontaneous acts without long-term benefits to the offenders, but organizational and corporate crimes rarely are. Indeed, much evidence indicates that corporate offenses—which, as noted in Chapter 3, are not captured in official data—are planned and executed over an extended period of time and are quite profitable for those who engage in them. As Beirne and Messerschmidt (2000) note, "Most criminologists would agree that persons with high levels of self-control who practice deferred gratification are precisely the individuals who engage in the numerous types of political, white-collar, and syndicated crime!" (p. 221).

Another criminological theory that has relied primarily on official data is that of Wilson and Herrnstein (1985; see also Herrnstein and Murray 1994) who, in their book *Crime and Human Nature: The Definitive Study of the Causes of Crime*, assert that "every study of crime using official data shows Blacks to be overrepresented among persons arrested, convicted, and imprisoned for street crimes. . . . No matter how one adjusts for other demographic factors, Blacks tend to be overrepresented by a factor of four to one among persons arrested for violent crimes, and by a factor of nearly three to one among those arrested for property crimes" (p. 461).

Wilson and Herrnstein (1985) examine four possible explanations for the racial differences in official crime data. "Economic deprivation" theories argue that blacks are more likely to be involved in crime because of reduced opportunities for them in society; "culture of poverty" theories imply that protracted poverty in black families results in poor socialization practices such that black children do not possess "either a sufficiently strong regard for the good opinion of others or a sufficiently long time horizon to make them value conventional norms or defer instant pleasures for delayed rewards" (p. 467). The "subculture of violence" theory asserts that blacks have a hostile view of the larger society, do not value legitimate goals, and thus are more likely to engage in crime. Wilson and Herrnstein essentially reject these sociological explanations and argue that black-white differences in crime are largely attributable to "constitutional factors"—in particular, differences in intelligence scores between blacks and whites. They claim that studies indicate that black IQ scores are, on the average, approximately 12 to 15 points lower than those of whites, and they reject the notion that the differences in IQ scores can be explained by social class differences or cultural biases in IQ tests. They conclude, "If lower measured intelligence is associated with crime independently of socio-economic status, and if Blacks, on the average, have much lower scores, than [sic] these facts may help explain some of the Black-White differences in crime rates" (p. 471).

Several criminologists have taken issue with Wilson and Herrnstein's explanation of these racial differences. Some suggest that the overrepresentation of blacks among arrestees is at least partially the result of police procedures, including the tendency for police to patrol black areas more frequently than white areas and the tendency to focus more on street crimes involving blacks more than white-collar and other forms of crime. Although Wilson and Herrnstein (1985) suggest that these factors cannot account for all or even most of the black overrepresentation in official statistics, emerging evidence indicates that racial biases in law enforcement are pervasive in the United States. This leads to a consideration of one of the emerging challenges in measuring crime in the context of official data: the issue of racial profiling.

Racial Profiling

All of our citizens are created equal and must be treated equally. Earlier today I asked John Ashcroft, the Attorney-General, to develop specific recommendations to end racial profiling. It is wrong, and we must end it. It's wrong, and we will end it in America. In so doing, we will not hinder the work of our nation's brave police officers. They protect us every day, often at great risk. But by stopping the abuses of a few, we will add to the public confidence our police officers earn and deserve. (President George W. Bush, address to a joint session of Congress, February 27, 2001; quoted in the *Atlanta Constitution* 2001)

In the late 1990s, there was a virtual explosion of media exposés on racial profiling by police departments in the United States. In a report prepared for the U.S. Department of Justice, Ramirez, McDevitt, and Farrell (2000) defined racial profiling as "any police-initiated action that relies on race, ethnicity, or national origin rather than the behavior of an individual or information that leads the police to a particular individual who has been identified as being, or having been, engaged in criminal activity" (p. 3).

Although evidence of racial profiling on the part of law enforcement was largely based on anecdotal information in the early 1990s, by the end of the decade, there was widespread concern over the issue, and a number of jurisdictions began to collect more detailed quantitative data. For example, a study analyzing 1995 and 1996 data from Maryland determined that 74.5 percent of speeders on highways in that state were white and 17.5 percent were black. However, blacks constituted almost 80 percent of drivers searched by the Maryland state police (Ramirez et al. 2000). Another study in New Jersey, focusing on data covering the years 1988 to 1991, found that blacks comprised 13.5 percent of drivers and 15 percent of speeding drivers on the New Jersey turnpike. However, blacks represented 35 percent of those stopped by the state patrol and more than 73 percent of those arrested. A later study from the same state, using data from 1997 and 1998, indicated that people of color constituted more than 40 percent of stops made on the turnpike. And although the overall proportion of individuals who were searched by the police was relatively small, blacks comprised more than 77 percent of those searched (Ramirez et al. 2000).

These and other preliminary data provide some indication of the pervasiveness of racial profiling, but as the report to the Department of Justice (Ramirez, McDevitt, and Farrell 2000) suggested, "The only way to move the discussions about racial profiling from rhetoric and accusation to a more rational dialogue about appropriate enforcement strategies is to collect the information that will either allay community concerns about the activities of the police or help communities ascertain the magnitude of the problem" (p. 13).

There are a number of important issues to consider here. How can officers determine the race or ethnicity of the individuals they stop in the least confrontational manner and without increasing the intrusiveness of the stop? Is it possible that collecting data on the race/ethnicity of those stopped will result in "disengagement"—leading police officers to reduce the number of legitimate stops and searches they conduct?[1] How can police departments ensure the accuracy of data collection procedures and be certain that the reporting requirements are not circumvented by officers who fail to file required reports or who deliberately report erroneous information? Can the data be analyzed and compared with an appropriate measure of the larger population of a jurisdiction (Ramirez et al. 2000:15)?

The report to the Department of Justice outlined the practices for collecting race data in five separate jurisdictions. In San Jose, California, it was determined that because the perception of the officers ultimately lead to the problem of racial profiling, the officers' perceptions were the appropriate method for ascertaining the race or ethnicity of the individuals they encounter. In that jurisdiction, officers were required to code into eight categories for race/ethnicity: Asian American, African American, Hispanic, Native American, Other, Pacific Islander, Middle Eastern/East Indian, and White.

In 1999 data, African Americans and Hispanics in San Jose were stopped by police at a rate exceeding their percentage in the population of the city. African Americans comprised 5 percent of San Jose's population but 7 percent of vehicle stops; Hispanics were 31 percent of the city's population but constituted 43 percent of the stops. However, San Jose police officials asserted that there were two reasons for these racial/ethnic disproportions in stops: (1) the number of officers per capita was higher in police districts that contained a higher percentage of minorities, and (2) socioeconomic factors in minority neighborhoods resulted in more calls for service and resultant interactions with police. These explanations suggest the possibility of a social structural dimension to racial profiling, indicating that, in order to properly analyze and draw conclusions from these data, detailed characteristics regarding the racial/ethnic composition of particular police precincts will be required.

In 2000, it was estimated that slightly more than 23 percent of San Diego's population were Hispanic, approximately 9 percent were black, and 5 percent were Asian. This city began collecting race-based traffic stop data in January 2000 and, similar to the decision in San Jose, opted to use the officer's perception of the driver's race or ethnicity. If officers were not sure, they were allowed to ask the driver. In San Diego, however, there are 18 racial/ethnic categories from which officers can choose: Other Asian, Black, Chinese, Cambodian, Filipino, Guamanian, Hispanic, Indian, Japanese, Korean, Laotian, Other, Pacific Islander, Samoan, Hawaiian, Vietnamese, White, and Asian Indian. One might question the ability of police officers to accurately code the race/ethnicity of those stopped, given the sheer number of categories listed. It is difficult enough for people to accurately distinguish between blacks and Hispanics, let alone Korean versus Japanese versus Laotian.

On the basis of the 1990 census, North Carolina's population of 6.5 million was approximately 76 percent white, 22 percent black, and 2 percent other racial groups. Legislation requiring law enforcement bodies to collect data on all routine traffic stops in the state was passed in 1999. The categories available were White, Black, Indian, Asian, or Other for race and

Hispanic or non-Hispanic for ethnicity. The scheme for coding race in that state is slightly different: police officers are required to use their best judgment regarding the race and ethnicity of those stopped, utilizing either (a) their perception of the race/ethnicity of the person stopped, (b) racial/ethnic information provided by the driver of the vehicle, or (c) backup racial and ethnic information collected by the state's Bureau of Motor Vehicles. Preliminary data from North Carolina indicate that black motorists were stopped in relative proportion to their representation in the state population but were disproportionately likely to be searched and arrested (Ramirez et al. 2000).

As of March 2001, more than 400 law enforcement agencies in the United States were gathering information on the race/ethnicity of those stopped, and it is highly probable that in the near future, the majority of jurisdictions in the country will be collecting such data. It is unlikely, however, that there will be consistency in how these data are collected. Thus, comparisons across jurisdictions and over time will be difficult to conduct.

The report to the Department of Justice (Ramirez et al. 2000) makes a number of recommendations with respect to the collection of these data. First, given the perception that young black males are disproportionately targeted by the police, there is a need to collect data on the gender and exact age of those stopped, in addition to their race/ethnicity. Second, the report recommends continuing the procedure of using the police officer's perception as the measure of those stopped. However, "to assist the officer in assessing the ethnicity of an individual, it is suggested that the officer assess and record any racial identification information after using the following subjective tools: visual, and verbal contact with the individual, and the surname of the individual." Third, the report recommends that jurisdictions consider whether an officer should be allowed to check two racial categories when the individual appears to be of mixed racial origin. The recommendations regarding the use of surnames and the possible coding of mixed race seems particularly problematic with respect to the reliability and validity of these data, however. Recognizing the possibility of inaccuracies in the categorization of race/ethnicity by these procedures, the report goes on to suggest that police departments should implement mechanisms for cross-checking the reliability of the data through periodic monitoring.

In his speech quoted at the beginning of this section, President Bush implied that racial profiling is primarily related to the biases and practices of individual officers. However, the studies conducted up to this point imply that the problem is also related to larger social structural issues. In order to adequately interpret the findings from racial profiling studies, additional data on the social class and economic characteristics of communities will need to be collected. As Matthew Zingraff, the lead researcher in a study of racial profiling in North Carolina has argued, "In the long run, I think we're going to learn that the disparity that does exist is a result of a lot of things other than active racial animus" (as quoted in Jonsson 2001). To conclude, the collection of race/ethnicity data by law enforcement constitutes one of the great challenges for official data in the 21st century.

Improving Police Statistics, Self-Reports, and Victim Surveys

The importance of accurate crime measurement has resulted in several recent developments designed to improve the quality and nature of crime data that derive from different methods. Major advances in official police reports, self-report measures, and victimization surveys are outlined below.

Advances in Police Reports of Criminal Incidents

Incident-based reporting systems in the United States are widely regarded as representing a major advance in the police recording of crime data. Although the development of this recording system has evolved slowly across jurisdictions, when implemented on a national basis, the National Incident-Based Reporting System (NIBRS) will dramatically alter the volume of official counts of crime. The wider array of information collected about the crime incident will also enhance the utility of these data for research purposes and the development of public policy.

The emergence of NIBRS data, however, will not eliminate the systemic problems that plague official measures of crime. Similar to the basic UCR data, the national representativeness of NIBRS data will ultimately depend on citizen reporting practices. If citizens do not report their victimizations to the police, no type of police data will accurately measure the true extent of crime.

Even with extensive training and standard coding rules, problems of unreliability in classifying and counting crime incidents are compounded under NIBRS procedures because of the greater complexity and diversity of the information collected. One unfortunate consequence of collecting more detailed information is the possibility of even greater disparity in its recording within and across jurisdictions.

NIBRS data are also not immune to political distortion and manipulation. In fact, the greater quantity of data that are collected under NIBRS may provide even greater opportunity for deception and fabrication. By emphasizing only particular NIBRS data elements that convey a positive spin on the effectiveness of police crime control activities and ignoring data that show contrary evidence, law enforcement agencies and other organizations may be able to pick and choose particular trends from these data that support their political positions. Even under the NIBRS procedures, reporting practices involve low visibility decisions that may be easily distorted for various purposes.

Advances in Self-Report Methodology

Reverse record checks and other types of cross-validation procedures have been widely used over the last two decades to assess and refine the methods of self-report surveys. Across various substantive domains (e.g., drug use, alcohol use, sexual behavior, income tax evasion), self-reports of criminal and conventional behavior have become a mainstay of basic social research and public surveys. Although there remains considerable suspicion about the accuracy of self-report measures of serious criminal behavior, self-report surveys of known offenders have been increasingly used to understand the nature of crime and decision-making processes underlying offenders' selection of crime victims.

One of the most interesting applications of self-report methods involves asking known offenders to describe their motives for particular offenses and the situational factors that influenced their criminal decision making. These studies often focus on interviews with incarcerated offenders. During the interview process, offenders are asked questions about target-selection factors and given visual cues that represent different crime situations. Through these self-reports of "attractive" crime situations, researchers have been able to identify key factors that underlie offenders' selection of victims. For example, the primary target-selection factors for burglaries identified in these self-report studies include signs of occupancy, convenience and familiarity, and the expected yield from the crime (see Bennett and Wright 1984; Cromwell, Olson, and Avery 1991; Miethe and McCorkle 2001). From a public policy perspective, these self-reports by known offenders become essential for developing reasonable situational crime prevention strategies and other crime control approaches.

As an approach for measuring the true extent and nature of crime, however, self-report studies continue to be limited by various methodological problems. Sample selection bias remains a serious problem, because those who participate in these surveys and report criminal behavior are probably a lot different from those who refuse to participate. Even when conditions of anonymity are guaranteed, the threat of legal liability for their answers still contributes to major underreporting of serious criminal acts among respondents.

Advances in Victimization Surveys

Major advances in victimization surveys have largely involved the development of more comprehensive screen questions. The screen questions in the NCVS have led to dramatic increases in the number of victimizations for particular types of crime (e.g., rapes, assaults, burglaries) identified in these surveys. In addition, the greater use of computer-assisted telephone interviewing with central monitoring of the interviews has also resulted in higher victimization rates derived from these surveys.

Although improvements in screening questions and survey methods are positive developments, these "advances" in victimization surveys may have an unintended consequence of increasing the number of less serious and even trivial offenses being recalled in victimization surveys. If a higher proportion of persons are reporting minor property offenses and alleged threats without injuries in victimization surveys, then the surveys may contribute to an overestimation of the crime problem. As a result of these changes, UCR and NCVS trends may also exhibit less convergence over time.

As a measure of crime prevalence, advances in victimization surveys are still unable to correct the major problems with this measurement approach. Regardless of whether or not new screens are used, victimization surveys cover only a small proportion of criminal behavior, and the results are susceptible to both sampling error and sampling bias. Problems with telescoping and the length of the reference period continue to adversely affect estimates of national victimization rates.

Summary and Conclusions

The major objective of this book has been to examine the most common methods for measuring crime. We have stressed the importance of accurate measurement of crime for evaluating criminological theory and public policy on crime control. On the basis of our review of the problems with each approach, it should be clear that neither police statistics, self-reports from offenders, nor surveys of victims provide a definitive and unequivocal measure of the nature and distribution of crime in society. Even with major advances in data collection and survey research technology, these three methods will continue to provide an incomplete and distorted picture of crime.

Given the limitations of current methods of counting crime, an important question involves whether these measures are "good enough" even if they are flawed. The answer to this question depends on the purposes to be served by these crime statistics. Police data on car thefts, for example, are probably adequate for most comparative purposes within and across jurisdictions, because a high proportion of these crimes are reported to the police by citizens. In contrast, rape statistics, regardless of their source, are notoriously inadequate for almost all purposes of theory testing and the evaluation of crime control policies. The adequacy of official and unofficial measures of other violent crimes other than murder and of property crimes falls somewhere between these two extremes.

Of the methods of counting crime examined here, the accuracy of police statistics on reported crimes is far less likely to be challenged in mass media stories, academic research, and general public discourse than either self-report or victimization results. In fact, through their connection with the FBI, UCR data have a unique aura of legitimacy that furthers their immunity to widespread scrutiny. Even when the shortcomings of police statistics are identified in media or academic accounts, UCR data are still treated as "objective" measures of the extent of crime. By identifying the various classification and counting problems with UCR data and their susceptibility to political manipulation and distortion, we hope our efforts will help curtail the uncritical acceptance of police statistics as an accurate measure of the extent and distribution of crime.

In conclusion, an enormous amount of money and energy has been directed at the measurement of crime. Methodological refinements in the type of information collected, question wording, and the development of standardized procedures for classifying and counting crimes have improved the quality of crime statistics. However, each technique for counting crime has serious flaws that are inherent in its basic design. By understanding the strengths and limitations of each approach, evaluators of criminological theory and crime control policies may be better informed of the various procedures and practices that underlie the social construction of crime statistics.

Note

1. Some evidence suggests that disengagement may be occurring in certain jurisdictions. For example, in Cincinnati, three months after riots related to alleged discriminatory practices on the part of the police occurred, the *Los Angeles Times* reported that "some police officers openly admit to slacking off on their jobs for fear that aggressive patrol work will set this tense city aflame once more" (Simon 2001). Similarly, the *Seattle Times* noted that police in that city were engaging in "de-policing, selective disengagement, [and] tactical detachment . . . [as a] logical reaction to chronic charges of police racism" (Tizon and Forgrave 2001).

References

Ageton, Suzanne S. 1983. "The Dynamics of Female Delinquency, 1976-1980." *Criminology* 21:555-84.

Akers, Ronald L. 1997. *Criminological Theories*. Los Angeles, CA: Roxbury.

Alphonso, Caroline. 2000. "Police Got Math Wrong: Record-Breaking Seizure of Ecstasy Not So Big After All." *Globe and Mail*, June 3.

Anderson, Margo J. and Stephen E. Fienberg. 1999. *Who Counts?—The Politics of Census-Taking in Modern America*. New York: Russell Sage.

Aquilino, William S. 1994. "Interview Mode Effects in Surveys of Drug and Alcohol Use." *Public Opinion Quarterly* 58:210-40.

Aquilino, William S. and Debra L. Wright. 1996. "Substance Use Estimates from RDD and Area Probability Samples: Impact of Differential Screening Methods and Unit Non-response." *Public Opinion Quarterly* 60:563-73.

Arrestee Drug Abuse Monitoring Program (ADAM). 2000. *1999 Annual Report on Drug Use Among Adult and Juvenile Arrestees*. Washington, DC: National Institute of Justice.

Atlanta Constitution. 2001. "Bush Addresses Congress." February 28.

Auerhahn, Kathleen. 1999. "Selective Incapacitation and the Problems of Prediction." *Criminology* 37:703-34.

Bachman, Ronet and Bruce M. Taylor. 1994. "The Measurement of Family Violence and Rape by the Redesigned National Crime Victimization Survey." *Justice Quarterly* 11:499-512.

Bearden, William O. 1998. "The Pool Is Drying Up." *Marketing Research* 10:26-33.

Beattie, R. H. 1941. "The Sources of Criminal Statistics." *American Academy of Political and Social Science* 217:19-28.

Beattie, Ronald H. 1960. "Criminal Statistics in the United States—1960." *Journal of Criminal Law, Criminology, and Police Science* 51:49-65.

Beirne, Piers and James Messerschmidt. 2000. *Criminology*. San Diego, CA: Harcourt Brace Jovanovich.

Bell, Daniel. 1967. *The End of Ideology*. New York: Free Press.

Belluck, Pam. 2001. "Detroit Casts Wide Net over Homicide Cases." *New York Times*, April 11.

Bendavid, Naftali. 2001. "Violent Crime Drops 15%, Hits New Low." *Chicago Tribune*, June 13.

Bennett, Trevor and Richard Wright. 1984. *Burglars on Burglary: Prevention and the Offender*. Hampshire, UK: Bower.

Bennett, William. 2001. "Advice for the Next Drug Czar." *Miami Herald*, March 5.

Berens, Michael J. and Todd Lighty. 2001. "Crime Rates off the Mark." *Chicago Tribune*, July 11.

Berk, Richard and Phyllis J. Newton. 1985. "Does Arrest Really Deter Wife Battery? An Effort to Replicate the Findings of the Minneapolis Spouse Abuse Experiment." *American Sociological Review* 50:253-62.

Biderman, Albert D. 1967. "Surveys of Population for Estimating Crime Incidence." *Annals of the American Academy of Political and Social Science* 374:16-33.

Biderman, Albert D. and David Cantor. 1984. "A Longitudinal Analysis of Bounding, Response Conditioning, and Mobility as Sources of Panel Bias in the National Crime Survey." Presented at the Annual Meeting of the American Statistical Association, Philadelphia, PA.

Biderman, Albert D. and James Lynch. 1991. *Understanding Crime Incidence Statistics: Why the UCR Diverges from the NCS*. New York: Springer-Verlag.

Biderman, Albert D. and Albert J. Reiss, Jr. 1967. "On Exploring the 'Dark Figure' of Crime." *Annals of the American Academy of Political and Social Science* 374:1-15.

Biemer, Paul P. and Michael Witt. 1997. "Repeated Measures Estimation of Measurement Bias for Self-Reported Drug Use with Applications to the National Household Survey on Drug Abuse." Pp. 439-476 in *The Validity of Self-Reported Drug Use: Improving the Accuracy of Survey Estimates* (NIDA Research Monograph 167), edited by Lana Harrison and Arthur Hughes. Rockville, MD: National Institute on Drug Abuse.

Bilchik, Shay. 1999. *Juvenile Offenders and Victims: 1999 National Report*. Washington, DC: U.S. Department of Justice, Office of Justice Programs.

Black, Donald. 1970. "Production of Crime Rates." *American Sociological Review* 35:733-48.

Bonger, William Adrian. 1916. *Criminality and Economic Conditions*. New York: Agathon.

Braithwaite, John. 1981. "The Myth of Social Class and Criminality Reconsidered." *American Sociological Review* 46:36-57.

Brantingham, Paul and Patricia Brantingham. 1984. *Patterns in Crime*. New York: Macmillan.

Browne, Malcolm. 2001. "Refining the Art of Measurement." *New York Times*, March 20.

Bullough, Vern L. 1998. "Alfred Kinsey and the Kinsey Report: Historical Overview and Lasting Contributions." *Journal of Sex Research* 35:127-31.

Bureau of Justice Statistics Bulletin. 1994. *Technical Background on the Redesigned National Crime Victimization Survey*. Washington, DC: U.S. Department of Justice, Office of Justice Programs, Bureau of Justice Statistics.

Butterfield, Fox. 2001a. "U.S. Crime Figures Held Steady Last Year, Ending an 8-Year Decline." *New York Times*, May 31.

Butterfield, Fox. 2001b. "Victim Poll on Violent Crime Finds 15% Drop Last Year." *New York Times*, June 14.

Cantor, David and James P. Lynch. 2000. "Self-Report Measures of Crime and Criminal Victimization." Pp. 85-138 in *Criminal Justice 2000*, vol. 4. Washington, DC: National Institute of Justice.

Caplow, Theodore, Louis Hicks, and Ben Wattenberg. 2000. *The First Measured Century: An Illustrated Guide to Trends in America*. Washington, DC: American Enterprise Institute for Public Policy Research.

Caulkins, Jonathan P. 2000. "Measurement and Analysis of Drug Problems and Drug Control Efforts." Pp. 85-138 in *Measurement and Analysis of Crime and Justice*, vol. 4, *Criminal Justice 2000*, edited by David Duffee. Washington, DC: National Institute of Justice.

Center for Criminal Justice Policy Research. 2000. *Improving the Quality and Accuracy of Bias Crime Statistics Nationally*. Boston, MA: Northeastern University.

Chaiken, Jan M. and Marcia R. Chaiken. 1982. *Varieties of Criminal Behavior*. National Institute of Justice Report R-2814-NIJ. Santa Monica, CA: Rand Corporation.

Chaiken, Jan M. and Marcia R. Chaiken. 1990. "Drugs and Predatory Crime." Pp. 203-39 in *Drugs and Crime*, vol. 13, *Crime and Justice: A Review of Research*, edited by Michael Tonry and James Q. Wilson. Chicago, IL: University of Chicago Press.

Chaiken, Marcia R. and Jan M. Chaiken. 1984. "Offender Types and Public Policy." *Crime and Delinquency* 30:195-226.

Chambliss, William J. 1984. *Criminal Law in Action*. New York: John Wiley.

Chang, Leslie. 2000. "In China, a Headache of a Head Count." *Wall Street Journal*, November 2.

Chicago Commission on Race Relations. 1922. *The Negro in Chicago: A Study of Race Relations and a Race Riot*. Chicago: University of Chicago Press.

Clark, John P. and Larry Tift. 1966. "Polygraph and Interview Validation of Self-Reported Delinquent Behavior." *American Sociological Review* 31:516-23.

Clelland, Donald and Timothy J. Carter. 1980. "The New Myth of Class and Crime. *Criminology* 18:319-36.

Cohen, Lawrence E. and Marcus Felson. 1979. "Social Change and Crime Rate Trend: A Routine Activity Approach." *American Sociological Review* 44:588-608.

Coleman, Clive and Jenny Moynihan. 1996. *Understanding Crime Data: Haunted by the Dark Figure*. Buckingham, UK: Open University Press.

Cromwell, Paul, James Olson, and D'Aunn Wester Avery. 1991. *Breaking and Entering: An Ethnographic Analysis of Burglary*. Newbury Park, CA: Sage.

Curran, Daniel J. and Claire M. Renzetti. 1994. *Theories of Crime*. Boston, MA: Allyn & Bacon.

deLeon, Virginia and Hannelore Sudermann. 2000. "Campus Crime Stats Deceiving, Officials Say—Inconsistencies in Reporting Standards Can Make Comparison Difficult." *Spokesman Review*, November 20.

Dillman, Don A. 2000. *Mail and Internet Surveys: The Tailored Design Method*. 2d ed. New York: John Wiley.

Dillman, Don A. and John Tarnai. 1991. "Mode Effects of Cognitively Designed Recall Questions: A Comparison of Answers to Telephone and Mail Surveys." Pp. 73-94 in *Measurement Errors in Surveys*, edited by P. P. Biemer, R. M. Groves, L. E. Lyberg, N. A. Mathiowetz, and S. Sudman. New York: John Wiley.

du Cane, E. F. 1893. "The Decrease of Crime." *The Nineteenth Century* 33:480-92.

Dunaway, R. Gregory, Francis T. Cullen, Velmer S. Burton, Jr., and T. David Evans. 2000. "The Myth of Social Class and Crime Revisited: An Examination of Class and Adult Criminality." *Criminology* 38:589-632.

Duncan, Otis Dudley. 1984. *Notes on Social Measurement*. New York: Russell Sage.

Dykema, Jennifer and Nora Cate Schaeffer. 2000. "Events, Instruments, and Reporting Errors." *American Sociological Review* 65:619-29.

Edwards, A. L. 1957. *The Social Desirability Variable in Personality Assessment and Research*. New York: Dryden.

Elliott, Delbert S. 1983. *National Youth Survey*. Boulder, CO: Behavioral Research Institute.

Elliott, Delbert S. and Suzanne S. Ageton. 1980. "Reconciling Race and Class Differences in Self-Reported and Official Estimates of Delinquency." *American Sociological Review* 45:95-110.

Elliott, Delbert S., David Huizinga, and Barbara Morse. 1986. "Self-Reported Violent Offending: A Descriptive Analysis of Juvenile Violent Offenders and Their Offending Careers." *Journal of Interpersonal Violence* 1:472-514.

Ellis, Lee and H. Hoffman. 1990. *Crime in Biological, Social, and Moral Contexts*. New York: Praeger.

Elmer, M. C. 1933. "Century-Old Ecological Studies in France." *American Journal of Sociology* 39:63-70.

Erickson, Maynard and Lamar T. Empey. 1963. "Court Records, Undetected Delinquency and Decision-Making." *Journal of Criminal Law, Criminology, and Police Science* 54:456-69.

Faziollah, Mark, Michael Matza, and Craig R. McCoy. 1999. "Police Checking into Old Sex Cases." *Philadelphia Inquirer*, October 29.

Federal Bureau of Investigation, 1984. *Uniform Crime Reporting Handbook*. Washington, DC: U.S. Government Printing Office.

Federal Bureau of Investigation, 1997. *National Incident-Based Reporting System*. Washington, DC: U.S. Government Printing Office.

Federal Bureau of Investigation, 1998. *Crime in the United States 1997*. Washington, DC: U.S. Government Printing Office.

Federal Bureau of Investigation. 1999. *Crime in the United States, 1998*. Washington, DC: U.S. Government Printing Office.

Federal Bureau of Investigation, 2000. *Crime in the United States, 1999*. Washington, DC: U.S. Government Printing Office.

Fendrich, Michael and Connie M. Vaughn. 1994. "Diminishing Lifetime Substance Use Over Time: An Inquiry into Differential Reporting." *Public Opinion Quarterly* 58:96-123.

Fitzpatrick, Clifford and Eugene Kanin. 1957. "Male Sex Aggression on a University Campus." *American Sociological Review* 22:52-8.

Freed, Dale Anne. 2000. "Officer Likes Sound of New Raves Bill." *Toronto Star*, May 17.

Garafalo, James. 1990. "The National Crime Survey, 1973-1986: Strengths and Limitations of a Very Large Data Set." Pp. 75-96 in *Measuring Crime: Large-Scale, Long-Range Efforts*, edited by Doris Layton McKenzie, Phyllis Jo Baunach, and Roy R. Roberg. Albany, NY: State University of New York Press.

Gfoerer, Joseph, Judith Lesser, and Teresa Parsley. 1997. "Studies of Nonresponse and Measurement Error in the National Household Survey on Drug Abuse." Pp. 273-95 in *The Validity of Self-Reported Drug Use: Improving the Accuracy of Survey Estimates* (NIDA Research Monograph 167), edited by Lana Harrison and Arthur Hughes. Rockville, MD: National Institute on Drug Abuse.

Gilbert, Neil. 1997. "Advocacy Research and Social Policy." Pp. 101-48 in *Crime and Justice: A Review of Research*. vol. 2, edited by Michael Tonry. Chicago: University of Chicago Press.

Glenn, John. 1978. "The Crime That's Burning America." *Journal of Insurance* 39:14-17.

Godfrey, Tom. 2000. "$5M in Ecstasy Seized at Airport." *Toronto Sun*, May 18.

Gold, Martin. 1966. "Undetected Delinquent Behavior." *Journal of Research in Crime and Delinquency* 3:27-46.

Gottfredson, Michael and Travis Hirschi. 1990. *A General Theory of Crime*. Stanford, CA: Stanford University Press.

Gove, Walter R., Michael Hughes, and Michael Geerken. 1985. "Are Uniform Crime Reports a Valid Indicator of the Index Crimes? An Affirmative Answer with Minor Qualifications." *Criminology* 23:451-501.

Green, Jack and Stephen Mastrofski. 1988. *Community Policing: Rhetoric or Reality?* New York: Praeger.

Grey, Colin. 2000. "Ecstasy Use Growing among Adults, Seniors." *National Post*, August 15.

Groves, R. M. 1989. *Survey Errors and Survey Costs*. New York: Wiley.

Groves, R. M. 1996. "How Do We Know What We Think Is Really What They Think?" In *Answering Questions: Methodology for Determining Cognitive and Communicative Processes in Survey Research*, edited by N. Schwarz and S. Sudman. San Francisco, CA: Jossey-Bass.

Gurr, Ted Robert. 1977. "Contemporary Crime in Historical Perspective: A Comparative Study of London, Stockholm, and Sydney." *Annals of the American Academy of Political and Social Science* 434:114-36.

Hagan, John. 1994. *Crime and Disrepute*. Thousand Oaks, CA: Pine Forge.

Harrell, Adele V. 1997. "The Validity of Self-Reported Drug Use Data: The Accuracy of Responses on Confidential Self-Administered Answer Sheets." Pp. 37-58 in *The Validity of Self-Reported Drug Use: Improving the Accuracy of Survey Estimates* (NIDA Research Monograph 167), edited by Lana Harrison and Arthur Hughes. Rockville, MD: National Institute on Drug Abuse.

Harrison, Lana. 1997. "The Validity of Self-Reported Drug Use in Survey Research: An Overview and Critique of Research Methods." Pp. 17-36 in *The Validity of Self-Reported Drug Use: Improving the Accuracy of Survey Estimates* (NIDA Research Monograph 167), edited by Lana Harrison and Arthur Hughes. Rockville, MD: National Institute on Drug Abuse.

Harrison, Lana and Arthur Hughes, eds. 1997. *The Validity of Self-Reported Drug Use: Improving the Accuracy of Survey Estimates* (NIDA Research Monograph 167). Rockville, MD: National Institute on Drug Abuse.

Harwood, John and Cynthia Crossen. 2000. "Head Count: Why Many New Polls Put Different Spins on Presidential Race." *Wall Street Journal*, September 29.

Hays, Tom. 2000. "Drug Seizures Suggest Ecstasy Flow Becoming Epidemic." *Associated Press*, April 3.

Heimer, Karen and Ross L. Matsueda. 1994. "Role-Taking, Role Commitment, and Delinquency: A Test of Differential Social Control." *American Sociological Review* 59:365-90.

Henry, Tamara. 1996. "Campus Crime Climbs—Better Enforcement is One Reason for Rise, Officials Say." *USA Today*, April 22.

Herrnstein, Richard J. and Charles Murray. 1994. *The Bell Curve*. New York: Free Press.

Hindelang, Michael J., Travis Hirschi, and Joseph G. Weis. 1979. "Correlates of Delinquency: The Illusion of Discrepancy Between Self-Report and Official Measures." *American Sociological Review* 44:995-1014.

Hindelang, Michael J., Travis Hirschi, and Joseph G. Weis. 1981. *Measuring Delinquency*. Beverly Hills, CA: Sage.

History of the United States Census. 2000. Retrieved March 2001 from (americanhistory.about.com/library/weekly/aa032700a.html).

Holmes, Steven. 2000. "Defying Forecasts, Census Response Ends Declining Trend." *New York Times*, September 20.

Holmes, Steven. 2001. "Census Officials Ponder Adjustments Crucial to Redistricting." *New York Times*, February 12.

Holsendoph, Ernest. 1974. "A City Raises Police Pay if Crime Goes Down." *New York Times*, November 10.

Huizinga, David and Delbert S. Elliott. 1986. "Reassessing the Reliability and Validity of Self-Report Delinquency Measures." *Journal of Quantitative Criminology* 2:293-327.

Huizinga, David and Delbert S. Elliott. 1987. "Juvenile Offenders: Prevalence, Offender Incidence, and Arrest Rates by Race." *Crime and Delinquency* 33:206-23.

International Association of Chiefs of Police. 1929. *Uniform Crime Reporting*. New York: Author.

Irwin, J. 1985. *The Jail: Managing the Underclass in American Society*. Berkeley, CA: University of California Press.

Jang, Sung Joon. 1999a. "Age-Varying Effects of Family, School, and Peers on Delinquency: A Multilevel Modeling Test of Interactional Theory." *Criminology* 37:643-85.

Jang, Sung Joon. 1999b. "Different Definitions, Different Modeling Decisions, and Different Interpretations: A Rejoinder to Lauritsen." *Criminology* 37:695-702.

Jang, Sung Joon and Byron R. Johnson. 2001. "Neighborhood Disorder, Individual Religiosity, and Adolescent Use of Illicit Drugs: A Test of Multilevel Hypotheses." *Criminology* 39:109-43.

Jenkins, Philip. 1994. *Using Murder: The Social Construction of Serial Homicide*. New York: Aldine de Gruyter.

Johnston, Denis F. and Michael J. Carley. 1981. "Social Measurement and Social Indicators." *Annals of the American Academy of Political and Social Science* 453:237-53.

Johnston, Lloyd D. and Patrick M. O'Malley. 1997. "The Recanting of Earlier Reported Drug Use by Young Adults." Pp. 59-80 in *The Validity of Self-Reported Drug Use: Improving the Accuracy of Survey Estimates* (NIDA Research Monograph 167), edited by Lana Harrison and Arthur Hughes. Rockville, MD: National Institute on Drug Abuse.

Johnston, Lloyd D., Patrick M. O'Malley, and Jerald G. Bachman. 1999. *National Survey Results on Drug Use from the Monitoring the Future Study, 1975-1988*, vol. 1, *Secondary School Students*, vol. 2, *College Students and Young Adults*. Bethesda, MD: National Institute on Drug Abuse.

Jones, Jeffery. 2001. "Two-Thirds of Americans Support the Death Penalty." Princeton, NJ: Gallup Organization.

Jonsson, Patrik. 2001. "With Racial Profiling, Even Research is Suspect." *Christian Science Monitor*, March 5.

Junger-Tas, Josine and Ineke Haen Marshall. 1999. "The Self-Report Methodology in Crime Research." Pp. 291-367 in *Crime and Justice: A Review of Research*, vol. 25, edited by Michael Tonry. Chicago, IL: University of Chicago Press.

Justice Magazine. 1972. "Police and Statistics." 1:1.

Kasindorf, Martin and Haya El Nasser. 2001. "Impact of Census' Race Data Debated." *USA Today*, March 13.

Kim, Julia Yun Soo, Michael Fendrich, and Joseph S. Wislar. 2000. "The Validity of Juvenile Arrestees' Drug Use Reporting: A Gender Comparison." *Journal of Research in Crime and Delinquency* 37:419-32.

Kindermann, Charles, James P. Lynch, and David Cantor. 1997. *The Effects of the Redesign on Victimization Estimates*. Washington, DC: U.S. Department of Justice, Bureau of Justice Statistics.

Kinsey, Alfred C., Wardell B. Pomeroy, Clyde E. Martin, and Paul H. Gebhard. 1953. *Sexual Behavior in the Human Female*. Philadelphia, PA: W. B. Saunders.

Kleck, Gary. 1982. "On the Use of Self-Report Data to Determine the Class Distribution of Criminal and Delinquent Behavior." *American Sociological Review*, 427-33.

Lauritsen, Janet L. 1999. "Limitations in the Use of Longitudinal Self-Report Data: A Comment." *Criminology* 37:687-94.

Leland, John. 2001. "Zero Tolerance Changes Life at One School." *New York Times*, April 8.

Lemert, Edwin. 1951. *Social Pathology*. New York: McGraw-Hill.

Lenhen, R. G. and A. J. Reiss, Jr. 1978. "Some Response Effects in the National Crime Survey." *Victimology* 3:110-24.

Leonard, A. E. 1954. "Crime Reporting as a Police Management Tool." *Annals of the American Academy of Political and Social Science* 291:127-34.

Lewis, Michael. 2000. "The Two Bucks a Minute Democracy." *New York Times Magazine*, November 5.

Lichtblau, Eric. 2001a. "Decade-Long Crime Drop Ends." *Seattle Times*, May 31.

Lichtblau, Eric. 2001b. "Crime Is: Up? Down? Who Knows?" *Seattle Times*, June 14.

Lindesmith Center. 2001. "Appropriate Sentencing Guidelines for MDMA." Retrieved March 23, 2001 (www.lindesmith.org).

Literary Digest. 1929. "Missouri's Boomerang Questionnaire." April 27.

Lott, John R., Jr. 2001. "Commentary: Zero Tolerance Equals Zero Thinking." *Los Angeles Times*, June 13.

Magura, Stephen and Sung-Yeon Kang. 1997. "The Validity of Self-Reported Cocaine Use in Two High Risk Populations." Pp. 227-46 in *The Validity of Self-Reported Drug Use: Improving the Accuracy of Survey Estimates* (NIDA Research Monograph 167), edited by Lana Harrison and Arthur Hughes. Rockville, MD: National Institute on Drug Abuse.

Maltz, Michael D. 1977. "Crime Statistics: A Historical Perspective." *Crime and Delinquency* 23:32-40.

Maltz, Michael D. 1999. "Bridging Gaps in Police Crime Data: A Discussion Paper from the Big Fellows Program. Washington, DC: U.S. Department of Justice, Office of Justice Programs, Bureau of Justice Statistics.

Martz, Ron. 1999. "Crime Stats: Questions Linger after Atlanta Audit." *Atlanta Journal-Constitution*, January 28.

Maxfield, Michael G. 1999. "The National Incident-Based Reporting System: Research and Policy Applications." *Journal of Quantitative Criminology* 15:119-49.

McCleary, Richard, Barbara C. Nienstedt, and James M. Erven. 1982. "Uniform Crime Reports as Organizational Outcomes: Three Time Series Experiments." *Social Problems* 29:361-72.

McCord, H. 1951. "Discovering the 'Confused' Respondent: A Possible Projective Method." *Public Opinion Quarterly* 15:363-6.

McCorkle, Richard C. and Terance D. Miethe. 2001. *Panic: The Social Construction of the Street Gang Problem*. Upper Saddle River, NJ: Prentice Hall.

McDonald, H. 2001. "Census Questions on Race Knocked." *Spokesman-Review*, April 1.

Mensch, Barbara S. and Denise B. Kandel. 1988. "Underreporting of Substance Use in a National Longitudinal Youth Cohort: Individual and Interviewer Effects." *Public Opinion Quarterly* 52:100-24.

Merton, Robert. 1957. "Social Structure and Anomie." Pp. 25-47 in *Social Theory and Social Structure*, edited by Robert Merton. New York: Free Press.

Miethe, Terance D. and Richard C. McCorkle. 2001. *Crime Profiles: The Anatomy of Dangerous Persons, Places, and Situations*. 2d ed. Los Angeles, CA: Roxbury.

Miethe, Terance D. and Robert F. Meier. 1994. *Crime and Its Social Context*. Albany, NY: State University of New York Press.

Miller, Peter V. 1997. "Is 'Up' Right? The National Household Survey on Drug Abuse." *Public Opinion Quarterly* 61:627-41.

Monkkonen, Eric. 1994. *Police Departments, Arrests and Crime in the United States, 1860-1920*. (Machine-readable data file). Eric Monkkonen, principal investigator. Ann Arbor, MI: Inter-university Consortium for Political and Social Research [distributor].

Morrison, William Douglas. 1892. "The Increase of Crime." *The Nineteenth Century* 31:950-7.

Mosher, Clayton. 2001. "Predicting Drug Arrest Rates: Conflict and Social Disorganization Perspectives." *Crime and Delinquency* 47:84-104.

Murphy, Fred J., Mary M. Shirley, and Helen M. Witmer. 1946. "The Incidence of Hidden Delinquency." *American Journal of Orthopsychiatry* 16:686-97.

Murphy, L. R. and R. W. Dodge. 1981. "The Baltimore Recall Study." Pp. 16-21 in *The National Crime Survey: Working Papers*, vol. 1, *Current and Historical Perspectives*, edited by R. G. Lenhen and W. G. Skogan. Washington, DC: U.S. Government Printing Office.

Myrdal, G. 1944. *An American Dilemma*. New York: Harper.

National Crime Victimization Survey. 2000. *Criminal Victimization in the United States, 1998*. Washington, DC: National Institute of Justice.

Nettler, Gwynn. 1978. *Explaining Crime*. New York: McGraw-Hill.

New York Times. 2001. "A Pennsylvania Town the Census Overlooked." March 18.

Newport, Frank, Lydia Saad, and David Moore. 1997. *Where America Stands*. New York: John Wiley.

NIBRS. 1997. *Implementing the National Incident-Based Reporting System: A Project Status Report*. Washington, DC: U.S. Department of Justice, Office of Justice Programs, Bureau of Justice Statistics.

Nicklin, Julie. 2000. "Inconsistencies Mar Web Site on Campus Crime." *Chronicle of Higher Education*, December 1.

Nye, F. Ivan and James F. Short, Jr. 1957. "Scaling Delinquent Behavior." *American Sociological Review* 22:326-31.

Nye, F. Ivan, James F. Short, Jr., and Virgil J. Olson. 1958. "Socioeconomic Status and Delinquent Behavior." *American Journal of Sociology* 63:381-89.

O'Brien, Robert M. 1985. *Crime and Victimization Data*. Beverly Hills, CA: Sage.

Oliver, Willard. 2001. *Community-Oriented Policing: A Systemic Approach to Policing*. Upper Saddle River, NJ: Prentice Hall.

Parry, H. J. and H. Crossley. 1950. "Validity of Responses to Survey Questions." *Public Opinion Quarterly* 14:61-80.

Pepinsky, Harold E. 1976. "The Growth of Crime in the United States." *Annals of the American Academy of Political and Social Science* 423:23-30.

Petersilia, Joan, Peter W. Greenwood, and Marvin Lavin. 1977. *Criminal Careers of Habitual Felons*. Department of Justice Report R-2144 DOJ. Santa Monica, CA: Rand Corporation.

Peterson, Karen. 2001. "Changes Boost Gay Household Tally." *USA Today*, July 7.

Peterson, Mark A. and Harriet B. Braiker. 1981. *Who Commits Crimes? A Survey of Prison Inmates*. Cambridge, MA: Oelgeschlager, Gunn, and Hain.

Phillips, Dretha M., Clayton J. Mosher, and Joseph R. Kabel. 2000. "Taking Measure of ADAM: Survey Methods and Self-Report Data in Jails." Paper presented at the Annual Meeting of the American Society of Criminology, November 2000, San Francisco, CA.

Pollack, Otto. 1951. *The Criminality of Women*. Philadelphia, PA: University of Pennsylvania Press.

Port, Bob and Ben Lesser. 1999. "The 25 Highest-Risk College Campus Neighborhoods." Retrieved November 10, 1999 (APBnews.com).

Porter, Theodore M. 1995. *Trust in Numbers*. Princeton, NJ: Princeton University Press.

Porterfield, Austin L. 1946. *Youth in Trouble*. Fort Worth, TX: Leo Potishman Foundation.

Porterfield, Austin L. and H. Ellison Salley. 1946. "Current Folkways of Sexual Behavior." *American Journal of Sociology* 52:209-16.

President's Commission on Law Enforcement and the Administration of Justice. 1968. *Crime in a Free Society*. Belmont, CA: Dickenson.

Public Broadcasting System, 2000. "The First Measured Century." Available at www.pbs.org.

Quetelet, L. A. J. 1842. *Treatise on Man and the Development of His Faculties*. Edinburgh, Scotland: S. W. and R. Chambers.

Quillian, Lincoln. 1996. "Group Threat and Regional Change in Attitudes Toward African-Americans." *American Journal of Sociology* 102:816-60.

Radzinowicz, L. 1945. "English Criminal Statistics: A Critical Appraisal." Pp. 174-94 in *The Modern Approach to Criminal Law*, edited by L. Radzinowicz and J. W. C. Turner. London: Macmillan.

Ramirez, Deborah, Jack McDevitt, and Amy Farrell. 2000. *A Resource Guide on Racial Profiling Data Collection Systems*. Washington, DC: U.S. Department of Justice.

Raphael, Mitchell. 2001. "Census Causes Identity Crisis for Transsexual." *National Post*, May 30.

Rashbaum, William K. 2000. "Drug Experts Report a Boom in Ecstasy Use." *New York Times*, February 26.

Rebovich, Donald J., Jenny Layne, with Wilson Jiandani and Scott Hage. 2000. *The National Public Survey on White-Collar Crime*. Morgantown, WV: National White Collar Crime Center.

Rennison, Callie Marie. 2001. *Criminal Victimization 2000*. Washington, DC: U.S. Department of Justice, Bureau of Justice Statistics.

Renshaw, Benjamin H. 1990. "Alternative Futures in Measuring Crime." Pp. 223-35 in *Measuring Crime: Large-Scale, Long-Range Efforts*, edited by Doris Layton MacKenzie, Phyllis Jo Baunach, and Roy R. Roberg. Albany, NY: State University of New York Press.

Rivera, Ray. 2000. "It's School as Usual at UW, Despite Attack on Campus." *Seattle Times*, September 25.

Rivera, Ray. 2001. "Drug Arrests at UW near Nation's Highest." *Seattle Times*, January 30.

Roberts, David J. 1997. *Implementing the National Incident-Based Reporting System: A Project Status Report*. Washington, DC: U.S. Department of Justice.

Robinson, Louis N. 1933. "History of Criminal Statistics (1908-1933)." *Journal of Criminal Law and Criminology* 24:125-39.

Robison, Sophia Moses. 1936. *Can Delinquency Be Measured?* New York: Columbia University Press.

Rozsa, Lori. 1998. "Sugarcoating? Officer Faked Boca Crime Statistics." *Miami Herald*, May 3.

Saad, Lydia. (1998) "Viagra a Popular Hit." Princeton, NJ: Gallup Organization.

Salant, Priscilla and Don A. Dillman. 1994. *How to Conduct Your Own Survey*. New York: John Wiley.

Sampson, R. 1986. "Effects of Socioeconomic Context on Official Reactions to Juvenile Delinquency." *American Sociological Review* 51:876-85.

SAMHSA. 1997. *National Household Survey on Drug Abuse: Main Findings, 1995*. Rockville, MD: Office of Applied Studies, Substance Abuse and Mental Health Services Administration.

SAMHSA. 2000. *Summary of Findings from the 1999 National Household Survey on Drug Abuse*. Rockville, MD: Office of Applied Studies, Substance Abuse and Mental Health Services Administration.

Schmitt, Eric. 2001. "U.S. Census Bureau Rejects Revision to Nation's Tally." *New York Times*, March 2.

Schneider, A. L. 1977. *The Portland Forward Records Check of Crime Victims: Final Report*. Eugene, OR: Institute for Policy Analysis.

Schoor, Daniel. 1996. "Playing the Numbers." *New Leader*, September 9.

Schwarz, Frederic D. 1997. "1947: The Kinsey Report." *American Heritage* 48:98-9.

Scott, Janny. 2001. "A Nation by the Numbers, Smudged." *New York Times*, July 1.

Seattle Post-Intelligencer. 1992. "Wisians are Unloved." January 8.

Secondary School Educators Newsletter, 2001. "Violence in Schools." Retrieved September 3, 2001 (http://7-12educators.about.com/library/weekly/aa041800a.htm).

Seidman, David and Michael Couzens. 1974. "Getting the Crime Rate Down: Political Pressure and Crime Reporting." *Law and Society Review* 8:457-93.

Sellin, Thorsten. 1928. "The Negro Criminal: A Statistical Note." *Annals of the American Academy of Political and Social Science* 139:52-64.

Sellin, Thorsten. 1931. "The Basis of a Crime Index." *Journal of the American Institute of Criminal Law and Criminology* 22:335-56.

Sellin, Thorsten and Marvin Wolfgang. 1964. *The Measurement of Crime and Delinquency*. New York: John Wiley.

Shaw, C. R. and H. D. McKay. 1931. *Social Factors in Juvenile Delinquency*. Washington, DC: U.S. Government Printing Office.

Shaw, C. R. and H. D. McKay. 1942. *Juvenile Delinquency and Urban Areas*. Chicago, IL: University of Chicago Press.

Sherman, Lawrence W. and Ellen G. Cohn. 1985. "The Impact of Research on Legal Policy: The Minneapolis Domestic Violence Experiment. *Law and Society* 23:117-44.

Short, James F., Jr. 1955. "The Study of Juvenile Delinquency by Reported Behavior—An Experiment in Method and Preliminary Findings." Paper presented at the Annual Meeting of the American Sociological Association, Washington, DC.

Short, James F., Jr. 1957. "Differential Association and Delinquency." *Social Problems* 4:233-9.

Short, James F., Jr. and Ivan Nye. 1957-58. "Reported Behavior as a Criterion of Deviant Behavior." *Social Problems* 5:207-13.

Short, James F., Jr. and Ivan Nye. 1958. "Extent of Unrecorded Juvenile Delinquency: Tentative Conclusions." *Journal of Criminal Law, Criminology, and Police Science* 49:296-302.

Simon, Stephanie. 2001. "Police Slow Down after Cincinnati Riots." *Los Angeles Times*, July 15.

Simpson, Janice. 1978. "Fighting the Fires." *Wall Street Journal*, April 10.

Singer, Eleanor and Stanley Presser. 1989. *Survey Research Methods: A Reader*. Chicago: University of Chicago Press.

Singleton, Royce A. and Bruce C. Straits. 1999. *Approaches to Social Research*. New York: Oxford University Press.

Skogan, Wesley. 1978. *Victimization Surveys and Criminal Justice Planning*. Washington, DC: Law Enforcement Assistance Administration.

Smith, D. 1986. "The Neighborhood Context of Police Behavior." In *Communities and Cities*, edited by A. Reiss and M. Tonry. Chicago, IL: University of Chicago Press.

Smith, Douglas A., Christy A. Visher, and G. Roger Jarjoura. 1991. "Dimensions of Delinquency: Exploring the Correlates of Participation, Frequency, and Persistence of Delinquent Behavior." *Journal of Research in Crime and Delinquency* 28:6-32.

Smith, Tom W. 1989. "That Which We Call Welfare by any other Name Would Smell Sweeter." Pp. 99-107 in *Survey Research Methods: A Reader*, edited by Eleanor Singer and Stanley Presser. Chicago, IL: University of Chicago Press.

Snyder, Howard N. 1999. "The Overrepresentation of Juvenile Crime Proportions in Robbery Clearance Statistics." *Journal of Quantitative Criminology* 15:151-61.

Snyder, Howard N. and Melissa Sickmund. 1999. *Juvenile Offenders and Victims: 1999 National Report*. Washington, DC: National Center for Juvenile Justice, U.S. Department of Justice.

Stevens, S. S. 1959. "Measurement, Psychophysics, and Utility." Pp. 18-63 in *Measurement: Definitions and Theories*, edited by C. W. Churchill and Philburn Ratoosh. New York: John Wiley.

Storey, Glenn R. 1997. "The Population of Ancient Rome." *Antiquity* 71:966-78.

Straus, Robert and Selden Bacon. 1953. *Drinking in College*. New Haven, CT: Yale University Press.

Sulok, Nancy J. 1998. "South Bend Crime Statistics Are Accurate, Police Chief Says." *South Bend Tribune*, November 2.

Sutherland, Edwin. 1940. "White-Collar Criminality." *American Sociological Review* 5:1-12.

Sutherland, Edwin. 1947. *Principles of Criminology*. 4th ed. Chicago, IL: J. P. Lippincott.

Tappan, Paul. 1947. "Who is the Criminal?" *American Sociological Review* 12:96-102.

Taranto, James. 2001. "Zero Tolerance Makes Zero Sense." *Wall Street Journal*, May 18.

Taylor, Bruce. 1989. *New Directions for the National Crime Survey*. Washington, DC: U.S. Department of Justice, Bureau of Justice Statistics.

Taylor, Bruce and Trevor Bennett. 1999. *Comparing Drug Use Rates of Detained Arrestees in the United States and England.* Washington, DC: National Institute of Justice.

The Civil Rights Project. 2000. "Opportunities Suspended: The Devastating Consequences of Zero Tolerance and School Discipline Policies." Cambridge, MA: Harvard University.

Thornberry, Terence P. and Marvin D. Krohn. 2000. "The Self-Report Method for Measuring Delinquency and Crime." Pp. 38-84 in *Measurement and Analysis of Crime and Justice,* vol. 4, *Criminal Justice 2000,* edited by David Duffee. Washington, DC: National Institute of Justice.

Tibbits, Clark. 1932. "Crime." *American Journal of Sociology* 37:963-69.

Time. 1936. "Studies for All." March 9.

Time. 2000. "Numbers." September 25.

Tittle, Charles. 1995. *Control Balance: Toward a General Theory of Deviance.* Boulder, CO: Westview.

Tittle, Charles R. and Robert F. Meier. 1990. "Specifying the SES/Delinquency Relationship." *Criminology* 28:271-99.

Tittle, Charles R., Wayne J. Villemez, and Douglas A. Smith. 1978. "The Myth of Social Class and Criminality: An Empirical Assessment of the Empirical Evidence." *American Sociological Review* 43:643-56.

Tittle, Charles R., Wayne J. Villemez, and Douglas A. Smith. 1982. "One Step Forward, Two Steps Back: More on the Class/Criminality Controversy." *American Sociological Review* 47:433-8.

Tizon, Alex and Reid Forgrave. 2001. "Wary of Racism Complaints, Police Look the Other Way in Black Neighborhoods." *Seattle Times,* June 26.

Tremblay, Pierre and Carlo Morselli. 2000. "Patterns in Criminal Achievement: Wilson and Abrahamse Revisited." *Criminology* 38:633-59.

Turner, A. G. 1972. *The San Jose Methods Test of Known Crime Victims.* National Criminal Justice Information and Statistics Service, Law Enforcement Administration. Washington, DC: U.S. Government Printing Office.

Turner, Charles F., Judith T. Lessler, and Joseph C. Gfoerer, eds. 1992. *Survey Measurement of Drug Use: Methodological Studies.* Publication No. (ADM) 92-1929. Rockville, MD: U.S. Department of Health & Human Services.

Uniform Crime Reports. (1984) *Uniform Crime Reporting Handbook.* Washington, DC: Federal Bureau of Investigation.

U.S. Bureau of the Census. 1999. *Statistical Abstract of the United States.* Washington, DC: Author.

USA Today, 1997. "Public Opinion Survey Responses are 'Guesses.'" October 3.

USA Today. 2001a. "Crackdown on Ecstasy." March 21.

USA Today. 2001b. "A Third of Teenage Violence Occurs in Schools." April 4.

U.S. News and World Report. 1962. "Who's to Blame for the Rising Wave of Crime?" January 1.

U.S. News and World Report. 1994. "Campus Crime: On the Rise." February 7.

Visher, Christy A. 1986. "The Rand Institute Survey: A Reanalysis." Pp. 161-211 in *Criminal Careers and "Career Criminals,"* vol. 2, edited by Alfred Blumenstein, Jacqueline Cohen, Jeffrey A. Roth, and Christy A. Visher. Washington, DC: National Academy Press.

Vold, George B. 1935. "The Amount and Nature of Crime." *American Journal of Sociology* 40:796-803.

Wallerstein, J. S. and C. J. Wyle. 1947. "Our Law-Abiding Law Breakers." *Probation* 25:107-12.

Washington Post. 2001. "Sentencing Guidelines Toughened for Ecstasy." March 21.

Weinraub, Benard. 1967. "Crime Reports up 72% Here in 1966, Actual Rise is 6.5%." *New York Times,* February 21.

Wellford, Charles and James Cronin. 2000. "Clearing Up Homicide Rates." *National Institute of Justice Journal*, April:307.

Williams, J. R. and M. Gold. 1972. "From Delinquent Behavior to Official Delinquency." *Social Problems* 20:209-29.

Wilson, James Q. and Allan Abrahamse. 1992. "Does Crime Pay?" *Justice Quarterly* 9:359-77.

Wilson, James Q. and Richard J. Herrnstein. 1985. *Crime and Human Nature*. New York: Simon & Schuster.

Wright, Douglas, Joseph Gfoerer, and Joan Epstein. 1997. "The Use of External Data Sources and Ratio Estimation to Improve Estimates of Hardcore Drug Use from the NHSDA." Pp. 477-97 in *The Validity of Self-Reported Drug Use: Improving the Accuracy of Survey Estimates*. NIDA Research Monograph 167, edited by Lana Harrison and Arthur Hughes. Rockville, MD: National Institute of Justice.

Wright, Scott W. 2000. "Campus Crimes Survey Angers HBCU Officials." *Black Issues in Higher Education*, March 2.

Zawitz, Marianne W., Patsy A. Klaus, Ronet Bachman, Lisa D. Bastian, Marshall M. Deberry, Michael R. Rand, and Bruce M. Taylor. 1993. *Highlights from 20 Years of Survey Crime Victims: The National Crime Victimization Survey, 1973-92*. Washington, DC: Bureau of Justice Statistics.

Zernike, Kate. 2001. "Crackdown on Threats in Schools Fails a Test." *New York Times*, May 17.

Zhang, Lening and Steven F. Messner. 2000. "The Effects of Alternative Measures of Delinquent Peers on Self-Reported Delinquency." *Journal of Research in Crime and Delinquency* 37:323-37.

Author Index

Subject Index

About the Authors

Clayton J. Mosher is Associate Professor of Sociology at Washington State University, Vancouver. He is the author of numerous articles in the areas of criminal sentencing, race, crime, criminal justice processing, and drug policies. His book *Discrimination and Denial* (1998) examines race and crime issues in Canada. His current work includes a book manuscript on Natives, crime, and criminal justice, and an evaluation of a drug treatment program for women offenders, funded by the National Institute of Justice

Terance D. Miethe is Professor of Criminal Justice at the University of Las Vegas, Nevada. He is the author of several books and articles in the areas of criminal victimization, violent crime, criminal processing, and legal decision making. His previous books include *Crime Profiles: The Anatomy of Dangerous Persons, Places, and Situations* (with Richard C. McCorkle, 2001), *Whistleblowing at Work: Tough Choices in Exposing Fraud, Waste, and Abuse on the Job* (1999), and *Crime and Its Social Context: Toward an Integrated Theory of Offenders, Victims, and Situations* (with Robert F. Meier, 1994).

Dretha M. Phillips is Senior Research Associate in the Social and Economic Sciences Research Center at Washington State University, Pullman. Her criminal justice/criminology research experience is wide ranging. It includes conducting face-to-face interviews with arrestees in jails, evaluating in-prison substance abuse treatment programs and community diversion initiatives for convicted offenders, and designing and analyzing data from public surveys on sex offender community notification laws.